CONFLICT OF LAWS

By

KERMIT ROOSEVELT, III

Professor of Law

University of Pennsylvania Law School

CONCEPTS AND INSIGHTS SERIES

FOUNDATION PRESS
2010

THOMSON REUTERS™

© 2010 By THOMSON REUTERS/FOUNDATION PRESS

    195 Broadway, 9th Floor

    New York, NY 10007

    Phone Toll Free 1–877–888–1330

    Fax (212) 367–6799

    foundation–press.com

Printed in the United States of America

ISBN 978–1–59941–788–2

Mat # 40903697

To Felicia Lewis

ACKNOWLEDGMENTS

I owe substantial debts of gratitude to the colleagues and students who have helped me refine my thinking about conflict of laws over the years. In particular, I am grateful to Herma Hill Kay, Larry Kramer, and the late David Currie, who invited me to join their casebook as a co-author. I have learned a tremendous amount from them. For assistance in the preparation of this book, I thank Jason Levine, Michael Packard, and Howard Wu, three Penn students who read the manuscript and warned me when it got abstruse.

September 2009
Philadelphia, PA

TABLE OF CONTENTS

TABLE OF CONTENTS

CONFLICT OF LAWS

Introduction

Conflict of laws, described most generally, is the field of law that deals with the situation that arises when the regulatory powers of different authorities overlap. So phrased, this description fits a wide range of circumstances. Indeed, one of the attractions of conflicts is that its insights can be applied to so many other areas—administrative law, for instance, or constitutional law, or many puzzles in federal-state relations not usually thought to present a conflicts issue.

As taught in law school, however, conflicts usually comprises the core area of choice of law and some subsidiary related fields, primarily judicial jurisdiction and recognition of judgments. This book focuses on those topics, though it will at times suggest some of the broader applications. It is in the nature of an opinionated guide to the conflict of laws. That is, it is designed primarily to be a useful aid for the student who is taking conflicts, or a reference for the student or attorney who has not, but it seeks also to evaluate different approaches and to demonstrate the value of looking at conflicts from a particular perspective.

Most centrally, the book presents the choice-of-law problem through the analytic lens of what I call the two-step model. A choice-of-law problem arises when a court must decide which of multiple candidate laws will supply the rule of decision for a case. In its most common form, this requires a court to choose between the laws of one or more states. Suppose, for example, that the parties are two residents of State A involved in a one-car accident in State B. Whose law should control whether the passenger can sue the driver, State A's or State B's?

The book suggests that the proper way to analyze this problem consists of two stages, which it calls **scope** and **priority**. First, the court must determine the scope of State A and State B law. It must determine, that is, whether State A and/or State B law reach these facts, whether they grant rights (claims or defenses) to the parties. Sometimes the problem can be resolved at this first stage, through scope analysis alone. If it turns out that only one state's law reaches the case, the case should obviously be decided under that law. If each state's law about passenger-driver suits stated that it applied "only to car accidents occurring in this state" then the accident would fall within the scope of State B's law and not State

A's.[1] If, however, the first stage analysis reveals that the case falls within the scope of both State A and State B law, and those laws conflict, the court must decide which of the two laws is to be given priority. It then decides the case under that law.

This description should not sound controversial. Indeed, I hope it sounds both fairly simple and fairly obvious. The choice-of-law theories that courts and scholars have developed over the years are neither simple nor obvious, but I believe that they will be easier to understand and evaluate if we consider them as attempts to answer the two questions of scope and priority.

Choice of law, unlike most other areas of law, has been very strongly influenced by the work of law professors. Perhaps not coincidentally, it is generally considered excessively complicated in theory and unsuccessful in practice. It is my hope that this book will show that things are not in fact so dire. The complexities are not as fearsome as they might seem at first blush, and the prospects for a successful choice-of-law system are greater than naysayers maintain.

The structure of the book is designed to follow that typically used in conflicts courses and in most of the leading casebooks. Its first part addresses the core topic of choice of law, starting with the traditional approach and moving on to more modern proposals. Having looked at choice of law from the internal perspective of a state wrestling with the problem, it then considers the external constraints that federal law and the Constitution place on the choice-of-law enterprise. Part Two deals with the topics of judicial jurisdiction and recognition of judgments, which are frequently covered in conflicts courses. It also offers an analysis of conflicts issues as presented in the specific substantive area of family law, and in the international setting.

---

1. Alert readers may wonder what happens if the accident falls within the scope of neither state's law. This problem will receive substantial discussion later.

Part I
CHOICE OF LAW
Chapter 1
THE TRADITIONAL APPROACH
I. Introduction

Choice of law has a long and rich history, about which volumes can and have been written. A quest for its origins could go back as far as ancient Egypt.[1] For our purposes, though, we can pick up the story in the United States in the early twentieth century with the work of Joseph Beale.

Beale was a Harvard law professor who went on to become the American Law Institute's Reporter for the First Restatement of Conflicts.[2] The choice-of-law approach that he championed has been called variously the "vested rights," "traditional," or "territorial" theory. (This book will use each name at times.) It was codified in the First Restatement (published in 1934) and dominant in the academy and the courts during the first half of the twentieth century.

Beale's approach can be presented as a set of rules governing particular kinds of cases, and the bulk of this chapter will be devoted to exposition and discussion of those rules. But for the most part, the rules follow logically from a few central principles, and so it is worth starting with those principles and the vision of choice of law that they reveal.

The master principle of Beale's system is that all laws are territorially bounded in their operation. (It is because of the centrality of the territorial principle that the vested rights system is also sometimes called territorialism.) What this means is that a state's law applies to all events that occur within a state, and to no events occurring outside it. As Beale put it, "[b]y its very nature law must apply to everything and must exclusively apply to every-

---

1. See Hessel E. Yntema, The Historic Bases of Private International Law, 2 Am. J. Comp. L. 297, 300–01 (1953).

2. The ALI is a group of judges, practitioners, and scholars which pub-

lishes Restatements of the Law, designed to clarify, modernize, and otherwise improve the law. See www.ali.org.

thing within the boundary of its jurisdiction."[3] (The reliance on the nature of law is a characteristic Beale move, and readers should note its use in place of argument or explanation.)

On Beale's account, when some event occurs, the legal system of the place where it occurs attaches consequences. In his terms, rights vest. A tort victim acquires a right to damages, a contract signatory acquires the rights granted by the contract, and so on. Once vested, these rights can be considered much like personal property. In particular, they are **transitory**: they can be taken into other states and sued upon. A party who suffers a tort in State A and thereby acquires rights under State A law, for instance, can take those State A rights into a State B court and ask for the remedy to which they entitle him.[4]

The idea of vested rights is easy to mock as metaphysical hogwash, and Beale's critics did not hold back.[5] But in fact the idea of vested rights still plays a fairly significant role in our legal system—for one thing, what Beale described is essentially the way we still treat judgments, which can be obtained in one state and enforced in another (as discussed in Chapter 7). The precise details of the vested rights theory are in any case less important than the master principle of territorialism.

One of the basic challenges for the traditional system is explaining where this territorial principle comes from. Beale tended to assert that it inhered in the nature of law, or sometimes in the Due Process Clause of the federal Constitution. Courts of the early twentieth century accepted both these assertions, to some extent, but eventually their persuasiveness declined. If the territorial principle is not a given, something imposed on states by nature or the Constitution, then it must be defended as a sensible choice that tends to achieve the goals for which a choice-of-law system aims.

Of course, people differ about what these goals are, and also their relative importance. (Standard desiderata include uniformity of result across forums, predictability, ease of application, fairness,

---

3. 1 JOSEPH H. BEALE, A TREATISE ON THE CONFLICT OF LAWS (1935) § 4.12 at 46.

4. According to Beale, the remedy would actually be granted under State B law, and the State B court would consider the existence of the State A rights as a fact entitling the plaintiff to a State B remedy. See 1 BEALE, supra note 3, § 5.4, at 53. Most modern states have dropped this distinction and consider remedy to come from foreign law. So did the First Restatement, as far as the

measure of damages is concerned. See Restatement of Conflict of Laws (1934) § 412.

5. See, e.g., David F. Cavers, *A Critique of the Choice-of-Law Problem*, 47 Harv. L. Rev. 173, 175–76 (1933) ("Indeed, one may now wonder how any juristic construct such as 'right' could have been accepted as fundamental in the explanation of any important aspect of judicial activity.")

and furtherance of state policies.) We will discuss this issue in more detail later, when it comes time to evaluate the traditional approach. The more immediate problem has to do not with the justification for the territorial principle but with its application. The vested rights model requires that every legal occurrence have a unique location, the place in which the rights vest. Identifying this location turns out to be harder than one might think.

The easy case for the vested rights theory is one in which all relevant events occur in a single state. If one party commits a tort against another in State A, or if the two parties make and perform a contract in State A, it is relatively clear on Beale's model that the rights should vest in State A and hence under State A law. This result does not change even if, for some reason, suit is later brought in State B. The plaintiff simply takes the rights that have vested in State A and presents them to the State B court, asking for a remedy based on rights created by the law of State A.

But matters can be considerably more complicated. Indeed, in a case that presents a choice-of-law question, they typically are. Such cases frequently involve cross-border events. A party may act negligently in State A and cause an injury in State B, or he may form a contract in A and breach it in B. How do we decide where the tort or the contract is located, as Beale's system requires?

There is no fully satisfactory answer to this question, but the one that Beale chose (the "last act rule") is at least plausible. He reasoned that since rights vested *when* some last necessary act or event occurred, they also vested *where* that event occurred. A tort, for instance, is not complete until an injury is inflicted. (You may remember from torts that "negligence in the air" is not actionable.) The injury is thus the crucial last act, and the tort occurs where the injury does. Similar rules apply for other causes of action.

Before we move to a discussion of these particular rules, it is worth pausing to ask how Beale's system looks from the perspective of the two-step model discussed in the introduction. The answer is that it is a scope-based system. The territorial principle is a rule of scope, which sets the reach of state laws equal to their geographical boundaries. (Importantly, it does so not only for the law of the forum, but for all laws. That is, a State A court applying Beale's approach will view not just State A law as territorially bounded, but the laws of States B and C as well.) It is an extremely powerful rule of scope because it also takes care of the problem of priority. Because state laws are territorially bounded, they can never overlap.

Within Beale's system, then, conflicts between state laws can never arise. This simplifies the analysis in some ways, because the question of how to resolve conflicts (the question of priority) need not be addressed. It also complicates it in some ways, because of the need to assign a unique location to each legal event. Whether the approach is appealing on the whole is a question that must be deferred for a bit. We will weigh its merits and demerits later. We turn now to the specific rules that implement Beale's system.

II. Traditional Theory: Jurisdiction–Selecting Rules

The traditional approach is what is sometimes called a jurisdiction-selecting approach. What this means is that it selects not a particular law but a particular jurisdiction, a state with the authority to regulate. It does so based on the territorial principle: the state with authority to regulate is the one in which the legal event occurred. Its law controls. One needn't ask, as we will see some modern approaches do, what purposes that law is intended to serve, or whom it is intended to benefit. One need only decide where the rights vested.

A. Torts

The rule that governs tort cases under the traditional approach is called *lex loci delicti*, Latin for "the law of the place of the wrong." It directs courts to decide tort cases according to the law of the place where the tort occurred—which, given the last act rule, is the place where the injury occurred. As Section 377 of the First Restatement puts it, "The place of wrong is in the state where the last event necessary to make an actor liable for an alleged tort takes place."

Once the place of injury is identified, the *lex loci delicti* rule controls the vast majority of issues. Some exceptions exist. The First Restatement contains a large number of specific rules detailing which issues are governed by the law of the place of injury and which are not.[6] Some of the former include whether a cognizable injury has been sustained (§ 378); whether liability is strict or governed by a negligence or intentional harm standard (§ 379); the applicability of the fellow servant rule (§ 386); and the existence of

---

6. A practitioner handling a tort case in a jurisdiction that follows *lex loci delicti* should consult the Restatement but should also be aware that local courts are unlikely to be familiar with its more specific rules and may disregard them if they seem to contradict common sense.

vicarious liability (§ 387). The most notable exceptions are the following.

First, Section 380(2) provides that if the issue is the "application of a standard of care," the application should be performed based on the law of the place of action, not that of injury. This is a very narrow exception, dealing with not the choice between different standards of care (which Section 379 commits to the law of the place of injury) but rather with the application of a single standard. As illustration, the Restatement advises that if both states X and Y impose liability on railroads for negligently causing fires, but only the law of Y makes failure to use a spark arrester negligence per se, a railroad acting in X without a spark arrester but with due care is not liable for a fire caused in Y. Second, Section 382 provides that acts taken pursuant to a legal privilege or duty in State X cannot be the basis for liability under State Y law even if they cause injury in Y. Last, Section 387 provides that the law of the state of injury controls the issue of vicarious liability only if the defendant authorized the individual who caused the injury to act for him in that state.

These exceptions aside, the *lex loci delicti* rule seems simple enough. As tends to be the case in law, it is possible to complicate matters. A victim of poisoning, for instance, might ingest poison in one state, feel queasy in another, realize he was seriously ill in a third, and die in a fourth. This course of events may strike you as unlikely, but the First Restatement took the possibility seriously enough to address it explicitly. For cases of poisoning, comment a to Section 377 provided, the controlling law is that of the place where "the deleterious substance takes effect upon the body," i.e., the location of the first illness. Somewhat oddly, this rule applies as well for wrongful death actions—the controlling law is the law of the place where the injury was inflicted, not where death occurred.[7] (This is somewhat odd since one might think that death is necessary for a wrongful death cause of action, and hence death would be the crucial last event.)

Still, in the vast majority of cases, applying the law of the place of injury will be a relatively straightforward process. Indeed, in the vast majority of cases act and injury will occur in the same state. The main criticism of *lex loci delicti* is not that it is unpredictable or difficult to apply but rather that its rigidity produces arbitrary and unfair results. *Alabama Great Southern Railroad v. Carroll*[8] is a classic example.

7. See Restatement § 377, note 1.   **8.** 97 Ala. 126, 11 So. 803 (1892).

W.D. Carroll was a brakeman for the Alabama Great Southern Railroad, which operated a line running from Chattanooga, Tennessee, through Alabama to Meridian, Mississippi. Ninety percent of the line was in Alabama. Carroll was an Alabama resident, his employer an Alabama corporation, and the contract of employment was formed in Alabama.

On a train from Birmingham, Alabama, to Meridian, Carroll suffered an injury when a defective link between two cars broke. The breakage and the injury occurred in Mississippi, but the negligence producing the injury (another employee's failure to discover the defect) occurred in Alabama. At common law, which Mississippi followed, the negligence of Carroll's "fellow servant" would not create liability for the railroad. Alabama, however, had abrogated the fellow servant rule by statute, and Carroll therefore could recover under Alabama, but not Mississippi, law.

What law should govern this case? *Carroll* is a favorite for casebook authors because it shows so starkly the consequences of focusing on one contact (the place of injury) alone. Everything about this case other than the injury is tied to Alabama, and the location of the injury is pure accident—the link could just as easily have broken before the train crossed the Mississippi border. Your intuition probably tells you that this case "belongs" to Alabama. But under the last act rule, the location of the injury is decisive, and Mississippi law governs.

Why should that be so? And if the traditional system and the last act rule produce such arbitrary consequences, should they be reconsidered? The modern answer is, perhaps—though we will need to think more about the tradeoffs between different choice-of-law values that reconsideration entails. For the Alabama Supreme Court in *Carroll*, though, the answer was that no alternative was possible. The Alabama statute allowing recovery "necessarily" was limited to injuries occurring within Alabama. It had to be interpreted, the court wrote "as if its operation has been expressly limited to this state, and as if its first line read as follows 'When a personal injury is received *in Alabama* by a servant or employe,' etc." *Carroll* thus also illustrates the status of the traditional system in the courts at the turn of the century. As Beale was so fond of saying, territorialism was simply part of the nature of law.

B. Contracts

Like torts, contracts is governed in the main by a principle encapsulated in a Latin phrase, this time *lex loci contractus*, the law of the place of contracting. As with a tort, it is possible to separate

8

the elements of a contract across state lines, with negotiation occurring in one state, offer in another, acceptance in a third, performance in a fourth, and so on. Again, therefore, territorialism demands a localizing rule that will fix a contract to a single place. Here, too, the traditional approach follows the last act rule. The last event necessary to the creation of contract rights is acceptance, so the place of contracting is the place of acceptance.

Alert readers might wonder why the last act rule does not indicate the place of breach, since breach is an element of a contract claim. The practical answer is that the place of breach is a clearly worse rule, since it is less predictable in operation and tends to greater arbitrariness. Beale could have offered a theoretical defense as well, however, on the grounds that contract rights are created by acceptance, and breach merely makes certain remedies available. Thus, under Section 332 of the First Restatement, the law of the place of contracting will govern issues such as "capacity to make the contract," "the mutual assent or consideration, if any, required to make a promise binding," and "fraud, illegality, or any other circumstances which make a promise void or voidable."

The First Restatement did, however, provide in Section 358 that the law of the place of performance governs some issues, including "the manner of performance," "the sufficiency of performance," and "excuse for non-performance." In consequence, a court deciding a contracts case under the First Restatement may resolve different issues under different states' laws. This practice, called **depecage,** is discussed in more detail in Chapter 3.

Most contract issues, including the especially important one of validity, will be determined by the law of the place of contracting, or more precisely the place of acceptance. But it turns out that *lex loci contractus* is not quite as easy to apply as *lex loci delicti*. Where an injury occurs is, or seems like, an ordinary question of fact.[9] But where acceptance occurs is more clearly a question of law, and that complicates matters. Another nineteenth century case, *Milliken v.*

---

9. Actually, it is not, because whether a legally cognizable injury has been suffered is a question of law as well—it depends on what the law deems an injury—and therefore it cannot be answered solely on the basis of fact. But the overlap between fact and law is so close here that it is easy to think that the location of an injury is a question of fact, particularly because state laws almost always assign the same location to an injury. To show that the location is indeed a question of law, we might imagine a State X law providing that a tort is not complete until the victim has requested an apology. Under this admittedly odd rule, a tort with an injury in State Y and an apology request in State X would occur in State X if the last act rule keys on State X tort law, but State Y if it keys on State Y law.

Pratt,[10] illustrates this point, showing both the operation and the complexities of the traditional approach.

The plaintiffs in *Milliken* were Maine businessmen shipping goods to customers both within and outside the state. The defendant was a Massachusetts woman, Sarah Pratt, who had guaranteed the debt of her husband Daniel. Under Massachusetts law at the time, married women were not allowed to guarantee their husbands' debt; under Maine law, they could. (The Massachusetts law is an offensive one that would now be unconstitutional, of course, but try not to be distracted by this fact. For purposes of analysis, you can suppose that the contractual disability is imposed not on married women but on minors, or some other group.) Sarah Pratt executed a guarantee in Massachusetts and sent it to the plaintiffs in Maine, whereupon they extended credit to Daniel and shipped goods to him in Massachusetts.

What is the place of contracting in *Milliken*? It is probably not immediately clear to you. What should be clear is that this is a legal question, not a factual one. It depends on how we characterize the contractual relationship between the parties, and perhaps also on intricacies of contract law such as the mailbox rule.

As it turned out, the Supreme Judicial Court of Massachusetts decided that the guarantee Sarah sent to Maine had been a unilateral offer—"extend credit to my husband and I will guarantee his debt." Unilateral offers, you may remember from contracts, are accepted by performance. So the place of acceptance, and the place of contracting, in *Milliken* is the place of performance. Plaintiffs performed, the Court said, by extending credit, which they did in Maine, and therefore Maine law governed.

Not every court would necessarily have agreed. Some might have thought that the contract was bilateral, or that performance was rendered by delivering goods, rather than extending credit. So *Milliken* shows that courts might differ about where a contract is formed, even if they are all following the traditional approach to choice of law. The point can be made more clearly still by considering the mailbox rule. When acceptance is transmitted by letter, the majority rule is that it is effective upon dispatch—when placed in the mailbox. Under that rule, a contract is formed at the time of dispatch, and, when we apply the last act rule, at the place of dispatch as well.

Some jurisdictions, however, follow a minority rule under which acceptance is not effective until received. Thus, under this

---

10.   125 Mass. 374 (1878).

rule, a contract is formed at the time and place of receipt. Here, clearly, we can see that the place of contracting depends upon substantive contract law: that law determines whether the last necessary act is dispatch or receipt. (Note, however, that the mailbox rule was created to answer questions about time, not place.)

Why does it matter if the place of contracting is determined by law rather than fact? It matters because while there is only one set of facts, there are many different laws. That is why we need conflicts. If these laws differ with respect to *where* they locate a contract, they will differ also in the law they select under the traditional approach.

Such differences create two problems. First, they threaten uniformity. If State A follows the mailbox rule and State B does not, an acceptance mailed from A to B will create a contract in State A according to A law and one in State B according to B law. Assuming that the courts of each state follow their own contract law in determining where the contract was created, they will disagree about the governing law. Each court, following *lex loci contractus*, will rule that the contract is governed by its own law. This disuniformity makes it harder for parties to structure their affairs and subjects defendants to forum-shopping, traditionally considered a bad thing.

Second, they make it hard for a court to perform a choice-of-law analysis in the first place. In the preceding paragraph, I assumed that each court would apply the law of its own state ("forum law") to decide where the contract was formed. But why should that be so? Given the territorial premise, if State B law by its terms creates a contract in State B, it is hard to see how a State A court has the authority to say that no such contract exists. But the same can be said about State A law: a contract has formed under that law, within State A, and according to territorialism, State A should have the last word on its existence. Despite the territorial rule of scope, a conflict has emerged within the traditional system, and the system has no resources to resolve it.

Beale, in the First Restatement, tried to avoid this problem by suggesting that contracts should be located with reference to "the general law of Contracts."[11] But what he invokes there is the general common law that the Supreme Court disavowed in *Erie Railroad v. Tompkins*.[12] Without its aid, there is no single law that

---

11. Comment (d) to § 311.

12. 304 U.S. 64 (1938). Coming only four years after the publication of the

can provide the answer. Forum law is the default, and there is no obvious alternative, but the disuniformity thus created reduces both the practical utility and the theoretical coherence of the traditional approach.

C. Other Traditional Rules

Torts and contracts are the bread and butter of choice-of-law analysis, but there are also other areas of substantive law where these issues arise. The traditional approach deals with them as you might expect given your exposure to it thus far: it uses territorial factors to identify the state with authority to regulate a particular transaction or relationship. Or in the words of the realtor, location, location, location.

i. *Property*

The treatment of property under the traditional approach depends on whether it is real or personal in nature. (This distinction is also sometimes phrased as "movable" (personal) vs. "immovable" (land or interests therein).) Real property is always governed by the law of the situs, the state where it is located. This rule follows quite obviously from the principle of territorial scope.

Because it follows so directly, it enjoyed great force under the traditional approach. For instance, as we will see in Chapter 7, courts are ordinarily required by the Constitution to grant effect to judgments issued in other states. Under the so-called "land taboo," however, a traditionalist State X court could disregard a State Y judgment purporting to affect interests in land located in State X.[13] The rule that situs law controls persists under modern conflicts approaches, as does the land taboo, in slightly attenuated form.

Personal property is also generally governed by the law of its location at the time of the relevant events. If a property owner in State X, for instance, transfers diamonds to an auctioneer in State Y and the auctioneer sells them below the stipulated reserve price, the law of State Y will determine whether the original owner can recover them from a purchaser. Put more generally, whether a

First Restatement, *Erie* must have been a nasty shock to Beale, who had spent over twenty years on the Restatement and relied on the general common law in numerous places.

13. For instance, in *In re Barrie's Estate*, 240 Iowa 431, 35 N.W.2d 658 (1949), the Iowa Supreme Court held that Iowa property owned by an Illinois decedent should be distributed according to the terms of a will valid under Iowa law, even though an Illinois court had rejected the will on the grounds that it had been revoked.

purchaser acquires good title to personal property will typically be determined by the law of the place of sale.

Two important exceptions exist, each of which looks to domicile rather than situs. Because domicile will be an important concept for the rest of this book, I pause now to explain it for those unfamiliar with the term. Domicile is the legal equivalent of the lay concept of residence. It identifies the state with which a person is most closely associated—and, we will see, the state which is supposed to have the paramount concern for that person's welfare. Acquiring new domicile requires that a person enter the new state with an intention to remain there for an indefinite period of time.[14] (For instance, a college student planning to leave the state where she attends school after graduation is not domiciled there.) These requirements of mental intent and physical presence are sometimes encapsulated in the phrase "mind and behind."

We will see that domicile plays a large role in modern approaches to choice of law. In the traditional system, it played a much lesser role, but it does control personal property in two circumstances. First, succession to personal property is governed by the law of the decedent's domicile, not of the property's location. Second, the rights of married couples to each other's personal property are determined by the law of the marital domicile, rather than situs law.

ii. Marriage

The general rule under the traditional system is what you would expect if you thought of marriage as a contract. The validity of a contract, remember, is determined by the law of the place of contracting. The validity of a marriage, likewise, is generally determined by the law of the place of its formation, usually called celebration. (The Latin phrase is *lex loci celebrationis*.)

The traditional approach recognized some exceptions, however. These exceptions appear to be based on the degree of antipathy felt towards a particular marriage. The First Restatement, uncharacteristically, did not offer exhaustive rules but merely illustrative examples. Thus, Section 132 provided that the law of either party's domicile could work to invalidate polygamous, incestuous, or interracial marriages. This last category has of course been superseded by the evolution of constitutional law, see *Loving v. Virginia*, 388 U.S. 1 (1967), but same-sex marriages are currently receiving a similar reception in most states. Marriage and other aspects of family law are dealt with in more detail in Chapter 8.

14. See, e.g., *White v. Tennant*, 31 W.Va. 790, 8 S.E. 596 (1888).

iii. Corporations

Like marriage, corporate law can largely be conceptualized as a species of contract, and the traditional approach treats it that way. The rights and obligations between members in the corporate venture—shareholders, officers, directors, and so on—are generally governed by the law of the state of incorporation, on the theory that the act of incorporation is essentially akin to the creation of a web of contracts. With respect to these matters, called the "internal affairs" of the corporation, courts would typically not only decline to apply forum law but decline to exercise jurisdiction at all, abstaining in favor of the courts of the state of incorporation. With respect to its dealings with outsiders, however, the traditional approach to choice of law treated the artificial person of the corporation much like a natural person: its torts and contracts would be governed by *lex loci delicti* or *lex loci contractus*. This general distinction between internal and external affairs continues to hold with the modern approaches, although of course they resolve external issues under modern rules rather than the traditional ones.

III. Traditional Practice: Escape Devices

As a matter of theory, the traditional approach is typically faulted for its rigidity and the arbitrary results that mechanical application of rules invariably produces in some number of cases. But in practice, the traditional approach has greater flexibility than the foregoing discussion might suggest. Courts have available several devices that can alter the outcome that traditional analysis would otherwise prescribe. Used appropriately, these "escape devices" can mitigate the vices of arbitrariness and inflexibility. Of course, they impose a corresponding cost on the virtues of predictability and uniformity, and there is also the possibility that they will be used for inappropriate reasons such as a desire to favor locals or sympathetic parties.

A. Characterization

The traditional approach works by applying a particular rule based on the nature of the claim presented. Thus, torts are governed by *lex loci delicti*, contracts by *lex loci contractus*, and so on. But there is of course a step preliminary to the application of the appropriate rule: the court must decide which rule is the appropriate one. It must decide whether the claim before it is a contract claim, or one that sounds in tort, and so on. It must *characterize* the cause of action.

Characterization is typically considered among the escape devices, but it deserves the name less than some of the others we will see later. Characterization is not simply an issue that a judge can bring up to change the outcome of a case; it is a real question that must be confronted in every case. Some cases will be relatively easy, of course, but some will be hard, and unfortunately the traditional approach offers very little in the way of guidance.

Carroll, introduced in the discussion of torts above, actually presented a characterization issue. That case, recall, involved a railroad brakeman injured in Mississippi. He and his employer were Alabama domiciliaries who had contracted in Alabama; the railroad operated primarily in Alabama; and the negligence that caused his injury occurred in Alabama. But because the injury occurred in Mississippi, the tort-specific rule of *lex loci delicti* directed the application of Mississippi law, which defeated Carroll's claim.

His lawyers realized this, and so they argued that the case was actually a contract suit. The Alabama statute that abrogated the fellow servant rule and allowed Carroll to sue his employer for an injury inflicted by another employee, they claimed, was incorporated into Carroll's contract of employment. And since he was suing to enforce a contract right, the applicable choice-of-law rule was *lex loci contractus*, which pointed to Alabama.

The court rejected this argument on the grounds that its effect would be to give Alabama tort law extraterritorial scope, something forbidden by the nature of law. Liability based on injuries received outside the state, the court wrote, "has not hitherto been suggested by any court or law writer, and ... to say the least, would be astounding to the profession." That may have been a slight overstatement, but in 1892 it was only a slight one. Times change, however, and eventually the nature of law no longer seemed a real barrier. Indeed, in 1928, the Alabama legislature amended the statute at issue in *Carroll* so that it applied to out-of-state injuries, so long as the employment contract was formed in Alabama. The legislative rejection of territorialism actually settled the issue for that statute, but it also showed that recharacterization was viable, and the question presented itself with increasing urgency in other cases.

A classic from the early days is *Levy v. Daniels' U–Drive Auto Renting Co.*[15] The defendant, a car rental agency doing business in Hartford, there rented a car to one Sack. The plaintiff, Levy, was a Hartford resident who was a passenger in the car. He was injured due to Sack's negligence, with the injury taking place in Massachu-

15. 108 Conn. 333, 143 A. 163 (1928).

setts. Connecticut, but not Massachusetts, had a statute imposing vicarious liability on rental agencies for injuries caused by the negligent operation of their vehicles.

Under the traditional system, *Levy* is an easy case once you get past the characterization step. If it is a contract case, *lex loci contractus* applies and directs Connecticut law, making the agency liable. If it is a tort, *lex loci delicti* points to Massachusetts law, and the agency is not liable. But how is a court to decide whether the case sounds in tort or contract?

The traditional approach offered no general principles to guide judges. The First Restatement gave some specific rules for particular issues. For instance, Section 387 provided that vicarious liability was a tort issue, meaning that Massachusetts law should govern in *Levy*. But the Restatement did not explain what theory, if any, lay behind its specific rules.

In the actual *Levy* case, the court decided that Connecticut's vicarious liability statute had been incorporated into the contract, and that the case therefore presented an issue of contract law rather than tort. It was not able to give much of an explanation why. The result, however, probably strikes most people as sensible. Like *Carroll*, *Levy* presented a situation where every relevant factor but the place of the injury pointed towards one state. If asked which state has the more legitimate claim to determine the liability of a Connecticut agency renting a car to a Connecticut resident in Connecticut, for an injury caused to another Connecticut resident, when the injury happens to occur in Massachusetts, most people would probably say Connecticut. The *Levy* court in fact gropes towards such a rationale by suggesting that this is the kind of case the Connecticut legislature sought to regulate. The "purpose of the statute," the court said, would be served by applying it in this case.

Levy thus presents an example of characterization used to reach a "sensible" outcome. This avoidance of arbitrary results produced by rigid application of the traditional system is the benign face of escape devices. But if the traditional approach is not fully in accord with our intuitions about sensible results, perhaps we would be better off trying to identify the principles that underlie those intuitions and developing a choice-of-law approach that promotes them directly. (In the next chapter, we will see an attempt to do just that with the idea of legislative purpose.)

The danger in relying on escape devices to mitigate arbitrariness is that they can be used for less lofty purposes. Professor Robert Leflar chronicles an extraordinary series of Arkansas decisions in which Arkansas courts, dealing with a cause of action for

16

mental anguish occasioned by failure to deliver a telegram, characterized the claim as tort when the failure to deliver occurred in Arkansas and as contract when the contract was formed there.[16] The rationale in these cases appears to have been simply whatever was necessary to decide them under Arkansas law.

Is there hope for a reasoned approach to characterization? In Chapter 3, I will suggest that while the characterization problem cannot be solved, we may be able to make it disappear if we address choice-of-law problems from the perspective of the two-step model. In a purely domestic case, after all, characterization does not pose the same sort of problem. A plaintiff can plead both a tort and a contract cause of action. He may in fact be able to state a claim on both theories, though he will not be allowed duplicative recovery. I will suggest that a similar approach can be used in the multistate case. A plaintiff can invoke whatever rights a state's law gives him. We do not need to "characterize the case" to decide what rights are available. We need only ask if the plaintiff can state a claim on a given theory under a given state's law. The appropriate question in *Levy*, then, would not be "Is this a tort or a contract case?" It would be "Can Levy state a claim under any law, on any theory?"

Narrowing down the possibilities is relatively easy. Levy cannot state a tort claim under Massachusetts law; that law does not provide for vicarious liability. He cannot state a contract claim under Massachusetts law either; under *lex loci contractus* that law is not available for a contract formed in Connecticut. Connecticut tort law is no help to him; under *lex loci delicti* it is not available for injuries suffered outside Connecticut. So we are left with the question of whether he can state a claim under Connecticut contract law. This may be a difficult question, but it is one that courts answer in ordinary cases. It requires no special "choice-of-law" analysis.

B. Substance vs. Procedure

The characterization problem discussed above asks courts to decide which substantive cause of action a case presents. The distinction between substance and procedure creates another characterization problem.

A forum will always apply its own procedural law. Under the traditional approach, the rationale for this rule is straightforward.

16. *Western Union Telegraph Co. v. Griffin*, 92 Ark. 219, 122 S.W. 489 (1909); *Western Union Telegraph Co. v. Chilton*, 100 Ark. 296, 140 S.W. 26 (1911). See R. Leflar, *The Law of Conflict of Laws* 95 (1962).

The rights that vest when, say, a tort is committed in State A are substantive rights under State A law. The plaintiff may then bring those rights into a State B court and seek a remedy, but there is no reason to suppose that State A procedure should operate in a State B court.

The rule is also fairly obviously a sensible one. No matter what you think is the reason for deciding a case under foreign substantive law, that reason is unlikely to apply to foreign procedural law. And since the parties must know which procedural rules to follow from the very start, before the court decides any choice-of-law issues, it makes good practical sense to reserve procedural matters to forum law.

But to say that a forum will always apply its own procedural law tells us nothing without some definition of the difference between substance and procedure. This distinction occurs repeatedly in the law—we will see it again in our discussion of the *Erie* doctrine—and the line is drawn in different places depending on the context. For purposes of choice of law, and from the perspective of the traditional approach, the best way to think about it is perhaps the following.

Substantive law is concerned with what people do outside of court, what is sometimes called "primary conduct." Substantive law places limits on what they can do, and when the limits are violated, it creates causes of action for injured parties. It is about what kinds of acts will create rights and liabilities. Procedural law is concerned with what people do inside court, litigating behavior, or what is sometimes called "secondary conduct." It is about how people enforce the rights and liabilities created by substantive law.

If we accept this formulation of the distinction, it should seem quite reasonable that courts apply forum procedure but foreign substantive law. But while describing the distinction this way may do a relatively good job of identifying the line we want to draw, it does not necessarily tell us on which side a given rule falls.

The First Restatement tried to help by providing a list of particular issues deemed procedural. These included some relatively obvious choices, such as forms of pleading (§ 592), competency of witnesses (§ 596), and admissibility of evidence (§ 597), and some more controversial ones, such as limitations periods (§ 603–605) and damage caps (§ 606). But for issues not on the list, the Restatement offered no general guidance. Courts have gone beyond the Restatement's list in finding issues they are willing to call procedural in appropriate cases, but they, too, seem to lack a general theory.

In *Grant v. McAuliffe*,[17] for instance, the California Supreme Court considered tort claims arising out of an Arizona car accident between Californians. The defendant died as a result of the accident. Under Arizona law, tort claims abate with the death of the tortfeasor, and the trial court accordingly dismissed the suit. The California Supreme Court, however, decided that survival of causes of action was a procedural issue, "not an essential part of the cause of action itself but relat[ing] to the procedures available for the enforcement of the legal claim for damages."

Like the application of Connecticut law in *Levy*, application of California law in *Grant* probably strikes you as sensible. If California wants to allow one of its residents to recover from the estate of another, based on conduct both states agree was wrongful, why should Arizona interfere? But the reason it appears sensible, assuming it does, is that California seems to have something at stake, while Arizona does not. This has no obvious connection to the characterization of survival as a procedural issue. Indeed, if the accident had involved only Arizona residents and suit, for some reason, was brought in California, the procedural characterization would *prevent* the sensible outcome. Thus, *Grant*'s use of characterization appears to be strategic rather than principled.

In *Grant*'s favor, one can at least say that the strategic deployment of the characterization argument is in service of a sensible result. But as noted above, the flexibility that escape devices lend courts can be used for all sorts of purposes. In *Kilberg v. Northeast Airlines Inc.*,[18] the New York Court of Appeals characterized a Massachusetts damage cap as procedural in order to allow full recovery for a New Yorker killed in a Massachusetts plane crash. A damages limitation, the court wrote "pertains to the remedy, rather than the right." Here, the motivation for the characterization seems to be simple parochialism, the desire to make a local whole.

C. Limitations Periods

Limitations periods present a particularly notable case of the substance/procedure characterization problem. According to the understanding of the distinction set out above, there is certainly a case to be made for calling them procedural. Filing a suit is litigating behavior, and time limits for that filing should accordingly come from forum law. Indeed, traditional choice-of-law theory classes them as procedural, and Sections 603 and 604 of the First

---

17. 41 Cal.2d 859, 264 P.2d 944 (1953).   **18.** 9 N.Y.2d 34, 211 N.Y.S.2d 133, 172 N.E.2d 526 (1961).

Restatement instruct courts to use the limitations period of the forum and disregard the foreign one.

However, there is the problem that the substance/procedure distinction is also conventionally associated with a distinction between important and not-so-important matters. (As any civil procedure professor can tell you, this association is misguided, but it exists). Limitations periods can be very important; they can be outcome-determinative, in the words of the *Erie* line of cases. And so there is also a temptation to say that they are substantive, as indeed they are for *Erie* purposes. (See Chapter 5).

The First Restatement in fact equivocates on the point. Section 605 provides that some foreign limitations periods should be heeded. If the limitations period is "made a condition of the right" so that the right "shall expire after a certain period of limitation has elapsed," then suit may not be maintained anywhere after that period.

This idea, too, should seem sensible. The state that creates a cause of action can surely give it an expiration date. In such a case, the limitations period is not so much a rule governing litigation behavior; it is a restriction on the right. But how are we to distinguish between the two sorts of limits? Or are there really two distinct sorts at all?

The problem is that limitations periods serve two different purposes, one which we can call procedural, and one which we can call substantive. The procedural purpose is to promote the litigation of fresh, rather than stale, claims by encouraging prompt filing. The interest at stake here is the interest in appropriate allocation of judicial resources, and it belongs to the forum where litigation takes place. The substantive purpose is to allow defendants peace of mind after some fixed period of time. That purpose requires balancing the value of repose against the gravity of the injury; it is part of the creation of the cause of action.

If limitations periods always serve both these interests, we should not expect much luck in distinguishing between the purported two types (usually called "statutes of limitation" and "statutes of repose.") The test that courts have developed asks whether the limitations period is "specifically directed" to the cause of action (in which case it is a condition of the right) or whether it is more general (in which case it is not).[19]

19. For an example, see *Bournias v. Atlantic Maritime Co., Ltd.,* 220 F.2d 152 (2d Cir. 1955).

The test has the virtue of being possible for courts to apply, but there is not much reason to think it does a very good job of distinguishing between limitations periods that are (primarily) concerned with stale claims and those that are (primarily) concerned with repose, even if such different types exist. Rather than attempting to refine or improve on the specificity test, the modern practice is either to provide that all limitations periods are deemed substantive, or to adopt "borrowing statutes" providing that claims must meet both local and foreign time limits. (In an interesting bit of parochialism, states frequently exempt forum residents from the operation of borrowing statutes.)

D. Renvoi

Renvoi is one of the most famous choice-of-law puzzles, and one of those responsible for giving the subject its air of esotericism and obscurity. The basic question can be stated quite simply, but it leads analysts quickly into a maze of complications. I will suggest in Chapter 3 that in fact the two-step model entirely eliminates the renvoi problem,[20] but in this section I will make only some preliminary steps towards that conclusion

The basic renvoi question is this. when a court decides to use the law of another state, should it use that state's choice-of-law rules, or only its "internal" law (substantive law excluding choice-of-law rules)? Using foreign choice-of-law rules is called "accepting the renvoi," ignoring them is called "rejecting" it. The terminology gets even more complicated, but there is no reason to pursue it.[21]

This simple question turns difficult for a number of reasons. The first is that there is no obvious basis on which to answer it. To resort to topics covered already, we might ask whether choice-of-law rules are substantive or procedural, since if they are procedural, that would give the forum a reason not to follow foreign choice of law. Like most substance/procedure characterization questions, this one is not entirely clear, but the better view is probably that choice-of-law rules are substantive. They are not intended to govern the behavior of parties in court; they operate to determine what substantive rights parties enjoy based on out-of-court behavior.

---

20. For a full statement of the argument, see Kermit Roosevelt III, *Resolving Renvoi: The Bewitchment of our Intelligence by Means of Language*, 80 Notre Dame L. Rev. 1821 (2005).

21. For those who are interested: if a court accepts the renvoi at finds that foreign choice-of-law rules direct it back to its own (forum) law, we have "remission." If the foreign choice-of-law rules point to a third state, we have "transmission." See Griswold, *Renvoi Revisited*, 51 Harv. L. Rev. 1165, 1166–70 (1938).

Can we then simply say that courts should accept the renvoi? This turns out not to be an entirely happy solution either. The second reason the renvoi question is difficult is that some attempts at answering it seem to lead to infinite recursions. If State A's choice-of-law rules point to State B, and State B's to State A, wholesale acceptance of the renvoi results not in the selection of a state's law but in an endless cycle.[22]

Most traditionalists argued that the renvoi should be rejected. In part this was no doubt because acceptance seems to lead to troubling results. Joseph Beale attempted to offer a theoretical justification, arguing that accepting the renvoi allowed foreign law to operate as law, when it should be consulted simply as fact. However persuasive the characterization of foreign law as fact might once have been (an issue discussed later in this chapter), the assertion is opaque at best. A State B choice-of-law rule that points to State A law says that the plaintiff has no rights under State B law. (Put in terms of the two-step model, it says that the case falls outside the scope of State B law and inside the scope of State A law.) If one can treat a State B law providing that the plaintiff has no rights because no vicarious liability exists under State B law as a fact, it is hard to see why accepting the same result through a choice-of-law rule involves treating it as law rather than fact.[23]

Scholars who advocated accepting the renvoi had a slightly easier time offering a theoretical justification for their position. If a State B court hearing a case would, following its choice-of-law rules, announce that the plaintiff has no rights under State B law, it is hard to see how a State A court can decide that he does. State B courts, one would think, should be the authority on who can claim rights under State B law.[24]

22. More esoteric terminology: if the renvoi is accepted and the foreign choice-of-law rule is taken to direct the court to another state's internal law, the renvoi is "partial." If the foreign choice-of-law rule is taken to direct the court to another state's whole law, including its choice-of-law rules, the renvoi is "total." It is the total renvoi that produces the infinite cycle.

23. It may be that Beale was objecting to the idea that State B choice-of-law rules can provide that a case falls within the scope of State A law, rather than just that it falls outside the scope of State B law. If that was his concern, he was on sounder ground, as discussed in Chapter 3.

24. To counter this argument, Walter Wheeler Cook came up with the theory that courts never actually apply foreign law; they just sometimes shape their own law to resemble it. Thus, a State A court can enforce rights under State A law that has been shaped to resemble State B law without worrying about whether a State B court would agree that State B rights actually exist. See W.W. Cook, The Logical and Legal Bases of the Conflict of Laws 239–51 (1942). This "local law theory" is yet another piece of conflicts esoterica that can be safely forgotten; one commentator has referred to it as "empty luggage." Hessel E. Yntema, *The Historic*

On the other hand, the advocates of renvoi had to face the problem of the infinite regress. Even the most brilliant theory will stumble if implementation is literally impossible. To get around the regress, renvoi proponents tended to assert that if the foreign choice-of-law rules point back to the forum, a court should simply accept the reference and decide the case under its own internal law. This worked as a practical matter but tended to undercut the theoretical superiority of the pro-renvoi side.

In practice, even Beale accepted the use of renvoi in certain limited circumstances, most notably those involving title to land and divorce decrees. In such cases, Beale suggested, the paramount importance of uniformity meant that when the First Restatement provided that they should be governed by the law of the situs and of the parties' domicile, respectively, that "law" included "the Conflict of Laws rules of that state."[25]

There is an apparent irony in the invocation of uniformity as a justification for accepting renvoi, namely, that it can run into the problem of infinite recurrence. If State A choice-of-law rules point to State B and vice-versa, and if the states agree that uniformity is important enough to warrant accepting the renvoi, they have stepped onto the treadmill. Dismounting requires one state to reject the renvoi, but it is hard to see how to decide which one should do so.

The irony is more apparent than real, however. What distinguishes the cases Beale identified as appropriate instances for renvoi is not just the importance of uniformity but the fact that the situs and domiciliary states have the dominant interest. (Beale, who did not think in terms of interests, did not say this, but if uniformity is the only relevant factor one would expect broader use of renvoi, since uniformity is always important to Beale. We will attempt to define "interest" more precisely in the next chapter.) What is important is not just that such cases be resolved uniformly but that they be resolved *as the courts of those states would resolve them*. It is unlikely, given their dominant interest, that the choice-of-law rules of the domiciliary or situs states would select a different state. It is even more unlikely that the domiciliary or situs states would deem it especially important to resolve the cases as the courts of the states their choice-of-law rules select would, which is what would lead them to accept the renvoi. Thus, the infinite recurrence should seldom arise.

Bases of Private International Law, 2 Am. J. Comp. L. 297, 316 (1953).

25. Restatement, Section 8.

So a limited use of renvoi can be incorporated into the traditional system without practical difficulty. The theoretical problems remain. And as we shall see, renvoi persists as a problem for the modern approaches. Indeed, a variant of the renvoi question is one of the fiercest battlegrounds within interest analysis. We will complete our discussion of renvoi in the next two chapters, in the context of those modern approaches.

E. Public Policy, Penal and Tax Laws

There exists one more group of ways to avoid the application of foreign law. Under both traditional and modern approaches, courts will not apply certain types of foreign law even if choice-of-law rules select them. These are penal laws, tax laws, and laws that sufficiently offend the forum's public policy.

i. Public Policy

The public policy exception is the broadest, at least potentially, and also the most controversial. In a choice-of-law case there will always be some difference between the policies of the states involved; otherwise there would presumably be no difference between their laws. A broadly conceived public policy "exception" could swallow the whole field of choice of law.

Under the traditional approach, several principles limited the scope of the public policy exception. First, it did not operate any time laws differed. Instead, it was limited to situations in which, as Judge Cardozo put it in an influential case, enforcing the foreign law "would violate some fundamental principle of justice, some prevalent conception of good morals, some deep-rooted tradition of the common weal."[26] (What precisely that means is open to interpretation, but it is something more than a mere difference of law.)

Second, it operated with respect to foreign claims, not defenses based on foreign law. As Justice Brandeis wrote,

> A state may, on occasion, decline to enforce a foreign cause of action. In so doing, it merely denies a remedy, leaving unimpaired the plaintiff's substantive right, so that he is free to enforce it elsewhere. But to refuse to give effect to a substantive defense under the applicable law of another State ... subjects the defendant to irremediable liability. This may not be done.[27]

26. *Loucks v. Standard Oil*, 224 N.Y. 99, 111, 120 N.E. 198 (1918).

27. *Bradford Elec. Light Co. v. Clapper*, 286 U.S. 145, 160 (1932).

Last, the consequence of the application of the public policy exception, as Justice Brandeis stated, was a dismissal without prejudice. The forum could decline to assist the plaintiff if it found his claim deeply offensive; it could, as it were, shut the courthouse doors and turn him away to seek a remedy elsewhere. It would not decide the case against him, and it would not apply forum law. The result of a public policy bar, on the traditional approach, was simply that the plaintiff had to find a different forum.

The second and third of these principles flow logically from the conceptual structure of the vested rights approach. The distinction between claims and defenses arises because the existence of a defense under foreign law, even a repugnant one, will prevent a right from vesting under that law. Put slightly differently, a plaintiff comes to court asserting (as a fact, Beale says) that foreign law entitles him to relief. But if a defense exists under foreign law, that law does not entitle him to relief. The forum cannot claim to be enforcing rights vested under foreign law if that law, viewed as a whole, does not grant the plaintiff a right to recover. (In slightly more modern terms, one might say that a court cannot claim to be applying foreign law if it only applies part of that law.)

The fact that dismissals are without prejudice likewise follows from the idea of transitory rights. If a plaintiff presents himself and seeks a remedy based on foreign rights, the court can either grant the remedy or refuse to do so. There is no logical basis on which it can ignore the foreign rights and rule for the defendant under forum law; forum law has nothing to say about the matter.

As the vested rights approach lost favor, these restrictions on the public policy exception have been increasingly disregarded. Modern courts will sometimes use public policy as a justification for selecting forum law, which makes very little sense from a theoretical perspective. (Formalism has its vices, but it does tend to produce analytical discipline.) In practical terms, the operation of the exception is somewhat unpredictable. At least, it is unpredictable if one tries to make sense of the decisions based on the repugnance of the foreign law alone. The New York Court of Appeals, for instance, refused to recognize Connecticut law permitting interspousal tort suits but (just one year later!) did recognize Hitler's Nuremberg laws, which required businesses to dismiss non-Aryan employees.

These decisions, *Mertz v. Mertz*[28] and *Holzer v. Deutsche Reichsbahn–Gesellschaft*[29] can be reconciled with two related obser-

28. 271 N.Y. 466, 3 N.E.2d 597 (1936).   **29.** 277 N.Y. 474, 14 N.E.2d 798 (1938).

vations, which together do have some predictive power for courts' use of the public policy exception. First, public policy may sometimes be used as an escape device not so much because the foreign cause of action is repugnant but because the court feels that the result under ordinary choice-of-law analysis is incorrect. Second, the repugnance of a foreign right has more to do with the way in which it is given effect in a particular case than with how intrinsically offensive it is.

A comparison of *Mertz* and *Holzer* illustrates both these points. We can see the first by noting that *Mertz* was a tort case decided when New York still followed *lex loci delicti*. Two New York spouses got into a car accident in Connecticut. The wife sued the husband, a claim permitted under Connecticut law but barred by the New York doctrine of interspousal tort immunity.

The New York Court of Appeals recognized that Connecticut law governed under the *lex loci delicti* rule, but, in a somewhat confusing discussion, it held that New York law controlled on the question of what remedies were available. We could call this a characterization argument exploiting the right-remedy distinction, or we could call it an aggressive use of the public policy exception. (Parts of *Mertz* suggest that since public policy is to be found in state laws, the exception can apply whenever laws differ, which is obviously overbroad.) In either case, what motivates it appears to be the sense that Connecticut has no business restructuring the spousal relationship of two New York domiciliaries—that is, that New York has the dominant interest in the issue, and it should be governed by New York law.[30]

In contrast to *Mertz*, *Holzer* does not look like a case where the issue is more appropriately controlled by New York. In *Holzer*, a fired German Jewish employee brought a wrongful discharge claim against his German employer. The New York Court of Appeals accepted the employer's defense that it had been required by law to fire him and dismissed the claim on the grounds that there is no liability for breach when performance has been made impossible by operation of law. Whatever we think of German law on that point, it is pretty clear that New York law should not control. The employment contract was formed and performed in Germany and the idea that New York law, rather than German, should govern rights and liabilities between employer and employee seems quite odd. In *Mertz*, then, the contacts with New York were much

---

30. The New York Court of Appeals later admitted as much in *Intercontinental Hotels Corp. v. Golden*, 15 N.Y.2d 9, 254 N.Y.S.2d 527, 203 N.E.2d 210 (1964), where it stated that "the language of the [*Mertz*] opinion indicates that the court was in reality there making a *choice-of-law* decision...."

stronger than they were in *Holzer*, and an implicit judicial sense that New York law should govern *Mertz* but not *Holzer* helps explain the different outcomes.

The second point is that recognizing foreign law may be more or less offensive depending on what recognition requires, and that in turn depends on what the connection of the litigation to the forum is. Applying Connecticut law in *Mertz* would have required the New York court to allow in New York precisely the conduct—an interspousal tort suit—that New York prohibited. In *Holzer*, by contrast, recognizing the validity of the Nuremberg laws, as they applied to an employer-employee relationship in Germany, would mean nothing more than denying recovery to the employee. Things would certainly have been different had the court been asked to allow a German company operating a factory in New York to fire its non-Aryan employees. Thus, the stronger the connections between a case and a forum, the more likely it is that giving effect to an odious foreign law will trigger the public policy exception.

A final difference between the two cases is that in *Holzer* the foreign law is offered as a defense. According to the traditional approach, this made it inappropriate to employ the public policy exception, for reasons of both fairness and logic. A plaintiff seeking to recover under German law—and Mr. Holzer's contract claims certainly did arise under the law of Germany, not New York—has to take the bitter with the sweet as far as German law is concerned; he cannot invoke one part and deny another. Likewise, if the task of the court is to enforce rights granted by German law, it is hardly doing its job if it ignores some elements of that law. Applying only the parts of German law that are consistent with New York policy is not really applying German law at all.

ii. Penal and Tax Laws

A last restriction on the operation of foreign law comes from the principle that one state will not enforce the penal or tax laws of another. Nor, of course, will it enforce another state's criminal laws, and the logic behind the penal and tax exception is essentially the same. States will open their courts to private individuals seeking to enforce foreign causes of action. Citizens of sister-states should have the privilege of litigation in the courts of each state, and they may in fact for various reasons not be able to bring the suit in their home state. But penal and tax laws, like criminal laws, do not present a dispute between private individuals; they implicate the relationship between an individual and a sovereign state. That state has its own courts and its own prosecutors, even if they take the form of private attorneys general, and it must use them to enforce its laws.

The reasoning behind the exclusion is fairly straightforward. Whether it is fully satisfactory is another issue, and in practice the prohibition on enforcement of tax laws has been abrogated by statute in many states. The more difficult issue is identifying such laws, particularly "penal" laws. Criminal laws are the easy case. Punitive damages certainly sound penal, and Section 611 of the First Restatement includes them in its list. Damage multipliers, which award a plaintiff double or treble damages, are harder to characterize and their treatment is inconsistent.

IV. The Traditional Flowchart; Pleading and Proving Foreign Law

Based on the preceding, we can summarize the process of deciding a choice-of-law issue under the traditional system. First, a court must **characterize**. It must segregate issues into the substantive and the procedural, and for the substantive it must decide what kind of claim (tort, contract, etc.) they present. Second, the court must **localize**. Having decided that the case presents a tort claim, for instance, it must decide where the tort occurred. (This is generally a matter of applying the last act rule.) Third, the court applies the rule appropriate to whatever type of claim is before it— *lex loci delicti* for a tort, *lex loci contractus* for a contract, and so on. This rule may direct the court to use foreign law; if so, it faces two other questions. First, should the foreign cause of action be rejected as offensive to the forum's public policy; and second, if the court decides to use foreign law, should it use foreign choice-of-law rules as well (the renvoi question).

If the public policy exception is not applied and the renvoi either is rejected or ends by pointing back to foreign law, the court decides the case under that foreign law. But how is it to establish the content of that law? Beale argued that foreign law is present as a fact in choice-of-law cases, and the traditional approach took this characterization seriously. Foreign law was proved to the jury, typically by expert testimony, and, like other jury findings, subject to only limited appellate reviews.

Finding this bizarre is not an inappropriate reaction. If we doubt the competence of juries to decide issues of law, making them decide issues of foreign law is surely no improvement, even if those issues are called issues of fact. Circumscribing appellate review just makes the problem worse.

Beale could not have been ignorant of these practical objections, but he went where his principles led him, and he reasoned that no other approach was possible. Since the territorial premise meant that only forum law could "operate as law" within the forum (whatever that means), foreign law simply had to be a fact. Some states have tried to ameliorate the difficulties through statutes authorizing or requiring courts to take judicial notice of the content of foreign law. In practice, the issue seldom arises; modern courts, whether through inadvertence or design, tend to treat the content of foreign law as a legal issue. (Choice-of-law issues in general are among the most likely to be overlooked in litigation, and within the choice-of-law analysis, the logical consequences of territorial principles more often than not go by the board.)

V. Evaluation

What should we think of the traditional approach? For Joseph Beale, the question did not really arise. No other system was possible. But once we abandon the idea that Beale's premises are commanded by the nature of law, his conclusions become debatable policy choices. It becomes possible to ask if the traditional approach does a good job of resolving choice-of-law problems.

In order to answer that question, we need first to decide what we want out of a choice-of-law system. Many different answers are possible, but they tend to share several features, which sometimes overlap. Put briefly and in somewhat general terms, the standard choice-of-law desiderata are the following. (This ranking is not in order of importance, since the hierarchy is highly debatable.)

Uniformity: It is generally thought a good thing if choice-of-law systems produce the same result regardless of where a case is brought. This concern may be couched in terms of unfairness to defendants, and sometimes that concern has weight. A defendant who is liable under some state's law no matter what he does is certainly in an untenable position. And perhaps there is even some unfairness in allowing a plaintiff to pick the most favorable from among several different state laws—though this intuition requires more argument to make it fully convincing. (We would not say it is unfair to allow a plaintiff to pick the most favorable of several different statutes from a single state, would we?) But at the least, we can say that forum shopping produces some inefficiencies, since the selection will be made for strategic advantage rather than ease of litigation.

Predictability: Predictability matters both outside of court and inside. On the outside, it is important for parties to be able to know which law will govern their conduct so that they can adjust their behavior accordingly. They should be able to know what laws they are subjecting themselves to, for reasons of both fairness and efficiency. For these reasons, it is good to have a choice-of-law system whose conclusions can be predicted by parties considering what to do outside court. Inside court, once litigation has begun, predictability still matters. Litigation is expensive, and reducing its cost is desirable, even if litigators might not think so. A predictable choice-of-law system makes the outcome of cases more predictable, which makes settlement more likely.

Ease of application: A choice-of-law system that is easy to apply is likely to be more predictable and do a better job of producing uniformity. A system that is perfectly predictable and uniform in theory will be neither in practice if applying it is so hard that courts and legal advisers routinely make mistakes. And a system that is easy to apply will reduce costs for parties planning transactions and for parties in court.

Fairness: People's intuitions about fairness certainly differ, but some results (for instance, application of a law the defendant could not have predicted) will strike many as unfair. Fairness is closely tied to predictability, and also, less closely, to uniformity.

Efficiency: All other things being equal, we presumably would like a choice-of-law system that accomplishes its aims as cheaply as possible. In large part, this can be achieved by making it easy to apply, but there may be situations in which efficiency is relevant in other ways. Some people argue that a choice-of-law system should "resolve cases efficiently" not just by doing so cheaply but by selecting an efficient law[31] or producing a utility-maximizing outcome as far as individual welfare is concerned.[32] I am skeptical of these arguments since they seem to be simply a way of using choice of law to elevate efficiency above the policy choices states have actually made. Efficiency is lovely, but it is not the only value, and to the extent that states have chosen to pursue something else, I do not see why the need for a choice of law analysis should be the

---

31. See generally Erin O'Hara & Larry E. Ribstein, The Law Market (2009).
32. See, e.g., Andrew Guzman, *Choice of Law: New Foundations*, 90 Georgetown L.J. 883 (2002); Erin O'Hara & Larry Ribstein, *From Politics to Efficiency in Choice of Law*, 67 U. Chi. L. Rev. 1151 (2000).

occasion for a judge to impose the contrary preferences of economists.

State Policies: States have laws for reasons, and they are intended to achieve certain results and avoid others. It should count as a credit to a choice of law system if it can maximize, in the aggregate and over time, the extent to which state laws are permitted to achieve their ends. (In other words, I believe in maximizing state policy satisfaction rather than individual utility.)

Advocates of the traditional approach typically claim that it delivers on the first three of these criteria. The claim should not be accepted uncritically. The traditional approach does not always give uniformity, and it is not always predictable. States may differ about where a tort or contract occurs, as the result of a difference of internal law (recall the discussion of the mailbox rule). Or judges may differ in their use of escape devices.

True, those problems may arise in only a small minority of cases. But there is another, more serious problem for uniformity: some states may decide not to follow the traditional approach. (Of course, methodological diversity will undermine uniformity for any system—uniformly, we could say. But since the traditional approach claims relative superiority, a uniform undermining is still significant.)

Moreover, it is clear that uniformity, predictability, and ease of application are not enough. "Always apply Alaska law" is a choice-of-law "system" that amply satisfies those three demands, but it is a pretty bad option. It is bad because it is arbitrary, unfair, and unresponsive to state policies. The traditional approach is not nearly as bad as "Always apply Alaska law," but it has these same defects to a lesser extent.

The disdain for state policies is the major flaw of the traditional approach and the reason that its results sometimes appear arbitrary and unfair. Using territoriality as a rule of scope is not always sensible, and sometimes it runs contrary to the wishes of state legislatures. (After *Carroll*, remember, the Alabama legislature amended the statute to make plain that it abrogated the fellow servant rule for out-of-state injuries if the employment contract was formed in Alabama.) In consequence, the traditional approach ends up deciding cases under the law of a state whose legislature might well disclaim any intent to regulate the transaction.

Such might be the case in *Carroll*. We have some evidence of what the Alabama legislature thought—they clearly did want to regulate, and they amended their law to do so. We do not know

31

what the Mississippi legislature thought, and it is quite possible that they would have had no reluctance to see Mississippi law applied. But imagine the legislatures of Mississippi and Alabama sitting together and negotiating about *Carroll* and what I will call a "mirror-image" case—one in which *Carroll*'s connecting factors are switched, so that the employer and employee are Mississippi residents, negligence is committed in Mississippi, and the injury fortuitously occurs in Alabama. Suppose the legislatures are told that one of these cases must be decided under Alabama law and one under the law of Mississippi. Is there any doubt that they would divide them the opposite of the way the traditional approach does, giving *Carroll* to Alabama and its mirror image to Mississippi? (A similar thought experiment should yield similar results for *Mertz*, *Grant*, and *Levy*. *Milliken* will be analyzed in great detail at the beginning of the next chapter.)

The fact that territoriality leads to results that seem arbitrary or needlessly contrary to state policy is a large reason for the creation and use of escape devices. Escape devices can mitigate arbitrariness if used wisely, but even then they undermine uniformity and predictability. And they are not always used wisely. The traditional approach should not be condemned—it has some definite virtues, and indeed it continues to be followed in a sizable minority of states.[33] But it is worth asking whether we can do better.

---

33. See Symeon C. Symeonides, *Choice of Law in the American Courts in 2008: Twenty-second Annual Survey*, 57 Am. J. Comp. L. (2009) (reporting that ten states follow the traditional approach for torts and twelve for contracts).

Chapter 2

MODERN APPROACHES I (INTEREST ANALYSIS)

I. Introduction

Almost from its inception, the First Restatement was subjected to fierce criticism. The attacks took two main forms. First, critics argued that particular results directed by the vested rights theory were arbitrary or undesirable. (Consider the *Carroll* case.) These objections could to some degree be met, and were, by minor adjustments within the theory that gave courts greater flexibility. Those adjustments are the escape devices surveyed in the previous chapter.

The second line of attack could not be dodged so easily. Critics took issue not with applications of the theory of vested rights but with the theory itself. They claimed that it was not a consequence of the nature of law, but rather a metaphysical assumption in need of justification. Piecemeal revisions could not meet this challenge; indeed, they made things worse. As the vested rights theory grew more riddled with exceptions, its status as a necessary truth appeared increasingly implausible.

Beale's system is one of the fullest flowerings of what is typically called Classical legal thought.[1] It relied on a number of principles associated with late nineteenth-and early twentieth-century legal thinking, among them the assertion that judges discover or "declare" the common law rather than making it, the related belief in the existence of a "general" common law, and an insistence on territoriality as a limit to state authority. In the 1930s and 1940s the Supreme Court weakened or outright knocked away some of the key supports on which Beale's system rested—the declaratory theory of law (in *Great Northern Railway v. Sunburst Oil & Refining Co.*),[2] the general common law (in *Erie Railroad v. Tompkins*),[3] and rigid territoriality, so far as personal jurisdiction was concerned (in *International Shoe Co. v. Washington*.)[4] With the vested rights system no longer holding a metaphysically privileged

---

1. See generally WILLIAM WIECEK, THE LOST WORLD OF CLASSICAL LEGAL THOUGHT: LAW AND IDEOLOGY IN AMERICA 1886–1937 (1998).

2. 287 U.S. 358 (1932).
3. 304 U.S. 64 (1938).
4. 326 U.S. 310 (1945).

status, it became possible to ask whether other approaches might be more desirable.

We can describe this situation most easily by reference to the two-step model set out in the introduction. The traditional approach, shorn of its metaphysical wool, worked basically by setting a territorial scope to state laws. Given this territorial scope, state laws could not conflict, and hence traditionalist thinkers never really had to confront the task of resolving conflicts between laws. The territorial rule of scope is very powerful. But is it sensible?

As long as territorial limits to legislative jurisdiction seemed part of the nature of law, or compelled by the Due Process Clause of the Constitution (see Chapter 4), they could be assumed rather than defended. But once the limits began to appear the product of choice rather the compulsion of nature or the Constitution, their proponents needed to argue that they were a *good* choice. The standard policy justification, we have seen, is that the traditional approach is certain and predictable. But predictability always involves a trade-off with arbitrariness in certain cases, and the escape devices designed to reduce the arbitrariness carried the cost of a corresponding decrease in predictability. Moreover, there are other values, notably state policies, that a choice-of-law regime should seek to promote. The basic question, phrased within the two-step model, is this: is there a better alternative to territorial rules of scope?

This chapter considers the main modern alternatives. It starts with the possibility of obtaining guidance from state legislatures and then considers the option of allowing parties to choose governing law. Both of these solutions are appealing in some circumstances, but neither will completely resolve the broad range of choice-of-law problems. And so the chapter then goes on to consider the modern approaches that have emerged as comprehensive alternatives to the traditional approach.

II.   Statutory Solutions

After the Alabama Supreme Court's territorialist decision in the *Carroll* case, the preceding chapter noted, the Alabama legislature amended the statute at issue to provide that it applied to cases in which an injury was received outside Alabama, so long as the employment contract was formed within the state. This sequence of events may suggest an easy solution to the whole choice-of-law problem: let the legislature decide.

Indeed, it is the rare choice-of-law thinker who denies that legislative guidance would be useful.[5] But there are two problems with relying on legislatures to solve choice-of-law problems for courts. First, legislatures seldom attempt to do so, and when they *do*, their solutions are limited. Second, it isn't clear that even their best efforts could solve the choice-of-law problem

As to the first problem, legislatures tend to think exclusively about the purely domestic case. How their statutes are supposed to operate in multistate cases typically receives no consideration. That is not to say that legislatures have made no efforts in this vein. They have acted to resolve some persistent problems in the operation of their choice-of-law systems. Many, as noted in Chapter 1, have adopted borrowing statutes in reaction to the traditional approach's characterization of limitations periods as procedural. Likewise, most states have adopted statutes that validate wills executed outside the state in which they are probated if they comply with the requirements of (i) the state of execution *or* (ii) the state of domicile at the time of execution *or* (iii) the state of domicile at the time of death, a more forgiving standard than the traditional approach would dictate.[6]

Helpful though they are, these interventions resolve only a narrow set of issues. The run-of-the mill choice of law case, such as a multistate tort, is seldom addressed. In any case, the second problem remains: it is not at all clear that legislation would or could completely solve the choice-of-law problem.

Think back to *Carroll* and its aftermath. The Alabama legislature evidently felt that the outcome of the case was wrong. The Alabama statute abrogating the fellow servant rule, they thought, should apply to cases where the employment contract was formed in Alabama. By amending the statute, they made this clear. To put it in terms of the two-step model, the Alabama legislature made clear that the facts of *Carroll* fell within the scope of Alabama law.

So far, so good. But what about Mississippi? As far as I know, Mississippi did not react to the Alabama statute. Indeed, if the matter had been brought to the attention of the Mississippi legislature, they might well have decided that the *Carroll* case should be decided under Alabama law. But *Carroll* is a case where the contacts point overwhelmingly to Alabama—that is what makes it

---

5. Some interest analysts, as discussed later in this chapter, did seem to think that analysts or judges should be able to override state legislatures as to the scope of state laws. A variant of that position has now been taken up by efficiency-oriented theorists who want to use choice-of-law as an occasion to evade inefficient state laws. See the discussion of party autonomy in Part II below.

6. See Uniform Probate Code, § 2–506, on which many state laws are modeled.

such a good illustration of the occasional perversity of the traditional approach. In other situations, where the contacts split more equally, legislative specification of scope will likely not lead to the consequence that the case falls within the scope of one state's law and not the other's. There will be at least some cases (the harder ones) that fall within the scope of both states' laws.

What guidance can a statute give then? Imagine that, for whatever reason, the Mississippi legislature took territoriality really seriously, and that after the Alabama legislature amended its statute, they did react. Imagine that they codified their fellow-servant rule and provided an explicit statement of scope: "This statute applies to all cases in which an injury is received in Mississippi."

Faced with these conflicting statutes, a court is only a little better off than with no legislative guidance. It is somewhat better off, because the legislatures have answered questions about the scope of the state laws under consideration. But those answers have left the court with the question of priority: given that the case falls within the scope of both states' laws, which is to prevail?

Statutory specification of scope will not answer that question. We could, of course, imagine an attempt to address the question of priority by statute as well. The Alabama legislature could add a clause saying "In case of conflict with the law of a sister state, this statute shall be given priority in all cases in which the injured party is a resident of this state." That would be tremendously helpful. We could imagine that Mississippi likewise enacted a rule of priority, and we might well find that the cases in which both states claimed priority were few and far between.

Mississippi might, for instance, similarly decide that when its law conflicted with that of another state, it wanted to assert priority when the employer was a Mississippi domiciliary. In this situation, a substantial number of cases could fall within the scope of both states' laws—all cases in which an employee whose contract was formed in Alabama received an injury in Mississippi. But in many of those cases, the states would actually agree about whose law should get priority. Disagreement about priority would exist only when the employer was from Mississippi and the employee from Alabama.[7]

---

7. In these truly intractable conflicts, we would probably expect a court to follow the directives of forum law. A disinterested forum (for example, Louisiana) would have to resolve the conflict on some other ground, perhaps by following the foreign rule of priority closest to forum law.

But all that is in the realm of imagining. State legislatures seldom think about scope, and they never think about priority as a separate issue. (It's hard to blame them; many choice-of-law scholars do not either.) We are not likely to get statute-by-statute specifications of either.

What are the other possibilities? There does exist a body where representatives of the several states gather to address issues that affect them all—the U.S. Congress. We might hope that Congress would offer some help in regulating choice of law. Congress certainly has the power to do so; the Full Faith and Credit Clause, in Article IV of the Constitution, gives it the authority to specify the "Effect" that the laws of one state shall have in another.

But just as state legislatures tend to ignore issues of scope, Congress tends to ignore choice of law. With the notable exception of the Defense of Marriage Act and a few other family law issues (discussed in Chapter 8), Congress has not been moved to exercise its power under the Full Faith and Credit Clause. When differing state policy choices cause friction between them, Congress is likely not to prescribe how the choice-of-law analysis should come out but rather to mandate a single substantive rule of law.

For example, the question of whether car rental agencies could be held vicariously liable for injuries caused by their vehicles generated a substantial number of choice-of-law cases. As of 2005, 19 states, including New York, imposed vicarious liability; the rest did not. Since rental cars frequently cross state lines and are rented by out-of-staters, courts confronted a dizzying variety of fact patterns. The issue received federal attention, but when Congress acted in 2005, it did not create a choice-of-law rule; it wiped out vicarious liability entirely.[8] That could be called a solution to the choice-of-law problem, but it is not a choice-of-law solution, and it "works" only in the sense that decapitation cures a headache. Assuming that federalism has some value, we should not hope for resolution of all choice-law-issues through federally-imposed substantive uniformity.

If neither Congress nor the states will provide choice-of-law solutions on a statute-by-statute basis, can we at least hope for attention to broader classes of cases? The Uniform Commercial Code, adopted in some form in every state, spells out such a regime for qualifying contracts. Section 1–105 of the Code provided that, with some exceptions, the parties to a contract could choose the governing law so long as the transaction "bears a reasonable relation" to the state whose law is chosen.

---

8. See 49 U.S.C. § 30106 (2005).

In 2001, the American Law Institute drafted a new choice-of-law provision, which ultimately became UCC § 1–301. This new section, as many scholars had urged, moved towards greater party autonomy by providing that the parties to a contract could choose the law even of a state that had no relation to the transaction.[9] Consumer contracts were excepted; they still required a reasonable relation between the transaction and the chosen state and even then could not deprive the consumer of non-waivable protections of his home law.[10] Last, an otherwise-effective choice of law would be invalidated if it selected a law whose application would be "contrary to a fundamental policy" of the state or country whose law would govern in the absence of the parties' choice.[11]

But a funny thing happened on the way to the law market. States adopting the revisions to Article 1 of the UCC overwhelmingly rejected the new provision, and in 2008 the ALI approved an official reversion to the text of the old § 1–105 (still designated § 1–301). The failure of the revision offers a useful context in which to think about another potential way to avoid a choice-of-law analysis: let the parties decide.

III.   Party Autonomy

Letting parties choose the law that governs their relationship is typically an option only in those cases where they have engaged in bargaining before litigation begins, which is to say, typically only in contract cases.[12] But in that narrow area it has exerted an increasingly powerful hold on the academic mind.

At the outset, it is important to distinguish between two different kinds of law selection. Letting parties choose the law according to which their contract will be interpreted is relatively unproblematic. If they are accustomed to drafting against the backdrop of, say, Louisiana rules of interpretation, there can be no objection to allowing them to stipulate that their contract should be so interpreted even if it is executed and performed in New York. They could, after all, have simply written out all of the Louisiana rules of interpretation in the contract, and there is no reason why they should not be able to incorporate those rules by reference.

9.   See U.C.C. § 1–305(c).

10.   Id. § 1–305(e)(1), (2)

11.   Id. § 1–305(f).

12.   If the parties agree on what law should govern during litigation, the court will generally not raise a choice-of-law question sua sponte. But of course parties will usually agree only when neither side sees an advantage in arguing for a different law, which is to say they will agree only when the choice-of-law analysis would not make a difference.

Questions of validity are different.[13] If a contract is invalid under the law that governs it (because, for example, it does not satisfy that law's requirements for consideration), the parties cannot add a clause providing that the consideration is sufficient or that the contract is binding nonetheless. Letting parties choose the law that governs the validity of the contract thus involves giving them a measure of power beyond what they can exercise without such a choice. If, in the above example, they are allowed to choose a law with lesser consideration requirements, the choice-of-law clause makes an otherwise unenforceable contract binding. For just this reason, early scholarship tended to reject the whole idea of contractual choice of law. Beale protested that it allowed parties to perform "a legislative act," which should be beyond their power.[14]

Other scholars, including both Beale's critics and some supporters, argued in favor of party autonomy.[15] As a solution to the choice-of-law problem, party autonomy seems to have much to recommend it. It offers great predictability and ease of enforcement, and perfect uniformity, so long as all states agree to enforce choice-of-law clauses. It also appeals to those who favor deregulation generally, for it allows parties to escape from state laws that are "inefficient" or otherwise undesirable.

Most modern choice-of-law approaches recognize at least a moderate degree of party autonomy. Parties may choose the law that governs their contract, under these approaches, so long as the state whose law is chosen meets some required standard of connection to the contract and its application does not contravene a fundamental policy of the state whose law would otherwise apply. (This standard is a rough paraphrase of the Second Restatement, considered in more detail below. The first UCC provision, as noted above, required a "reasonable relation" but had no public policy exception.)

The requirement of some connection between the contract and the chosen law is the line that separates the moderates from the extreme proponents of party autonomy. Some people—notably the academic champions of efficiency—argue that this requirement

---

13. The Second Restatement, as we shall see, draws a similar distinction between issues that "the parties could have resolved by an explicit provision" (such as rules of interpretation) and those that they could not have resolved (such as the validity of the contract).

14. Joseph H. Beale, *What Law Governs the Validity of a Contract*, 23 Harv. L. Rev. 260, 260 (1910).

15. See, e.g., Hessel Yntema, *Contract and Conflict of Laws: "Autonomy" in Choice of Law in the United States*, 1 N.Y.L.F. 46 (1955); Friedrich Juenger, *American Conflicts Scholarship and the New Law Merchant*, 28 Vand. J. Transnat'l L. 487 (1995).

should be lifted, that parties should be able to choose any law they like. (With some significant exceptions, this was the approach embodied in the revised UCC.)

This extreme approach would certainly serve the goal of party autonomy, and perhaps that of efficiency as well. The problem is that neither contract law nor conflicts is devoted solely to autonomy and efficiency. States restrict contractual freedom to serve policies they have chosen, and one of the desirable features of a choice-of-law system is that it respect the policies of the states that have legitimate claims to regulatory authority. Allowing the parties to choose the law of one of several states with legitimate claims may thwart some of those states' policies, but the policy it promotes will also be that of a state with a legitimate claim. In the moderate regime, party autonomy operates only as a tiebreaker between such states.

But if the parties are able to choose the law of a state with no connection to the transaction, and hence no legitimate claim of regulatory authority, the link to state policy has vanished. And once state policy is out of the picture, there is no longer any connection between autonomy and the traditional understanding of choice of law as a means of allocating authority between co-equal sovereigns.[16] If the choice-of-law goal of furthering the policies of states with legitimate claims drops out and autonomy is our sole desideratum, there is no reason to limit autonomy to multistate cases. Parties to purely domestic contracts should be able to choose whatever law they want, just like parties to multistate contracts. Indeed, there is no reason why they should have to choose the law of a state at all. They should be able to choose "laws" drafted by think-tanks or business associations as well. More simply, the extreme approach suggests that they should be able to contract for whatever they want.

When the matter is put this way, it should be clear that the involvement of choice of law is purely accidental, or rather expedient. The unbridled drive for party autonomy is more about deregulation than choice of law. (Thus, I would say, the requirement of some connection to the chosen law separates the choice-of-law theorists from the deregulators.) And that, presumably, is why the revised UCC met such resistance: states did not want to nullify

16. The title of one of the articles in this movement, *From Politics to Efficiency in Choice of Law*, says it well: choice of law changes from a means of allocating authority to a tool to promote efficiency. The question is whether this is a proper use of the field, and my view is that it is not. States that favor deregulation should simply adopt that position as a matter of their substantive contract law.

their restrictions on freedom of contract for reasons unrelated to multistate coordination. Deregulation may be good or bad as a policy matter. But that question should be debated on its own merits rather than advanced under cover of choice of law.[17] As a choice-of-law doctrine, total party autonomy has essentially the same virtues as "Always apply Alaska law"—and many of the same vices. It is perfectly uniform and predictable, but it is arbitrary as far as state policies are concerned.

IV. Interest Analysis

A. Introduction: Critics of the First Restatement

The Legal Realists offered quite telling criticisms of the First Restatement. But they did not do much in the way of providing a better solution to the choice-of-law puzzle. No truly compelling alternative to the traditional approach emerged until Brainerd Currie's interest analysis, which he developed in a series of articles in the late 1950s and early 1960s. It is worth starting, however, with a consideration of what the Realists thought a choice-of-law theory should look like.

Walter Wheeler Cook, in the midst of attacks on Joseph Beale, commented that choice-of-law problems should be resolved "by the same methods actually used in deciding cases involving purely domestic torts, contracts, property, etc."[18]—that is, that they should not be thought of as presenting issues different in kind from those raised by purely domestic cases.

What would this mean in practice? Cook never elaborated, but let us try to develop the idea. We have seen that a choice-of-law problem can be reduced to two distinct questions. First, what is the scope of the laws at issue? Second, if there is a conflict between the laws, which law is to be given priority? To see if a choice-of-law problem can be resolved by the tools of ordinary legal analysis, we must ask if purely domestic cases present these questions.

Imagine that you represent a New York resident negligently injured by another New Yorker in a traffic accident in New York. The accident takes place on the on-ramp to I–95, and a state statute provides for treble damages for accidents "on an interstate

---

17. Regardless of how that debate comes out, parties may be able to opt out of state regulatory schemes through the clever use of arbitration agreements and forum-selection clauses. For a how-to guide, see THE LAW MARKET.

18. WALTER WHEELER COOK, THE LOGICAL AND LEGAL BASES OF THE CONFLICT OF LAWS 43 (1942).

highway." You want your client to benefit from this statute, but it is unclear whether he can. The court will have to determine whether the statute gives him a right to treble damages on these facts. This is, it should be evident, precisely the same question that arises at the first step of choice-of-law analysis: whether the case falls within the scope of the laws the parties invoke.

How is this question resolved in a purely domestic case? Faced with a set of facts that lie on the margin of a statute, courts will typically try to identify the purpose of the statute and ask whether its application to these facts will promote its purpose. (They may use other approaches; statutory interpretation is a complicated subject.[19] But what I describe here is probably the most common approach.) As a lawyer, you would want to convince the court that the legislature had a goal that will be served by applying the statute to your client's case. (Perhaps research reveals that federal highway funding is affected by the number of accidents on a given stretch of highway, and that accidents occurring on on-ramps are included in the calculations.)

At the first step, then, we can see that domestic cases do indeed present scope issues similar to those of choice-of-law cases, and the analysis employed in the domestic context may prove a useful guide if we want to determine the scope of state laws in multistate cases. We will pursue that question in a moment. What about the second step, that of priority? Can we imagine a conflict between laws in a purely domestic case?

We can, though the analogy will not prove quite as close. We might imagine, for instance, that the plaintiff has suffered $50,000 in damages and requests a judgment for that amount. The defendant might respond that the plaintiff was 40% at fault and that, under the comparative negligence regime prevailing (let's assume) in New York, the damages should therefore be only $30,000. Here there is definitely some sort of interaction between the two laws— the general tort right to recover and the more specialized comparative negligence defense. But it is not quite the same as a conflict between sister-state laws, for both laws here are part of a single unified body of New York tort law, and an award of $30,000 gives effect to both.

A starker conflict can be produced if we suppose that the defendant invokes a statute that actually bars recovery—perhaps he is a police officer acting in the course of his duties and the

---

19. See generally WILLIAM N. ESK-RIDGE, ET AL, LEGISLATION AND STATUTORY INTERPRETATION (2000).

legislature has immunized such people for ordinary negligence. Now there is a conflict between the tort law right of recovery and the statutory immunity. To resolve this conflict we need what I have called a **rule of priority.** In this hypothetical case, the relevant rule of priority is clear: statutes prevail over contrary common law rules. This and other similar rules create a relatively simple hierarchy of laws within a single state. Statutes prevail over common law, recent statutes over older ones, and state constitutions over state statutes. In the interaction between state and federal law, the topic of Chapter 5, we have some similarly clear rules of priority. Federal law prevails in a conflict with state law by virtue of the Supremacy Clause of Article VI, and the federal constitution prevails over federal statutes.

Resolving conflicts between the laws of sister states is more difficult. States are co-equal sovereigns within our federal system; no state can claim a privileged position with respect to the laws and policies of the others. As we shall see in Chapter 4, some provisions of Article IV of the Constitution enforce this understanding of state equality, though the extent and manner of enforcement is a matter of dispute. The problem of determining the relative priority of conflicting sister state laws is perhaps the hardest problem in choice of law, for the analogy to the purely domestic context provides no solution and the constitutional constraints have turned out to be quite weak.

What consideration of the domestic case shows, then, is that the supposedly distinctive "choice-of-law" questions of scope and priority do indeed arise in ordinary cases. As far as scope goes, the analysis employed in domestic cases may prove quite useful as a guide to multistate choice of law. With respect to priority, however, the domestic case can rely on resources not available in the multistate arena, and choice-of-law theorists will have to be more creative.

B. Brainerd Currie

Brainerd Currie's **governmental interest analysis** has been the subject of innumerable law review articles. Indeed, its status as an object of scholarly study has come to rival, if not surpass, its status as a method of resolving conflicts. There are almost as many articles attacking, defending, or reinterpreting interest analysis as there are articles applying it, and the correct understanding of interest analysis is a matter of heated dispute. In this Chapter I will take a position on several of these disputed questions, but I will also do my best to give an accurate picture of contending positions in the academic literature. At the beginning, though, I intend to let Currie speak for himself.

The best way to get a sense of Currie's approach is to read his articles, and among those articles the best place to start is *Married Women's Contracts: A Study in Conflict–of–Laws Method*. This article offers Currie's views on the case of *Milliken v. Pratt*, the unilateral contracts case from Chapter 1. There, recall, Massachusetts law prohibited married women from entering into surety contracts on behalf of their husbands (that is, it made such contracts unenforceable), while Maine law permitted them to do so. (As I said in Chapter 1, this is an offensive law which would now be unconstitutional, but try to put that from your minds.)

In the real case, Massachusetts had eliminated this contractual disability by the time of litigation. To sharpen the conflict, Currie imagines instead that the Massachusetts legislature had voted to reaffirm it. So the two laws do reflect contrary policies, each of which enjoys the current support of its respective state legislature. How should a judge think about the situation thus created?

The first thing to do, Currie suggests, is to determine the scope of these laws. He starts with Massachusetts. Does the Massachusetts legislature, he asks, intend for its contractual disability to apply to a wholly foreign contract—one executed and performed in Maine, between Maine residents? Unquestionably no, he answers. And they unquestionably did intend it to apply to the wholly domestic contract, one between two Massachusetts parties executed and performed in Massachusetts. In between are the intermediate cases, which have some connection with Maine and some with Massachusetts. We do not immediately know whether the Massachusetts law is intended to cover them, and likewise with the Maine law. The words of the statutes do not tell us; legislatures write in majestic generalities, but they do not intend universal scope. How then should we decide what the limits are?

Currie's answer is the one proposed by the Legal Realists. We decide the limits as we would in a purely domestic case: we construct the policy behind the law and ask whether application of the law to a particular set of facts would promote that policy. As he put it, "we may inquire what policy can reasonably be attributed to the legislature, and how it can best be effectuated by the courts in their handling of mixed cases." This is how we proceeded in the on-ramp accident hypothetical.

What are the policies behind these two laws? Massachusetts evidently thinks that married women require special protection. Currie describes the law as creating a "particular, favored class of debtors." One might well ask whether being prevented from making an enforceable contract puts them in a favored class or not, but leaving that issue aside, it is clear that the Massachusetts law embodies a view that some married women should not be allowed to make certain contracts. Now comes the key question: which married women?

Currie's answer is, those with whose welfare the Massachusetts legislature is concerned—Massachusetts married women, of course. The "of course" here should serve as a warning sign to the alert reader. Just as Joseph Beale covered gaps in his argument with repeated pronouncements that violation of the territorial principle were "impossible," Currie here moves quickly over an important and difficult question. In Currie's defense, he notes that for the purpose of simplicity he posits a "selfish state," interested only in the welfare of its domiciliaries. States may, he grants, choose to be more high-minded—but deciding that they have made this choice in the absence of an explicit legislative direction will turn out to be quite difficult. We will return to this point later when we consider critiques of interest analysis. For now, assume with Currie that the Massachusetts protective policy is intended to operate for the benefit of Massachusetts married women, and them alone.

How about Maine? Maine has ordinary contract law, and its overriding policy is to allow the making of enforceable contracts. As with Massachusetts, we must now ask to which cases this policy extends. Currie's answer is that it applies to all cases in which a Maine resident is a creditor. He does not support this conclusion with an "of course," but again we might ask how confident we can be, or how to move beyond the "selfish state" assumption in an actual case.

Having set out the state policies, the next step is to categorize the universe of potential cases. Currie identifies as potentially relevant four contacts between the states and a possible case: the domicile of the creditor, the domicile of the married woman, the place of contracting, and the location of the forum. From the perspective of a Massachusetts court, the possibilities are as follows (D indicates Domestic, or Massachusetts, and F Foreign, or Maine):

	Residence of Creditor	Residence of Married Woman	Place of Contracting	Forum
1	D	D	D	D
2	F	D	D	D
3	D	F	D	D
4	D	D	F	D
5	D	D	D	F

	Residence of Creditor	Residence of Married Woman	Place of Contracting	Forum
6	F	F	D	D
7	D	F	F	D
8	D	D	F	F
9	F	D	D	F
10	F	D	F	D
11	D	F	D	F
12	F	F	F	D
13	F	F	D	F
14	F	D	F	F
15	D	F	F	F
16	F	F	F	F

Cases one and sixteen can be eliminated; they are the purely domestic and purely foreign possibilities and they pose no real difficulty: everyone agrees that Massachusetts law should govern the purely domestic case and Maine law the purely foreign one. Currie's analysis is devoted to the remaining fourteen, and it aims to highlight the arbitrariness of the traditional approach and to propose a more sensible alternative.

The demonstration of arbitrariness is achieved by comparing the prescriptions of the traditional approach to the results of policy analysis. We have concluded already that the Massachusetts protective policy is at stake whenever the married woman is from Massachusetts, and the Maine policy whenever the creditor is from Maine. In Currie's terminology, each state will be **interested** when those contacts are present.

It is worth pausing a moment to clarify what Currie meant by the assertion that a state is interested in a case. It might sound as though the meaning is that the state somehow cares about the outcome of the case—that a public opinion poll would reveal strong preferences, or that the legislature would vote overwhelmingly for a particular outcome, or that some outcome would benefit the state. However, as just noted, the phrase is simply shorthand for the proposition that the policy behind a particular law would be advanced by its application to the case, and we should not go too far beyond that definition. We might say, as we would in a purely domestic case, that the facts fall within the scope of the state's law, or that the law is intended to reach the case. But we need not personify the state to talk about its interests, and as we shall see the tendency to personify has created some confusion.

Return to the table of possibilities. Looking at it from the perspective of interest analysis lets us see when the two states' policies are at stake. Massachusetts is interested in cases 2, 4, 5, 8, 9, 10, and 14. Maine is interested in cases 2, 6, 9, 10, 12, 13, and 14.

Case No.	2	3	4	5	6	7	8	9	10	11	12	13	14	15
MA Interest?	Y		Y	Y			Y	Y	Y				Y	
ME Interest?	Y				Y			Y	Y		Y	Y	Y	

There are three possibilities as far as the interests are concerned. One state may be interested, or both, or neither. Currie's analysis works by comparing the prescriptions of the traditional approach with his suggestion in each category. Start with the one-interest cases. Here, Currie suggests, the appropriate solution is clear. Applying the law of the only interested state advances that state's policy at no cost to any other state's policies.

There are six of these: cases 4, 5, 6, 8, 12, and 13. The traditional approach decides all of them by applying the law of the place of contracting, which does not relate to whether a state is interested or not. It picks Massachusetts law in cases 5, 6, and 13, and Maine law in cases 4, 8, and 12.

If we look at these outcomes with the states' interests in mind, we see that the traditional approach picks the law of the only interested state only two times out of six—not even half, worse than chance! (If you are wondering how that can be, the answer is that we did not count cases one and sixteen, which are also cases in which only one state is interested. The traditional approach gets both of those right from the interest analysis perspective, making it four for eight overall—which is what you would expect from an approach that does not consider state interests.) Currie thinks that these outcomes show the wrongheadedness of the traditional approach: it is "incredibly perverse" and "merely meddling" to apply the law of an uninterested state rather than an interested one.

Then there are the cases where both states are interested: cases 2, 9, 10, and 14. In these cases the court must make a choice between the states' policies; one must give way. Each state's law is intended to reach these facts, and they prescribe contrary results: there is a conflict.

The traditional approach again resolves these by applying the law of the place of contracting, Massachusetts law in 2 and 9, Maine law in 10 and 14. Currie views these outcomes as peculiar. Thinking in terms of interests, the resolution looks random, because there is as yet no reason to prefer one law over the other. The place of contracting, Currie believes, should not be the factor

47

resolving the conflict because it has no connection to the policies at stake.

What then should a court do? The resolution of "true conflicts" is a complicated topic, and Currie's thinking on it underwent some evolution. In his *Milliken v. Pratt* article, he suggested that the "sensible and clearly constitutional" thing to do was to apply the law of the forum. That way, the court could at least be sure it was advancing some state's policy.

One consequence of this forum-preference, compared to the traditional approach, should leap out at you: it destroys uniformity. Currie concedes this, and he admits that the uniformity of the traditional approach is considered a major selling point. His response is that uniformity exists in the traditional approach only if several conditions are met: if the possible forums (i) characterize the case the same way, (ii) apply the same conflicts rule, (iii) agree on where the contract was executed, and (iv) do not use any escape device. Whatever uniformity is left, Currie says, is not worth the price paid, which is that in a substantial number of cases (4, 6, 8, and 13) the traditional approach subverts one state's interest without advancing the other's.[20]

There remain cases 3, 7, 11, and 15. Here the immediate reaction is to say that neither state has an interest in the application of its law. Maine has no interest in enforcing its contract law against a Maine woman in favor of a Massachusetts creditor, and Massachusetts has no interest in extending the benefit of its contractual disability defense to a Maine woman against a Massachusetts creditor. Currie's analysis avoids this conclusion, arguing instead that Massachusetts also has an interest in the security of transactions, which makes it interested in enforcing the contract when the creditor is from Massachusetts and the married woman from Maine.

This is, however, an unusual kind of interest. Massachusetts, personified, might have some preference that the Massachusetts creditor recover, but it is not an interest in deciding the case under Massachusetts law, because under Massachusetts law the creditor *can't* recover—unless for some reason the Maine married woman cannot invoke the contractual disability. That is, the creditor can only recover if Massachusetts offers him its general contract law

---

20. Currie actually thought the traditional approach did even worse than this, because as discussed below he did not believe that there were any cases where neither state was interested. According to his analysis, the traditional approach needlessly thwarted a Massachusetts interest in two more cases, producing a failure rate of six out of fourteen.

(because he is a local) but withholds its more specific contract defense from an out-of-stater (because she is an out-of-stater).

That would be an example of **depecage**, the application of different states' laws to different issues within a single case. We encountered depecage briefly in the discussion of substance and procedure in Chapter 1, and we shall return to it in our consideration of pervasive problems in Chapter 3. For the purposes of introducing interest analysis, we may ignore the twist for the moment and suppose that neither state has an interest in applying its law. The traditional approach gives us Massachusetts law in cases 3 and 11, and Maine law in cases 7 and 15. These results cannot be faulted in terms of needlessly thwarting state interests, but neither can they be applauded as consistent with some reasonable policy analysis; they are essentially random as far as policies are concerned. Because he relied on the subsidiary Massachusetts interest in the security of contracts, Currie did not confront the no-interest cases in his *Milliken v. Pratt* article, but when he did consider them he advocated instead the application of forum law.

Where does all this leave us? There are six cases in which only one state is interested, four in which both are, and four in which neither is. Each category of case will come to have a name. If only one state is interested, the case is a **False Conflict.** If both are interested, it is a **True Conflict.** And if neither is interested, it is an **Unprovided-for Case.** The traditional approach resolves the cases randomly as far as state interests are concerned, with the result that in some false conflicts, one state's interest is thwarted without advancing the other's. Currie recommends instead that courts apply the law of the only interested state in false conflicts, and forum law in other cases.

The basic picture you should take from this introductory discussion is the following. The traditional approach ignores the content of laws. It uses the territorial rule of scope to eliminate conflicts by allocating authority to a single territorially-appropriate state. Interest analysis departs from the traditional approach because its preeminent focus is on the content of the contending laws.

As a result, interest analysis rejects territoriality as a rule of scope. Instead, it determines scope by examining the content of the laws at issue. If application of a particular law in a particular case is consistent with the policies and purposes of the law, then the court should assume the law was meant to apply. This is, as Currie realized, just what courts do in purely domestic cases. That is why he sometimes says that the idea of conflicts as a specialized field has created more problems than it solves.

Demonstrating those problems is the aim of the analysis we just worked through. The basic point is that, at least for contracts cases, the territorial rule is arbitrary. It has no relation to the purposes the state laws are intended to serve. Following *lex loci contractus* thus leads courts to sacrifice those purposes even when they do not need to. Currie's basic claim is that we can get better results, in some of these cases, if we pay attention to the laws' purposes. At the least, he argues, interest analysis offers a clearly superior solution to false conflicts. We will continue our discussion of interest analysis with a closer look at that claim. The other categories of cases are the subjects of subsequent sections. They will prove more difficult, but they will also allow us to delve a bit deeper into the underlying structure of Currie's theory.

C. False Conflicts

The false conflict is generally considered the crowning glory of interest analysis. In these cases, only one state is interested, and therefore applying its law advances its policies without harm to the policies of any other state. Here, at least, the proponents of interest analysis claim, Currie's approach is clearly superior to the traditional one.

As a theoretical matter, this seems right. If such cases do exist, and if they can be reliably identified, then the solution proposed by Currie (apply the law of the only interested state) seems superior to that dictated by the traditional approach, which focuses on a territorial connecting factor that has no policy significance. But does this theoretical description fit the facts of the real world? We can try to answer that question by considering two of the classic false conflict cases.

i. *Tooker v. Lopez*[21]

Two New York domiciliaries, Catherine Tooker and Marcia Lopez, attended college in Michigan. Tooker and Lopez were traveling together in Michigan, in Lopez's New York-registered car. Lopez, the driver, lost control, and both were killed. Tooker's estate sued Lopez.

At the time, Michigan had a guest statute providing that passengers in an automobile could recover against the driver only upon a showing of gross negligence or willful misconduct. New York had no such law. Should the Michigan guest statute operate to block Tooker's claim?

21.   24 N.Y.2d 569, 301 N.Y.S.2d 519, 249 N.E.2d 394 (1969).

The New York Court of Appeals reasoned that the purposes of the guest statute were to protect insurers against fraudulent and collusive claims and to protect drivers from suits by ungrateful passengers. Which insurers and drivers? Michiganders, of course. Thus, the purposes could not be furthered by applying the statute in a case where the driver and insurer were from New York. The case is a false conflict: New York has an interest in compensating its injured domiciliary, Tooker, and Michigan has no interest in blocking Tooker's recovery.

ii. *Schultz v. Boy Scouts of America, Inc.*[22]

Two New Jersey boys were molested by their scoutmaster during trips to New York, and one later committed suicide. Their parents sued the Boy Scouts for negligence in hiring and supervision. The Boy Scouts of America was a New Jersey domiciliary at the time of the molestation, but had relocated its national headquarters to Texas by the time of litigation. New Jersey grants charities immunity for negligence; New York does not.

The New York Court of Appeals again found a false conflict. New Jersey's policy was that charities should not bear the costs of their negligence, and this policy would be promoted by applying New Jersey law to protect the Boy Scouts. New York had no interest in the application of its no-immunity rule because the injured parties were not New Yorkers.

Are you persuaded that these cases present false conflicts? Start with *Tooker*. As an initial matter, it is not entirely clear what the purpose of a guest statute is—is it to protect drivers from ungrateful guests, to protect insurance companies from collusive suits, or something else altogether? The New York Court of Appeals changed its mind on this over the course of several cases, and the Michigan Supreme Court eventually struck down its guest statute on the grounds that it was not a rational means of promoting any legitimate state purpose.[23] Still, it is hard to conjure a Michigan policy that would be served by preventing a New York passenger from recovering against the New York driver of a New York car in *Tooker*.

So *Tooker* is a good example for proponents of interest analysis. *Schultz* is a harder case. (In fact, *Schultz* also featured a claim against the Franciscan Brothers, another employer of the scoutmaster, which raised even more difficult questions.) Does New York

---

22. 65 N.Y.2d 189, 491 N.Y.S.2d 90, 480 N.E.2d 679 (1985).

23. See *Manistee Bank & Trust Co. v. McGowan*, 394 Mich. 655, 232 N.W.2d 636 (1975).

really have no interest in providing recovery to out-of-staters injured within its borders?

The reason the Court of Appeals deemed *Schultz* a false conflict is that it thought the legal rule at issue was about loss allocation rather than conduct regulation. The distinction between these two types of rule crops up repeatedly in conflicts cases and the scholarly literature, and it provides a useful analytic structure with which to examine interest analysis, so it is worth spending a moment to explain.

A **conduct-regulating rule**, as the name suggests, is designed to affect conduct. It identifies some acts as wrongful and directs people not to commit them. A tort cause of action for negligence is a conduct-regulating rule, and a speed limit is an even clearer example. A **loss-allocating rule,** by contrast, does not identify conduct as permitted or wrongful. It is concerned with allocating loss regardless of whether a wrong has been committed—typically, it immunizes some actor against liability for concededly wrongful conduct or allows recovery against an actor who did not directly cause the harm. The guest statute at issue in *Tooker* and the charitable immunity in *Schultz* are both examples of loss-allocating rules; vicarious liability is another.

For purposes of interest analysis, the significant difference between a loss-allocating rule and a conduct-regulating one is the kind of connecting factor that will create an interest in the application of that rule. Generally speaking, states have an interest in applying a conduct-regulating rule when the proscribed conduct occurs within their borders or causes injury there, or (somewhat less obviously) when it injures their domiciliaries, no matter where the injury occurs. By contrast, an interest in the application of a loss-allocating rule typically exists when the rule will *benefit* a domiciliary—when, for instance, it will protect a local charity or a local driver or insurance company.[24] That is, the contacts that create interests for conduct-regulating rules are (largely) *territorial*, while the contacts that create interests for loss-allocating rules are (largely) *domiciliary*.

The classic false conflict tort case arises when there is a suit between co-domiciliaries, or domiciliaries of states with an identical loss-allocating rule, and the location of the tort is not the state of

---

24. These general rules do not always hold. In *Schultz*, for instance, the New York Court of Appeals decided that New Jersey had an interest in applying its loss-allocating charitable immunity to protect a foreign charity (the Franciscan Brothers) against a claim by New Jersey residents. This reading of the scope of charitable immunity may make sense, for reasons discussed later in this chapter.

domicile. This, of course, is the pattern of both *Tooker* and *Schultz*. (If you think back to earlier cases, it is also the pattern of *Grant v. McAuliffe*, *Carroll*, and *Levy v. Daniels U–Drive*. There is a reason for that: the cases that the traditional approach handles poorly tend to be false conflicts. Thus, false conflicts are useful to illustrate the occasional perversity of the traditional approach (*Carroll*) or the escape devices that judges use to avoid it (*Grant* and *Levy*).) In this kind of case, courts tend to conclude that the conflict is false because the state of domicile has an interest in the application of its loss-allocating rule but the locus state does not. (The locus state does have an interest in the application of its conduct-regulating rule, but no conflict exists there as both states agree a wrong has been committed.)

We can refine the analysis further by drawing one more distinction: the loss-allocating rule of the shared domicile can be one that allows recovery when locus law does not, or it can be one that bars recovery when locus law allows it. *Tooker* is an example of the first subcategory, as are *Grant*, *Carroll*, and *Levy*; *Schultz* is an example of the second.

This difference is what makes *Schultz* a harder case than *Tooker*. In cases where the shared domicile bars recovery, its loss-allocating rule seems to conflict with the conduct-regulating rule of the locus state. In *Schultz*, that is, New Jersey's policy about loss-allocation (that charities should not bear the costs of their negligence) comes into conflict with a New York policy that is in part about loss-allocation (New York believes that charities should bear the costs of their negligence, just like anyone else) but also in part about conduct-regulation (New York seeks to deter negligence even if the responsible party is a charity). In consequence, deciding that New York has no interest in *Schultz* is harder than deciding that Michigan has none in *Tooker*. In short, the set of very easy false conflicts is quite narrow: it is not all common-domicile cases where loss-allocating rules are at issue; it is only those cases in which the law of the common domicile grants recovery while the law of the locus state bars it.

The conduct-regulating/loss-allocating distinction is only one way of identifying false conflicts, but it is probably the most important. What we think about whether the distinction is real and whether courts can effectively draw it in practice will thus have significant consequences for our overall view of interest analysis.

Like most distinctions, this one will break down under enough analytical pressure. Many of the rules conventionally deemed loss-allocating are clearly intended to affect behavior. The abrogation of the fellow servant rule at issue in *Carroll* gives employers an extra incentive to ensure workplace safety. The vicarious liability at issue in *Levy* was intended to make rental agencies exercise care in deciding to whom they would rent. Even charitable immunity is intended to make charities more willing to perform good works.

These conduct-regulating elements of purportedly loss-allocating rules do undermine the theoretical purity of the distinction. But they may not detract substantially from its utility for choice-of-law purposes. The "loss-allocating" rules of Alabama in *Carroll* and Connecticut in *Levy* do aim to influence conduct, but the conduct they target (coworker negligence and the decision to rent to Mr. Sack) took place in Alabama and Connecticut. Applying the rules would actually further those states' interests in regulating conduct within their borders.[25] (This would in fact always be the case with the Connecticut law, though not the Alabama one.) Thus, the fact that a state's "loss-allocating" rule also aims to influence conduct needn't upset the analysis as long as the conduct it regulates takes place within the state.

Supposing that the distinction is in fact workable in theory, there remains the question of whether courts can actually apply it. There are some alarming indicators that they cannot. If one is seeking an example of a pure loss-allocating rule, it is hard to find a better example than the choice of strict liability rather than negligence. If negligence is measured by the Learned Hand test, so that a party is negligent only if he fails to take cost-justified precautions (those whose reduction in expected harm exceeds their cost), it can be shown that the switch from negligence to strict liability does not affect behavior. (Briefly, this is so because strict liability will still not induce a party to take non-cost-justified precautions, since it is cheaper on an expected basis simply to pay the costs of accidents.)[26]

---

25. Put another way, if we focus on the behavior of the rental agency and the employer, *Carroll* and *Levy* look like cross-border torts, with conduct in one state and injury in another. In such cases, the state where the conduct occurred does have an interest in applying a rule directed to that conduct, especially when the consequence is injury to a domiciliary. (*Carroll*, in fact, is a cross-border tort even when viewed more conventionally because the negligence that caused Carroll's injury took place in Alabama. This is one reason why the allocation of regulatory authority to Mississippi seems arbitrary.)

26. Longer explanation: imagine that there is an accident that has a 10% chance of occurring and, if it occurs, will cause $100 worth of harm. The expected cost of this accident is $10. If a precaution will reduce the chance of occurrence to 0, then under the Learned Hand test a party is negligent not to take that precaution if it costs less than $10 but not if it costs more. Under this rule, the party will take a precaution that costs (for example) $5 to avoid the expected $10 cost of the accident. He will not take a more expensive precaution (say, $15) because failing to do so is not negligence and he will not have to pay the cost of the accident if it occurs.

54

In *Padula v. Lilarn Properties*,[27] the New York Court of Appeals faced precisely this situation—the clearest possible example of a rule that has no effect on behavior—and still got the distinction wrong. The New York-domiciled employee of a New York employer was injured while working on a construction site in Massachusetts. New York, but not Massachusetts, imposed strict liability on scaffold owners in such circumstances. The Court of Appeals decided that the New York choice of strict liability was "primarily conduct-regulating" and decided the case under Massachusetts law.

Even if courts could distinguish between conduct-regulating and loss-allocating rules, determining the scope of loss-allocating rules presents another problem. We can use charitable immunity as an example. The first-cut analysis suggests that states should be interested in applying their immunities to all charities domiciled within the state. That would make sense if the policy behind the immunity was simply that charities were good organizations that shouldn't have to pay damages. But it's more likely that the policy is to encourage charitable works. In that case, the policy will be implicated when charities are engaged in activities within the state. Or will it? Perhaps it is more precise to draw the line around activities that benefit the state's domiciliaries?

It is hard to be confident about exactly what the legislature aimed to achieve, and in fact legislatures probably often have multiple and perhaps conflicting goals. Finding false conflicts in these circumstances requires a degree of willful blindness on the part of judges, since with a variety of policies behind most laws, most contacts will be enough to trigger an interest.[28]

Still, that degree of blindness is nothing compared to the blindness of the traditional approach. And if judges finding false conflicts are construing away inconvenient policies, they are least presumably doing so to less significant policies. That may not be so bad, because less significant policies are the ones that are likely to give way in a priority analysis. That is, even if it is an oversimplification to call a case such as *Schultz* a false conflict, it may well be the case that the outcome is correct, and clearly so. If New York and New Jersey had to divide up *Schultz* and its mirror image, a case in which a New York youth was molested in New Jersey by the employee of a New York charity, it is pretty clear that New York

---

Now switch to strict liability. The party will still take the $5 precaution; nothing has changed there. Less obviously, he will still *not* take the $15 precaution, because the expected cost of the accident is less than that, so on an ex ante basis

it is cheaper to pay the cost of the accident if it happens.

27. 84 N.Y.2d 519, 620 N.Y.S.2d 310, 644 N.E.2d 1001 (1994).

28. See Joseph Singer, *Real Conflicts*, 69 B.U. L. Rev. 1 (1989).

would want to give its law priority in the mirror-image case, and not in *Schultz*, while New Jersey would want to claim priority in *Schultz* and not the mirror-image.

The category of false conflicts is not one that interest analysis handles perfectly. But no approach handles any category of cases perfectly. It does seem that interest analysis reaches more sensible results in most of the false conflict cases than the rigid traditional approach, and it reaches them with more candor and explanation than the traditional approach supplemented by escape devices. In any event, false conflicts are the category that shows interest analysis at its best. The other categories, we shall see, generate substantially greater difficulties.

D. The Unprovided–For Case

Currie's approach is at its most persuasive in dealing with false conflicts. That true conflicts—cases in which more than one state is interested—are difficult should surprise no one. What is likely more surprising is that unprovided-for cases, in which no state is interested, were taken to pose an even greater challenge for the theory. Professor Aaron Twerski pronounced that the existence of unprovided-for cases opened interest analysis to "the strongest ridicule."[29] Currie himself seemed at least mildly troubled, admitting that "[t]raditionalists may stand aghast at this anomaly...."[30]

Why was the unprovided-for case taken as an indicator of problems with interest analysis? If you think of a choice-of-law system as akin to a machine into which we feed data about a case and which then spits out the governing law, the reaction is understandable. With the unprovided-for case, the machine receives the data and then just sits there whirring. It does not give an answer, at least not one of the form we were expecting. The unprovided-for case, on this description, looks much like renvoi did within the traditional approach: a set of circumstances in which the system breaks down.

When we discuss renvoi in the next chapter, I will suggest that the similarity is no coincidence: renvoi is indeed a special instance of the unprovided-for case. What is important now is to understand the unprovided-for case from the perspective of interest analysis. As an example, we can use the facts of *Erwin v. Thomas*.[31]

---

29. Aaron Twerski, Neumeier v. Kuehner: *Where are the Emperor's Clothes?*, 1 Hofstra L. Rev. 104, 107 (1973).

30. CURRIE, SELECTED ESSAYS ON THE CONFLICT OF LAWS 152 (1963).

31. 264 Or. 454, 506 P.2d 494 (1973).

Erwin was a Washington resident. He was injured, in Washington, by Thomas, an Oregon resident. Erwin's wife sued Thomas for loss of consortium. This cause of action existed under Oregon law, but not under Washington law.

It is relatively easy to reach the conclusion that this case is unprovided-for, from Currie's perspective. Oregon has a policy of compensating wives for injuries to their husbands. Which wives? Oregonians, of course, and possibly also the wives of men injured in Oregon, to avoid discriminating against out-of-staters with respect to injuries suffered within the state. (We will consider the issue of discrimination in more detail later, in Chapter 4.) But Mrs. Erwin fits in neither category, so Oregon's policy will not be advanced by allowing recovery under Oregon law.

Washington is not interested either. It does not have a policy of compensating wives whose husbands are injured, so that policy could not be advanced: Mrs. Erwin does not have a cause of action under Washington law. It is also probably the case that it does not have a policy of protecting people who injure husbands, so there is no policy that can be advanced by protecting Thomas: he cannot claim a defense under Washington law.

What is harder is figuring out what to do with the case once we have decided that neither state is interested. Mrs. Erwin brought her suit in Oregon, and after some hemming and hawing the court decided that it should do "what comes naturally" and apply Oregon law. In this it followed Currie, who suggested that the forum should apply its own law "simply on the ground that that is the more convenient disposition...."[32]

Traditionalists should find this outcome troubling. By making the governing law dependent on the forum, it destroys uniformity and predictability, two of the traditionalists' chief concerns. But interest analysts should be troubled too, for there is something fundamentally flawed in the idea of applying the law of an uninterested state.

Interest analysis, recall, uses the concept of a state interest to set the scope of a state's law, in the same way that the traditional approach used territoriality. If an event occurred outside the geographic boundaries of a state, traditionalists believed, that state's law simply had nothing to say on the subject: it created no rights or liabilities. So too with interest analysis. If a state is uninterested, its law does not apply to the case. It creates no rights or liabilities. To say that, having determined that neither state is interested, we

---

32. Currie, Selected Essays at 184.

will simply apply forum law, then, is tantamount to saying that we will apply forum law even though we have just determined that it does not apply.

Why did Currie not see this? It is impossible to be sure, but my guess is that he was misled by the notion that a court must apply some state's law in order to decide a case. On its face this seems sensible—a case must be decided under some law. But it conceals a slippage between two different senses of the word "apply" and two different visions of choice of law. This confusion pervades both the caselaw and the academic commentary, and so it is worth devoting a bit of time to an attempt to straighten things out.

The problem arises because we can mean two very different things when we talk about a law "applying." We can mean that *the law gives rights or imposes obligations*, as in the assertion "Title VII applies to all businesses with fifteen or more employees." This is the ordinary usage. But we can also mean that *the case will be decided under a particular law, regardless of whether it creates rights or obligations*, as in the assertion "In *Erwin*, the court decided to apply Oregon law."

What happens in *Erwin* is an unnoticed move from the second of these senses to the first. Neither state is interested, the court reasons, but the case must be decided under some law, and Oregon law is the natural choice. Here the court is using the second sense, and thus far there is nothing objectionable. But then the court decides that because it is going to "apply" Oregon law in this second sense, Oregon law must "apply" in the first sense. That is why it concluded that Mrs. Erwin could invoke all the rights granted by Oregon law, including the cause of action for loss of consortium. Now the court has moved to the first sense—it has gone from "I will apply Oregon law" to "Oregon law applies"—and it has done so without any justification. In fact, it has contradicted itself, because the earlier decision that Oregon is not interested means that its law does not "apply" in the first sense: it does not give Mrs. Erwin a cause of action.

A slightly different way of putting this is the following. The *Erwin* court seems to think that choice-of-law analysis is akin to picking a particular set of glasses. Your choice-of-law methodology selects the appropriate pair, you put them on, and thereafter you view the case through their lenses. You put on Oregon glasses, for instance, and after that you treat the case as though it were a purely domestic Oregon case—and therefore Mrs. Erwin can avail herself of all the rights created by Oregon law.

This may be a way of doing choice of law, but it is not interest analysis, properly understood.[33] That becomes clear if we think in terms of the two-step model and the analogy to ordinary cases. The concept of a state interest tells us whether a case falls within the scope of a state's law. If it falls outside, that law does not attach legal consequences. It creates neither causes of action nor defenses. When we determine that a state is not interested, we determine that its law does not reach the case, just as if we were considering the scope of Title VII and we realized that the employer had only ten employees.

It would be obvious nonsense to say that although Title VII does not apply, the case must be decided under some law, and Title VII is convenient. It makes no more sense to say that although neither state is interested, we will nonetheless decide the case under one of their laws as though it were a purely domestic case.

I believe this confusion comes from careless use of the word "applies," and I try to avoid it for that reason, or at least to be conscious about in which sense I am using it. Once the confusion is dispelled, the unprovided-for case does not pose a challenge for interest analysis. It is very easy. In an unprovided-for case, we reach the conclusion that no state's law creates rights or obligations. And what that means is simple: the plaintiff has failed to state a claim and the case should be dismissed.

This view has not caught on in the courts. Those states that have adopted interest analysis tend to follow Currie on the correct disposition of unprovided-for cases: they apply forum law, just as in *Erwin*. The view does have a significant place in the academic literature, however, most notably in Larry Kramer's pathbreaking article *The Myth of the Unprovided-for Case*.[34] As we shall see, the proper understanding of interest analysis is still a topic of debate in academic circles, but my view is that Kramer is fundamentally correct, and my own work employs a similar perspective.

E. True Conflicts

The appeal of interest analysis stems from the fact that its rule of scope seems more sensible. If we ask what state legislatures would want in the multistate context, it is more plausible to

---

33. Indeed, it is rather more like the traditional approach; it works by choosing jurisdictions, not laws. Currie criticized traditionalists for applying states' laws when doing so did not advance their underlying policies, but this is exactly what his solution to the unprovid- ed-for case does. For the earliest statement of this insight, see Larry Kramer, *The Myth of the Unprovided-for Case*, 75 Va. L. Rev. 1045 (1989).

34. 75 Va. L. Rev. 1045 (1989).

suppose that they would want their laws applied when doing so furthered the underlying policies, than to suppose that they would want rigid territorialism. This is most obvious in the false conflict case, where the traditional approach on occasion frustrates one state's interest without advancing another's.

In the unprovided-for case, Currie's version of interest analysis is not obviously superior to the traditional approach. It is just as arbitrary to apply forum law as it is to pick law according to a territorial connecting factor that has no policy significance. Indeed, Currie's solution is arguably worse because it sacrifices uniformity for no identifiable gain. Here interest analysis could be improved by staying closer to the domestic analogue and realizing that when no state is interested, the plaintiff cannot state a claim.

What about the remaining possibility, when more than one state is interested? Here we have a conflict between state laws and we need a way to decide which one shall prevail; we need what I call a **rule of priority.** Currie did not claim that interest analysis offered one. True conflicts, he believed, were fundamentally insoluble, at least by courts. "[A]ssessment of the respective values of the competing legitimate interests of two sovereign states in order to determine which is to prevail, is a political function of a very high order ... that should not be committed to courts in a democracy." What then should judges do when faced with a true conflict? In his early work, the answer he offered was essentially the same as that suggested for the unprovided-for case: apply forum law, since there is no reason to prefer any other.

While courts do tend to follow Currie's advice for unprovided-for cases, the forum-favoring rule of priority has not caught on as a resolution to true conflicts.[35] That is not surprising. Like his answer for the unprovided-for case, it sacrifices uniformity for no gain. Worse, it is unabashedly parochial in just the way that would be expected to exacerbate interstate tensions.

In fact, Currie himself later came up with an alternative to pure forum-preference. Others followed suit. In the remainder of this section, we will consider several different suggestions for rules of priority within interest analysis—different ways, that is, to resolve true conflicts. These approaches can be grouped into two

---

35. Michigan has a preference for forum law, but no other state explicitly admits to it. Whether judges tend to favor forum law even when applying facially neutral approaches is another question. Patrick Borchers has attempted to answer it through an empirical analysis of case outcomes. See Patrick J. Borchers, *The Choice-of-Law Revolution: An Empirical Study*, 49 Wash. & Lee L. Rev. 357 (1992). His results suggest that interest analysis does not lead to greater preference for forum law than any other modern approach.

categories, because the true conflict presents courts with two basic options. First, they can renounce the attempt to "solve" it by finding the "right" answer. Rather than trying to decide which state's interest should prevail, courts taking this approach will try to promote systemic values such as uniformity and predictability. Second, courts can take up the challenge of finding the right answer and try to figure out which state's law should be given priority. We will see examples of each of these approaches.

i. Moderate and Restrained Interpretation

Currie's initial approach to true conflicts was to deny the ability of courts to resolve them. Congress might offer solutions, he suggested, but in the meantime courts could do nothing but apply forum law.[36] Later, however, he suggested that a court discovering a true conflict could in fact do something: it could think twice about whether the conflict was real. It could ask, that is, whether "a more moderate and restrained interpretation" of the forum's policy and "the circumstances in which it must be applied to effectuate the forum's legitimate purpose" might eliminate the conflict.[37]

I have already suggested that *Schultz* looks a bit like an example of this approach. New York certainly could have asserted an interest in the application of its law. Indeed, when we discuss the constitutional limits on choice of law we will see that there may well be constitutional difficulties with a system under which New York withholds from out-of-state visitors the rights it grants to locals. To say that New York is not interested in *Schultz* is probably best understood as shorthand for the assertion that New York would almost certainly be willing to subordinate its interest to that of New Jersey.[38]

Currie had a different exemplar, *Bernkrant v. Fowler*.[39] The Bernkrants, Nevada residents, owed John Granrud $24,000 on the purchase of a Nevada apartment building. At a meeting in Las Vegas, apparently inspired by the location, he orally offered them what he called "a sporting proposition" whereby in exchange for partial payment and refinancing, he would add a provision to his will forgiving any debt remaining at the time of his death. The Bernkrants accepted. Coincidentally, one hopes, Granrud died a year and a half later. He had not gotten around to making the

---

36. See CURRIE, SELECTED ESSAYS at 182.

37. Currie, The Disinterested Third State, 28 L. & Contemp. Probs. 754, 757 (1963).

38. This is especially true if, as I will argue, the Constitution allows a state to demand priority for its law in only one of a pair of mirror-image cases

39. 55 Cal.2d 588, 12 Cal.Rptr. 266, 360 P.2d 906 (1961).

promised change to his will. At the time of his death he was a California domiciliary, and the Bernkrants sued his estate in California.

Under California's statute of frauds, a promise to make a provision by will, or a promise not to be performed within the lifetime of the promissory, must be in writing. Nevada law, the California Supreme Court believed, would hold the contract enforceable. The case thus seems to present a true conflict: Nevada law favors the Nevada domiciliaries, and California law favors the California estate.

But would it be reasonable for California to assert an interest on these facts? Probably not, the court reasoned. At the time the contract was executed, the parties would reasonably have assumed that it was governed by Nevada law. (Granrud's domicile at the time of contracting was unknown. The court's argument is stronger if he was a Nevada domiciliary then, but the court noted that even if he were domiciled in California, the result would be the same.) To anticipate that California's statute of frauds would end up governing the contract, they would have had to have known that Granrud would be a California resident at the time of his death. That, of course, was highly unlikely, and the court reasoned that unpredictable application of the California statute of frauds would not serve its purpose. Hence California was not interested and the case presented a false conflict.

Bernkrant is likely one of the best examples for the moderate and restrained interpretation (Currie termed it "brilliant"), for on reflection it does indeed seem that applying the statute of frauds will not serve its purpose. Presumably, the statute reflects a legislative view that enforcing certain kinds of contracts without their expression in writing will lead to excessive error in upholding "contracts" that were not in fact formed. But applying the writing requirement to parties who were not aware of its existence will obviously produce tremendous error in the other direction, and a legislature might well not want to do so—as long as the ignorance was reasonable and involved a class of cases that could readily be segregated, so that knowledge would not become an issue in every case.[40]

40. For analogy, one might look to the Supreme Court's retroactivity jurisprudence, where the Court has frequently observed that applying a new rule to parties who were not on notice of it will not promote the rule's purpose. *Miranda* is a striking example: applying its warning requirement to statements made before the case was decided will exclude many perfectly voluntary confessions, and for essentially that reason the Court declined to do so.

If those conditions were not met, the legislature might well have wanted the rule applied even in some cases in which application would not serve its purpose, just in order to simplify things. Many rules are overbroad but are applied nonetheless. The requirement of the *Miranda* warning, for instance, can exclude voluntary confessions. Even if the legislature would opt for uniform enforcement, however, we could understand "moderate and restrained interpretation" as a rule that if two laws conflict and one applies only because it is deliberately overbroad (i.e., it has a prophylactic scope and the particular case is not one in which the law's purpose would be served), then that overbroad law should yield. At this point, though, we begin to edge towards a balancing of interests.

In other cases, like *Schultz*, what is going on seems even more like balancing in disguise. If the use of moderate and restrained interpretation is limited to cases in which an apparent interest can be made to vanish completely, its applicability will likely be quite limited. But taking a shortcut around balancing may be relatively unobjectionable, and so long as the disguise is limited to truly easy cases, not much turns on the description. Still, if, like Currie, you believe that evaluation of the magnitude of an interest is categorically beyond the competence of courts, avoiding balancing by construing an interest to nothingness is a bit of a dodge. In terms of the two approaches to true conflicts mentioned above, it is an attempt to find a right answer while denying that one is doing anything of the sort.

ii. Territorial Tiebreakers

The next solution is admittedly arbitrary in terms of the question of which state's law should prevail, but it serves systemic values of uniformity and ease of application. It is the use of a territorial connecting factor as a tiebreaker. New York's *Neumeier* rules do a bit more than resolve true conflicts, but in essence they produce interest analysis with a territorial tiebreaker.

The *Neumeier* rules have their origin in *Neumeier v. Kuehner*,[41] a guest statute case featuring a New York driver and an Ontario passenger killed in an accident in Ontario. Ontario had a guest statute; New York did not. The New York Court of Appeals took the opportunity to endorse three rules first set out in Chief Judge Fuld's concurring opinion in *Tooker v. Lopez*. (The rules have been restated in several other cases, notably *Cooney v. Osgood Machinery*.)[42]

---

41. 31 N.Y.2d 121, 335 N.Y.S.2d 64, 286 N.E.2d 454 (1972).

42. 81 N.Y.2d 66, 612 N.E.2d 277, 595 N.Y.S.2d 919 (1993).

The rules apply to loss-allocating issues in tort cases, and they divide cases into categories primarily according to the domicile of the parties. The first rule applies to cases in which the parties share a domicile[43] and provides that in such cases, the law of the common domicile should govern. We have seen examples of such cases, including *Carroll, Grant v. McAuliffe, Levy v. Daniels*, and of course *Tooker*.

The second rule applies to cases in which the parties are domiciled in different states, each party is favored by the law of his home state, and the tort occurs in one party's home state. In these cases, the second rule directs courts to apply the law of the state where the tort occurred.

Neumeier's third rule covers other split-domicile cases. It provides that the governing law will usually be the law of the place of the accident unless displacing it will "advance the relevant substantive law purposes without impairing the smooth working of the multistate system or producing great uncertainty for litigants."[44]

We can see that the *Neumeier* rules work like interest analysis with a territorial tiebreaker if we translate the *Neumeier* categories into their interest-analysis equivalents. Cases that fall under the first rule (common domicile) will generally be false conflicts. Sometimes they will be easier false conflicts, like *Tooker*, and sometimes harder ones, like *Schultz*, but from the perspective of interest analysis, they are all false conflicts, and *Neumeier*'s first rule handles them as interest analysis prescribes. It applies the law of the shared domicile, which will be the only interested state.

The second rule deals with true conflicts in which the accident occurs in one party's home state. It uses the location of the accident as a tiebreaker to pick between the two interested states. A diehard proponent of interest analysis might object to the use of a territorial connecting factor on the grounds that the location of the accident is "mere fortuity" (a phrase frequently used to denigrate the significance of a disfavored contact). But having essentially thrown up its hands at true conflicts, interest analysis is not in a position to cast stones. And there is something to be said for the territorial tiebreaker. Both parties have chosen to associate them-

---

43. What if the parties are from different states but those states have the same loss-allocating rule? Probably this kind of case also falls under the first *Neumeier* rule, though it is not mentioned in most formulations. Otherwise the third rule applies, but a case in which the parties' separate domiciles share a loss-allocating rule is the clear-est case for the application of the third rule's exception, so the outcome should be application of the shared domiciliary law in any case. See *Dargahi v. Hymas*, 2007 WL 2274861 (S.D.N.Y. 2007) (discussing cases applying the first *Neumeier* rule to such situations).

44. *Neumeier*, 31 N.Y.2d at 128.

selves with the place of the accident; it is a neutral choice that will not exacerbate interstate tensions in the way that a rule of forum-preference might; and, unlike forum preference, it preserves uniformity.[45]

What counts as an "other" split-domicile case that would call the third rule into play? The most obvious example is probably an unprovided-for case. As with true conflicts, the third rule's prescription amounts to the substitution of a territorial tiebreaker for interest analysis's recommendation of forum preference, and the same arguments can be mustered in its favor.

The third rule will also govern true conflicts in which the accident takes place in a third state, so that a territorial tiebreaker would not select one of the domiciliary states. For these cases, *Neumeier*'s third rule suggests using territoriality anyway. This is not as arbitrary as it might seem at first blush, since the selected law will usually be identical or at least substantially similar to the law of one of the domiciliary states. (We are usually dealing with recovery vs. no-recovery rules.) Moreover, the third rule qualifies its prescription with the somewhat opaque caveat that the territorial suggestion may be displaced in appropriate circumstances.

This exception tends to be invoked in cases that feature true conflicts with injury in neither party's home state. Like any escape device, it allows courts to avoid arbitrary results but reintroduces unpredictability. In practice, self-confident judges seem to take it as an invitation to balance interests when the territorial solution would result in application of the law of an uninterested state.[46]

A territorial tiebreaker does not provide the "right" answer to a true conflict. But it does have some points in its favor, especially when compared to a rule of forum-preference: it is uniform, non-parochial, and at least modestly justifiable in terms of the parties' choice to associate themselves with a particular state. It might, in fact, be the best we can do if true conflicts are truly insoluble. But is there a way to find the right answer? The approaches examined in the following sections attempt to do so.

---

45. See *Cooney v. Osgood Machinery Inc.*, 81 N.Y.2d 66, 595 N.Y.S.2d 919, 612 N.E.2d 277 (1993) (making these points).

46. See, e.g., *Gilbert v. Seton Hall University*, 332 F.3d 105 (2d Cir. 2003) (applying exception to case involving charitable immunity in suit by Connecticut-domiciled student against New Jersey university for injury suffered in New York rugby match).

iii. Balancing and Comparative Impairment

Our first task, of course, is to figure out what a right answer would look like. From the perspective of interest analysis, this is actually a relatively easy question. The problem with the traditional approach, interest analysis argues, is that it disregards state policies and thwarts them needlessly. It performs poorly in terms of maximizing the aggregate satisfaction of state policies over the long run of cases. A good system of choice of law is one that takes state policies into account. And the ideal resolution of true conflicts is presumably the one that maximizes state policy satisfaction.

The obvious way to do this, in any individual case, would be to grant priority to the law reflecting the "greater" interest or the "more significant" policy. But two questions immediately present themselves. What does it even mean for an interest to be greater or a policy more significant? And supposing we can figure that out, can a court really pick the winner in a given case?

The first question is in fact a little tricky. If we understand interest analysis as a means for promoting policies chosen by the states (this is a contested characterization, as we will see) then it should be clear that a court cannot simply decide which policy is more important in some abstract or objective sense. It would have to attempt to figure out which policy is subjectively more deeply-held.

Intersubjective comparisons raise knotty philosophical problems. (Do I feel pain more intensely than you, or am I just more of a crybaby?) But given that states are co-equal sovereigns within our constitutional system, there are thought-experiments that can get us at least in the neighborhood of what we are looking for. We might imagine, for instance, a game in which each state starts with 100 points. States allocate these points to different laws in order to indicate their relative importance, and in a true conflict the court should give priority to the policy that has more points behind it.

That is balancing, which Currie argued courts should not do in a democracy and were not equipped for in any event. It was, he wrote "a political function of a very high order" requiring information that courts could not obtain from "even a very ponderous Brandeis brief."[47] But courts do many things for which they are imperfectly equipped, and many things that are at least superficially problematic in a democracy. (Leaving judicial review aside, it is "antidemocratic" to have them interpret statutes.) It is not clear why balancing state interests is uniquely objectionable, and letting courts make the effort seems likely to do better than forum-preference in terms of policy satisfaction. In fact, balancing is

---

47. CURRIE, SELECTED ESSAYS at 182.

frequently invoked in the caselaw, where many judges apply the law of the state with the "greater interest," even when they are supposed to do something else.[48] Among academics it is considered a little naïve, because it turns out that there is a better way to maximize state policy satisfaction—at least in theory.

The better way is comparative impairment, created by Professor William Baxter.[49] Baxter's insight is that maximizing policy satisfaction requires courts to consider not just how important a state's interest is, but how it will be affected if the state's law is not used to decide the case. For illustrative purposes, suppose that we have a true conflict between the laws of States A and B. Deciding the case under State A law will give A 10 units of policy satisfaction; deciding it under B law will give B 7 units. (The precise quantification is of course unrealistic, but it is convenient to illustrate the idea behind comparative impairment.)

Simple balancing would tell a court to give priority to A law. Baxter's point is that we also need to ask what the payoff to the states is when their law is *not* given priority. A will not get the full ten units of policy satisfaction if B law gets priority, but will its payoff be reduced to zero? Probably not; probably its policy will not be completely thwarted. Let us suppose the A payoff is reduced to 6. We perform (somehow) the same analysis for B and find that giving priority to A law knocks B's payoff down to 2. The following diagram illustrates the analysis.

	A payoff	B payoff	Total payoff
Apply A Law	10	2	12
Apply B Law	6	7	13

Now we can see that balancing would in fact have led us astray. The *total* payoff from giving priority to A law is 10 + 2 = 12, while the payoff from giving priority to B law is 7 + 6 = 13. Giving priority to B law will actually maximize aggregate policy satisfaction. Courts should not pick the more important policy; they should pick the one that would be more impaired if it were not followed.

Baxter's insight is actually a fairly good one. It is arithmetically sound, as the demonstration above shows, but more important, it

48. See, e.g., *Padula v. Lilarn Properties Corp.*, 84 N.Y.2d 519, 521, 620 N.Y.S.2d 310, 644 N.E.2d 1001 (1994) ("New York utilizes interest analysis to determine which of two competing jurisdictions has the greater interest in having its law applied").

49. See William Baxter, *Choice of Law and the Federal System*, 16 Stan. L.Rev. 1 (1963).

captures something about actual cases. Recall *Schultz*, in which the New York court was willing to construe away New York's interest in holding a New Jersey charity liable for negligent hiring that caused injury to a New Jersey domiciliary in New York. Saying that New York has no interest probably overstates the matter, but it seems relatively clear that if we have to divide *Schultz* and its mirror-image between the two interested states, *Schultz* should go to New Jersey and the mirror-image to New York.

The reason for this is not that the New York policy at stake in *Schultz* is objectively unimportant or subjectively not deeply-held. It is that both parties are out-of-staters and giving priority to New Jersey law leads not to a statement that the conduct New York condemns is acceptable but merely to a conclusion that the loss should lie where it fell. New York's policy is impaired in only a relatively minor way, and that is perhaps the best explanation for *Schultz*.

The operation of the public policy escape device, described in Chapter 1, provides a useful parallel. What courts seem to find important, we saw there, is not simply how offensive the foreign law is, but rather to what extent recognizing it would require the forum to embrace the underlying policy—to what extent the forum's contrary policy would be impaired. In resolving true conflicts, likewise, there is a place for asking not just how important the states' policies are, but how thoroughly they are compromised by giving priority to another state's law.

One could, of course, attempt to capture this insight within the framework of balancing. One would ask, then, not simply how important or deeply-held a state policy was, but how directly it was at stake in a particular case, measuring this by the difference in payoffs between the use of that state's law and another's. One could even describe Currie's moderate and restrained interpretation as a limiting case of this analysis: sometimes, Currie suggested, further reflection will show that the policy is not at stake at all.

However it is described, the evaluation will probably be the same. Comparative impairment is a nice idea, and if it could be done easily and consistently, it would have much to recommend it. Unfortunately, arithmetical demonstrations notwithstanding, it seems quite unlikely that this is possible. In practice, judges tend to ignore or misunderstand even quite basic features of most choice-of-law approaches, and the difference between comparative impairment and balancing is likely to escape them entirely.

The result of adopting comparative impairment would most likely be an ad hoc and quite standardless weighing of interests.

This might do better than either forum preference or territorial tiebreaking in terms of maximizing state policy satisfaction, but it would be quite unpredictable and probably not uniform.[50] Still, policy maximization seems to be aiming at the right target. The question it raises is whether we can aim at that target in a more rule-bound way, without leaving so much to judicial discretion. The next two sections consider attempts to do just that.

iv. Principles of Preference

Professor David Cavers took a slightly different perspective. Baxter derived his approach by imagining what would happen if states were able to bargain over the allocation of authority in true conflicts. Cavers instead asked what would happen if states were compelled to come up with rules for resolving true conflicts without knowing what their policies were—if negotiations were conducted behind what the philosopher John Rawls called "the veil of ignorance."[51] Cavers suggested that this negotiation might lead to something like what he called "principles of preference" to govern true conflicts.[52]

In *The Choice of Law Process*, Cavers offered seven of these principles. His formulations are complicated and it is unlikely that you will ever be called upon to state or apply them. A few samples give the general flavor. A standard tort true conflict arises when a defendant whose home state has a less protective law injures a plaintiff whose home state has a more protective law. Cavers' first principle provides that if the law of the place of injury is more protective than the law of the place where the defendant resides or acted, the law of the place of injury should prevail, "at least where the person injured was not so related to the person causing the injury that the question should be relegated to the law governing their relationship."[53] If the conduct and injury take place in a state with less protective laws, Cavers' second principle provides that the

---

50. Surveys of decisions under comparative impairment tend to support this dim prognosis. See, e.g., Kay, *The Use of Comparative Impairment to Resolve True Conflicts: An Evaluation of the California Experience*, 68 Cal. L. Rev. 577 (1980); Kanowitz, *Comparative Impairment and Better Law: Grand Illusions in the Conflict of Laws*, 30 Hastings L.J. 255 (1978).

51. DAVID CAVERS, THE CHOICE OF LAW PROCESS 130–131 (1965). It is not entirely clear as a theoretical matter that hypothetical veil-of-ignorance bargaining should produce different results than hypothetical fully-informed bargaining, and the differences between Cavers and Baxter may in fact have more to do with their intuitions than their methodologies.

52. Id. at 121–22.

53. Id. at 139.

law of the place of injury should again prevail, with the same caveat about the parties' relationship.[54]

For contracts, Cavers generally favored party autonomy but would apply protective restrictions on capacity to contract for transactions involving a state's domiciliary that were "centered there."[55] Boiled down, the principles of preference amount to a qualified endorsement of territoriality based largely on intuitions about what seems fair—and hence what states would agree to when negotiating behind the veil of ignorance. They will be persuasive to the extent that the reader shares Cavers' intuitions about fairness.[56]

v. Kramer's Canons

Professor Larry Kramer suggests that aggregate policy satisfaction can be advanced through the application of "policy-selecting rules" that resolve true conflicts by appeal to generally shared policies.[57] For instance, states generally share the policy that substantive law takes priority over procedure. If a true conflict features a clash between the substantive law of one state and the procedural law of another, it will likely maximize state policy satisfaction in the long run to give priority to substantive law.

To some extent, then, Kramer suggests resolving multistate conflicts in the same way as domestic ones, by looking at the hierarchy of laws constructed in purely domestic cases. That is where the substance over procedure rule comes from. Continuing on in the same vein could lead to the conclusion that statutes should prevail over common law in true conflicts, constitutions over statutes, and perhaps even recent statutes over older ones. These are not all sensible rules, but the idea that information about multistate priority can be gleaned from the domestic case is a useful insight. Indeed, some version of it is at work in the principle that a law with current vitality should prevail over an obsolete one, a principle Kramer endorses.[58]

---

54. Id. at 146.

55. Id. at 181.

56. This is not meant as a dismissal. Cavers derived his principles after years of discussion with his students, which suggests that there is indeed some consistency among intuitions as an empirical matter. Moreover, the extent to which one state's policy is impaired by not applying its law also seems to be determined on a more or less intuitive basis under Baxter's approach—certainly there is no obvious objective method of quantifying impairment.

57. See Larry Kramer, *Rethinking Choice of Law*, 90 Colum. L. Rev. 277, 311–344 (1990).

58. See, e.g., *Offshore Rental Co. v. Continental Oil Co.*, 22 Cal.3d 157, 148 Cal.Rptr. 867, 583 P.2d 721 (1978), where the California Supreme Court, while performing comparative impairment, decided to favor a "prevalent and progressive" Louisiana law rather than

When finding a shared rule of priority is not possible, Kramer suggests that courts should look for a shared substantive policy that can be advanced. Even if courts cannot advance the ball by trying to choose between the two policies directly at stake (thus ruling out balancing and comparative impairment), they can still enhance policy satisfaction in the long run by trying to advance these shared third policies. Giving priority to a law actually relied on by the parties, for instance, will advance the shared policy of fairness.

vi. Others

The preceding sections cover most of the major suggestions for resolving true conflicts. There are, however, some others, most notably "better law" and the Second Restatement, the approaches we will consider in the next chapter. They get a separate discussion because they were designed not as rules of priority to be plugged into interest analysis in case of true conflicts but as complete approaches in their own right. It is worth remembering, however, that any self-sufficient system can also be used as a plug-in for true conflicts. Indeed, such use of the Second Restatement is not un-heard-of. Pennsylvania and New Jersey both follow interest analysis and resort to the Second Restatement to resolve true conflicts, although New Jersey may be shifting to a pure Second Restatement analysis.[59]

F. Evaluation

So what can we conclude about interest analysis? Currie's writings have been enormously influential among academics, but less so among judges. Interest analysis is now expressly used in only two jurisdictions, California and the District of Columbia.[60] But its lack of popularity among judges does not seem to be a consequence of its indeterminacy or manipulability; the most popular approach (the Second Restatement, considered below) is even worse on those grounds. Moreover, focusing on the number of states that expressly endorse interest analysis certainly understates Currie's influence, for the Second Restatement and other modern approaches adopted many of the insights of interest analysis and in the hands of some judges can operate almost indistinguishably.

---

an "unusual and outmoded" California one.

59. See *Lacey v. Cessna Aircraft Co.,* 932 F.2d 170, 187 (3d Cir.1991) (explaining Pennsylvania's "hybrid" approach); *P.V. ex rel. T.V. v. Camp Jaycee,* 197 N.J. 132, 962 A.2d 453 (2008) (apparent-

ly shifting to use of Second Restatement as a stand-alone).

60. See Symeon C. Symeonides, *Choice of Law in the American Courts in 2008: Twenty-second Annual Survey,* 57 Am. J. Comp. L. (2009).

Evaluating interest analysis from a theoretical perspective is difficult because different people have starkly different views about what interest analysis is, or should be. The most significant division has been between those who consider state interests as "objective" entities—discernible by judges or interest analysts regardless of what state legislatures say—and those who think them "subjective"—within the control of state legislatures. Some scholars maintain that interests should be understood objectively,[61] and others assert that the matter "is not completely clear."[62]

There is obviously disagreement on this issue, but to me the objective/subjective question is an easy one. What a state's policy is or should be is a question within the control of the state legislature, and it is not subject to second-guessing by scholars. Currie's basic insight is that the task of determining the scope of a state's law is not fundamentally different in a multistate case than it is in a purely domestic case. And in a purely domestic case, no one would question that the legislature decides to which sets of facts the law applies, and to which it does not.[63]

So state interests are subjective. Case closed—or is it? That a court should defer to what its own legislature says about the purpose or the scope of its laws may seem relatively obvious, but granting that interests are subjective in this sense has further consequences. If a State A court accepts what the State A legislature says about the scope of State A law, it should presumably also accept what a State B legislature says about the scope of State B law—and if the legislature has not spoken, what the State B courts have said.

This second step proved vexing for interest analysts. It implied that in determining whether a foreign state was interested—that is, determining the scope of foreign law—the forum should defer to statements of the foreign legislature and courts. There is no problem doing this if the courts or legislature have spoken in terms of the policy behind a particular law—if they have announced, for instance, that their guest statute is intended to protect insurers from fraudulent suits, and not to protect drivers from ungrateful

---

61. See, e.g., *Comment, False Conflicts*, 55 Cal. L.Rev. 74, 85 (1967); Herma Hill Kay, *Comment on* Reich v. Purcell, 15 U.C.L.A. L. Rev. 584, 589 n.31 (1968).

62. Lea Brilmayer, Conflict of Laws 81 (1995). Brilmayer herself does seem to believe that the better understanding of interest analysis takes interests to be subjective. See Lea Brilmayer, *The Other* *State's Interests*, 24 Cornell Int'l L.J. 233, 241 (1991).

63. As Currie put it, the interest analyst's assessments of state interests "are tentative and subject to modification on the advice of those who know better"—namely, state courts and legislatures. Currie, Selected Essays, at 592.

guests. But what if the foreign courts or legislature have not spoken the language of policy and have not spoken about an individual law? What if they have said something about the scope of all the foreign state's laws—what if they have adopted a choice-of-law system?

Granting that interests are subjective seems to imply that the forum should consult the foreign state's choice-of-law rules in order to decide whether the foreign state is interested. "Interests" are just a way of divining scope in the absence of explicit guidance, and choice-of-law rules provide explicit guidance. But this means that forums following interest analysis may find themselves forced to respect the territorial approaches of more traditional states. That might be convenient on occasion—it might turn true conflicts into false ones. But it would be awkward in others, when it did the reverse. Interest analysts tended to be willing to consider foreign choice-of-law rules in the former situation, but they balked at the latter and sought to avoid it. Foreign choice-of-law rules (at least traditional ones), did not actually reflect state interests, they protested. And therefore they need not be respected (at least when doing so made analysis harder).[64]

It is certainly true that a territorial choice-of-law rule is not drawn from a consideration of the purpose of a particular law. It is unlikely to direct application of that law in those cases in which application would serve the purposes for which it was enacted. In that respect, territorialism does not reflect state interests as interest analysis ordinarily constructs them. But does that really mean that foreign traditional choice-of-law rules can be disregarded?

I think not. I think, again, that this is an easy question if we keep in mind upon the basic insight of interest analysis, that choice-of-law problems are not different in kind from those presented by purely domestic cases. Interest analysis is simply a way of determining the scope of a potentially applicable law. Nothing in the methodology elevates it above explicit direction from the local legislature, or from the legislature or courts of a foreign state.

When a legislature speaks to the scope of state law, it has spoken; the matter is settled. After the post-*Carroll* Alabama legislature announced that its abrogation of the fellow-servant rule applied to cases where the employment contract was formed in Alabama, neither an Alabama court nor a Mississippi one, no matter how enlightened, could decide that the statute was territori-

---

64. See Arthur T. Von Mehren, *The Renvoi and Its Relation to Various Approaches to the Choice-of-Law Problem,* in XXTH CENTURY COMPARATIVE AND CONFLICTS LAW 380 (1961).

al instead. If *Carroll* had gone the other way, with the Alabama Supreme Court deciding that abrogation was linked to contract formation, not injury, and the legislature had responded by setting a territorial scope, that legislative direction would have been equally controlling. And if the legislature had decided to set the scope of all state statutes at once—if it had adopted a territorial choice-of-law rule—that would be binding too.[65] Interests are subjective, and so is the scope of state law: subject only to constitutional constraints, it is up to the state's legislature and, in the absence of legislative action, its courts.

I understand interest analysis, then, as driven by this basic insight, that choice of law has no distinctive problems and needs no distinctive solutions. Choice of law simply requires a court to perform the two-step process of scope and priority described in the introduction. The court must decide which of various arguably applicable laws actually do apply—which reach the facts of the case—and then resolve any conflicts it finds. Interest analysis is a method of performing the first step of determining scope: it tells courts that in the absence of explicit direction, they should determine scope by considering the policies behind a law and asking whether application in the case before them would promote those policies. Explicit direction from a court's own legislature will trump the results of interest analysis, and so will similar direction from a foreign legislature or foreign high court.

This statement of interest analysis implies the correct resolution for false conflicts and unprovided-for cases. In false conflicts, only one law creates rights or obligations, and obviously those should be enforced. In unprovided-for cases, no law creates rights or obligations, and therefore the plaintiff cannot recover. These results do not obtain because they are good policy solutions to the "problems" of false conflicts and unprovided-for cases; they follow directly from the understanding of interest analysis outlined above. No such solution follows for true conflicts; there courts must resort to some rule of priority selected on policy grounds. Since I attempt here only to set out the conceptual structure of interest analysis, I make no recommendations for a rule of priority.

Let us try to evaluate interest analysis as I have described it. There are essentially two major challenges. The first is whether the construction of state interests can in fact be performed, or whether it is so malleable as to amount nothing more than a convenient cover for judicial whim. The second is whether, even if possible,

---

65. The rule is no less binding if adopted by a state's courts.

74

interest analysis is a game worth the candle: is it so hard and so unpredictable that we would be better off with a simpler approach?

On the first question, the interest analysts' standard answer is that while deciding whether application in a multistate case will further a statute's purpose may be a difficult task, it is the same task that courts perform in hard domestic cases—and, as we shall see, in federal preemption cases as well. Certainly that is how Currie describes his method. But further reflection and consideration of his examples introduce some doubts.

Consider first the marginal domestic case. Imagine that you are a judge confronted with a statute of indefinite scope: it provides treble damages for "pedestrians" injured by cars. A person injured while rollerblading invokes the treble damages provision. How will you approach the case?

You might, of course, decide that you are a formalist or a textualist and try to follow the majority of contemporaneous dictionaries. But it is more likely that you believe the purpose of the statute is relevant—purposive interpretation is the most common method among judges. So you would ask why the legislature singled out pedestrians for special treatment, and if you could figure out that reason, you would ask whether it applied to rollerbladers as well. (Perhaps the legislature wanted to encourage non-motorized travel to reduce carbon emissions and promote physical fitness.)

Is the process of interest analysis like this kind of interpretation? Consider Currie's analysis of *Milliken v. Pratt*. He spends a fair amount of time working through the policies underlying contract law in general and contractual disabilities in particular. But when he comes to the question of scope—whose contracts Maine intends to validate, and which married women Massachusetts intends to "protect"—his interpretive process changes. There is no close study of these policies; there is only the assertion that—"of course"—Maine and Massachusetts are concerned with the welfare of their domiciliaries and not out-of-staters.

At a high level of generality, this analysis could be called similar to interpretation of the pedestrian statute. There is a core case to which the law clearly applies—a purely domestic contract case, for the Maine or Massachusetts law, and a person walking on foot for the pedestrian statute. To decide whether the law reaches a marginal case, we ask what attributes of the core case place it within the scope of the law, and then we ask whether the marginal case shares those attributes to a sufficient degree. The significant difference is that the determination of relevant attributes in the pedestrian hypothetical comes from a consideration of that precise statute and cannot necessarily be applied to other statutes, even those that also use the word "pedestrian." In Currie's example, the determination that the scope of the states' laws is drawn to protect their residents appears like lightning from the pregnant cloud "of course." And it applies to all laws.

Interest analysis, at least as practiced in the essay on *Milliken*, does not really interpret a specific statute to determine scope. It answers a broader question about whom state laws are designed to protect or benefit. That is not a question that can be answered by delving deeper into the text, structure, or history of a statute; it requires us to consider other values as well. It is, essentially, the question of what choice-of-law rules a legislature would want.[66]

The answer offered in Currie's analysis of *Milliken*—that the legislature would want its laws to have the scope that offers the greatest immediate benefit to local residents—is a possible answer, but it is certainly not the only one. To his credit, Currie explicitly acknowledged this; for the purposes of analysis he asked the reader to "[a]ssume a quite selfish state, ... blind to consequences and interested only in short-run gains."[67] "Determination of the policy expressed in a state's law, and of the state's interest in applying that policy to cases involving foreign elements," he added later, "is not distinctively the task of the conflict-of-laws technician. ... The distinctive task of the conflict of laws technician ... is to take the state court's determination of policy and interest as given...."[68]

Later advocates of interest analysis tend to give this disclaimer short shrift and to proceed as though the selfish state is, if not the truth, at least an invariant assumption. There is a reason for that; the assumption makes interest analysis much easier to apply. If we release that restriction on state interests, the analysis becomes unbearably indeterminate. A legislature might want its laws applied to benefit its citizens. But it might also believe that its solutions are best and want its laws applied whenever they can be. Or it might think that uniformity and predictability require territorial limits, even though these values come at some cost to the policies behind particular laws. Without some limiting assumptions, it is hard to see how a court could have any confidence in its ability to divine what the legislature would have wanted.

Where the traditional approach faced a tradeoff between uniformity and predictability, on the one hand, and arbitrariness on the other, interest analysis faces a very similar dilemma. With the

---

66. David Cavers makes essentially this point in THE CHOICE OF LAW PROCESS, at 97.

67. CURRIE, SELECTED ESSAYS at 89.

68. Id. at 591–592.

selfish state assumption it achieves a fair degree of uniformity and predictability, but at the cost of unpleasant parochialism and, in all likelihood, significant divergence from actual legislative preferences. But take away that assumption and courts are adrift with almost no meaningful guidance. Inevitably, they will set scope by making policy rather than interpreting laws.

The above might make things look bleak for interest analysis, but there are a few things to be said in its defense. First, judicial policymaking or guesses as to appropriate scope may be very unlikely to match what a legislature would decide if it considered the question. But territorialism is also unlikely to do that, and judicial guessing will probably come closer. Second, even a wrong guess may be useful if it prompts legislative response—though territorialism can do this too, as the response to *Carroll* shows. Last, interest analysis at least gets the conceptual structure of choice of law right. Territorialism, in its traditional form, did not; it asserted that territorial scope inhered in the nature of law and had no answers for the conflicts that emerged when this principle was overthrown.

The second question remains. Even granting that interest analysis has the conceptual structure right, and that judicial guesses as to appropriate scope are likelier to do better than a blanket territorial rule, is it worth imposing the costs of this complicated and indeterminate analysis on judges, litigants, and individuals or corporations trying to assess their exposure to different laws? Might it be better simply to have clear rules?

The debate between advocates of rules and those of standards exists throughout the law. A few points recur, though their significance will vary from one context to another, and thus there can be no single answer to the debate. That is, what we think of the following considerations may depend on whether we are trying to choose between a rule and a standard in the context of a speed limit (55 m.p.h vs. "drive prudently, all things considered") or an approach to choice of law.

In general, the standard considerations are these. Rules do a better job of letting people predict the consequence of their actions and conform their behavior to the law. They simplify the task of judges and litigants, and they constrain judicial discretion to avoid the influence of undesirable or illegitimate considerations. Application of clear rules should come out the same way in all courts, enhancing uniformity. And such rules should produce fewer appeals, easing the burden on appellate courts and sparing parties the expense of another round of litigation. They are, in short, quick, easy, and cheap.

However, rules tend to have imperfect fit: following a rule will almost always lead to some cases coming out wrong in terms of the purpose of the rule. Standards allow for perfect fit; they can, in theory, get all the cases right.

In the context of choice of law, the rules vs. standards debate appears primarily as a choice between the First Restatement and the modern approaches. In theory, the difference should not be that great, for the modern approaches aspire to be at least reasonably determinate. In practice, however, what courts do with them is dramatically unpredictable. The fact that escape devices and simple error render the First Restatement somewhat unpredictable in practice narrows the gap but does not close it.

One might hope that time will bring greater predictability to the modern approaches, and perhaps it will. In the meantime, each major choice of law approach has its strengths and its weaknesses. The traditional approach will sometimes produce results that seem arbitrary, needlessly thwarting the policies of one or another state. How frequently it will do this is not clear. The tables accompanying Currie's analysis of *Milliken* suggest that it occurs in four out of the sixteen categories. In four of the six false conflicts, that is, the traditional approach fails to apply the law of the only interested state. But since we do not know the relative frequency with which cases fall into each of these categories, the four out of sixteen figure is largely meaningless.[69] If, for instance, it almost never happens that a Massachusetts married woman contracts with a Massachusetts creditor in Maine (one of Currie's examples of the perversity of the traditional approach), the fact that the traditional approach gets this wrong and interest analysis right means little. The traditional approach can also gain the flexibility to avoid perverse results through the judicious use of escape devices. But to the extent escape devices are available, uniformity and predictability decline.

Interest analysis does a better job of avoiding perverse results. But it offers less in the way of uniformity and predictability— perhaps not as a matter of theory, but certainly in practice. If the selfish state assumption is relaxed, interest analysis becomes even more indeterminate. Relaxing the assumption may be the road to progress—it is down that road that refinements such as the distinc-

---

69. This too is a point of which Currie was aware. See SELECTED ESSAYS at 587.

tion between conduct-regulating and loss-allocating rules lie—but as the methodology becomes more complicated, it demands more of judges, and errors and deliberate misapplications will increase. Anyone who doubts this point should spend a few hours comparing the complex academic "solutions" for true conflicts to actual decisions.

The fact that the states have not settled on a single approach to choice of law is as good evidence as there can be that each approach has its appeal. Which one you prefer will depend largely on the relative significance you assign to particular desiderata and the extent of your confidence in judges; it will say more about you than it does about choice of law. I will not make a recommendation. At places in the book I do argue for the theoretical superiority of one or another approach, or more frequently of a particular way of thinking about a problem. But generally speaking, I am not trying to convince you that one approach is more desirable than another as a practical matter. I aspire instead to offer a clear view of the strengths and weaknesses of each.

Chapter 3

MODERN APPROACHES II (THE SECOND RESTATEMENT AND BETTER LAW)

I. The Second Restatement

As the choice-of-law revolution, inspired by academic writings like those of Currie, got underway in the courts, the members of the American Law Institute were also at work. Recognizing the force of the criticisms of the First Restatement, they began drafting a Second Restatement of Conflict of Laws in 1953. Like the United States Constitution, the Second Restatement was originally conceived as an attempt to amend its predecessor but ended up as a wholesale rethinking.

The Second Restatement was completed in 1971. Seventeen-plus years of labor allowed for the airing of a wide range of views. One might also think the years would afford time to pick and choose among competing theories, but this seems not to have been the case. Instead, the Second Restatement offers something for everyone. In the end, it advises courts to apply the law of the state with "the most significant relationship" to a particular issue.

The heart of the Second Restatement is § 6, which sets out what the Restatement calls "choice-of-law principles." These principles, with some modifications, guide analysis or provide a default backdrop in essentially all substantive areas of law. Section 6 provides, first, that a court should "follow a statutory directive of its own state." The second part of § 6 provides a non-exclusive list of "factors relevant to the choice of the applicable rule of law." They are:

a) the needs of the interstate and international systems,

b) the relevant policies of the forum,

c) the relevant policies of other interested states and the relative interests of those states in the determination of the particular issue,

d) the protection of justified expectations,

e) the basic policies underlying the particular field of law,

f) certainty, predictability, and uniformity of result, and

g) ease in the determination and application of the law to be applied.[1]

None of these factors should surprise you. They are the virtues that the approaches we have seen so far either possess or are criticized for lacking. The evident aim of § 6 is to provide an approach that takes all relevant considerations into account and accords them their proper weight. The uncharitable might wonder why it took seventeen years to come up with that idea, or why it was not expressed more concisely ("A court should apply the law that is appropriate, giving all relevant considerations due weight"). But the Second Restatement does aim to guide judicial discretion; it both suggests when different factors should be given greater or lesser weight and offers specific guidance for most areas of law.

The explanation of the relevant factors is provided largely in the comments to § 6. There, the drafters inform us that factor a), the needs of the interstate and international system, is relevant because choice-of-law rules "should seek to further harmonious relations between states and to facilitate commercial intercourse between them."[2] That aspiration provides very little guidance, however, and factor a) turns out to have minimal independent significance. Comment d) concludes with the observation that that choice-of-law rules chosen with due "regard for the needs and policies of other states and of the community of states ... are likely to commend themselves to other states and be adopted," leading, ideally, to uniformity in choice-of-law rules. A consummation devoutly to be wished, to be sure, but not much help for a judge facing a particular case.

Factors b) and c) essentially incorporate interest analysis: that is what the reference to policies and "interested states" means. As comment e) explains, "If the purposes sought to be achieved by a local statute or common law rule would be furthered by its application to out-of-state facts, this is a weighty reason why such application should be made."[3] Comment f) goes on to make a similar pitch for "the relevant policies of all other interested states."[4] Breaking from Currie, the Second Restatement does seem to contemplate some form of weighing of interests, for factor c) refers to the "relative interests" of the states. "Relative" could be taken to direct simple balancing, or it could be implemented via one of the more complicated approaches such as comparative impairment.

1. Restatement, Second, of Conflict of Laws § 6(2) (1971).

2. Id. comment d.

3. Id. comment e.

4. Id. comment f.

Comment f) refers to "the state whose interests are most deeply affected,"[5] which in fact sounds a bit like comparative impairment.

Factor d), the protection of justified expectations "is an important value in all fields of the law, including choice of law."[6] Within choice of law, however, it is more important in some areas than others. A desire to protect justified expectations is one of the factors underlying the relatively broad freedom the Second Restatement gives contracting parties to choose the governing law. It also underlies the rule that courts should select the law that validates a trust of movable property if possible. But on some occasions, comment g) explains, "particularly in the area of negligence, ... the parties act without giving thought to the legal consequences of their conduct or to the law that may be applied." In those situations, factor d) plays no role.

Factor e) suggests a solution to some true conflicts. When "the policies of the interested states are largely the same but ... there are nevertheless minor differences between their relevant local law rules,"[7] factor e) advises courts to choose the law whose application would best achieve the basic policy underlying the field of law. For contracts, this will generally mean validating the contract, as comment h) explains. To some extent, this factor resembles Kramer's canons, though it is much more limited in scope.

Factor f) (certainty, predictability, and uniformity) again identifies values thought desirable across a wide range of legal fields. Comment i) notes that they are desirable in choice of law as a means to reduce forum-shopping.[8] Reflecting the influence of critics of the First Restatement, however, the comment then backpedals, noting that the values "can ... be purchased at too great a price" and that in "a rapidly developing area, such as choice of law, it is often more important that good rules be developed than that predictability and uniformity of result should be assured by adherence to existing rules."[9] Factor g), ease in the determination and application of the law to be applied, is similar to uniformity and predictability, and it receives similar treatment. Perhaps abashed by Currie's observation that "Always apply Alaska law" is ideal from that perspective, comment j) states that the value of simple rules "should not be overemphasized, since it is obviously of greater importance that choice-of-law rules lead to desirable results."[10]

5. Ibid.
6. Id. comment g.
7. Id. comment h.
8. Id. comment i.

9. Ibid.
10. Id. comment j.

One might quibble with some elements of the commentary. If we adopted a rule that contracting parties could not choose the law to govern their contract, expectations would presumably adjust to that rule, or would be unjustified if they did not. Potentially negligent tortfeasors probably do give some thought to the applicable law when deciding how much care to exercise. Forum-shopping may not be as inherently evil as most assume, and the value of simple rules is perhaps greater than the comments admit. Still, the commentary presumably leaves courts at least a bit better off in terms of understanding and applying the factors.

The bulk of the Second Restatement's guidance, however, comes in the small number of sections that address particular fields of law and the large number of "presumptive" rules for specific legal issues. Frequently, these rules are those of the First Restatement.[11] Thus, for instance, § 146 provides that in a suit for personal injuries, "the local law of the state where the injury occurred determines the rights and liabilities of the parties, unless, with respect to the particular issue, some other state has a more significant relationship under the principles stated in § 6...."[12] Sometimes they are not; for intra-family immunity, for instance, the presumptive law is that of the parties' domicile.[13]

These presumptions could provide substantial guidance, if they were given significant weight, but the phrasing of the Second Restatement suggests to the contrary that they are to be given no weight if the § 6 analysis points in a different direction. The value of presumptive rules that carry no weight is rather unclear, since this means that cases should always be decided as § 6 analysis indicates. Some of the rules are even more cryptic; several state that governing law for a particular issue is to be selected by application of the general rule for torts and then add that the applicable law will "usually" be the law of some identified state.[14] The use of "usually" suggests something about statistical likelihood but again does not seem to be intended to carry normative weight.

---

11. The Second Restatement also resembles the First in its treatment of the public policy exception, § 90. That section provides that courts may dismiss without prejudice suits relying on foreign laws that offend a strong forum policy. It distinguishes between dismissing a case and deciding under forum law on grounds of forum policy, and also notes that public policy does not justify striking down a foreign defense—that is, it follows the traditional version of the public policy exception.

12. Id. § 146.

13. Id. § 169.

14. See, e.g., id. § 165 (providing that the law determining whether assumption of risk bars recovery is to be determined by the general tort rule but will usually be the law of the state where the injury occurred).

There are a few other general points worth making about the Second Restatement before delving into its application to particular fields of law. First, because it offers different general rules for different kinds of cases (torts, contracts, property, etc.), it retains the characterization problem of the First Restatement, which interest analysis largely avoids.[15] Second, unlike the First Restatement, the Second embraces **depecage**: it specifically directs courts to perform their analysis on an issue-by-issue basis. Last, and most generally, the Second Restatement lacks an underlying theory. It advises courts, for each issue, to apply the law of the state with "the most significant relationship" to the transaction and the parties with respect to that issue. Section 6 sets out the factors that are relevant to finding the most significant relationship, and other sections, considered below, explain which contacts are likely to trigger those factors in particular kinds of cases. But the Second Restatement nowhere explains what it means to have the most significant relationship—and in consequence, courts are left to grapple with the Section 6 factors on an ad hoc and intuitive basis. They cannot rank the factors in general, because their appropriate weight will vary across different categories of cases. Within those categories, however, the possibility remains that greater guidance can be given.

A. Torts

The general principle for torts is set out in § 145, which provides that a tort issue should be decided under the local law of the state "which, with respect to that issue, has the most significant relationship to the occurrence and the parties under the principles stated in § 6."[16] Somewhat more helpfully, § 145 then goes on to give a non-exhaustive list of contacts "to be taken into account in applying the principles of § 6 . . . ." They are:

a) the place where the injury occurred,

b) the place where the conduct causing the injury occurred,

c) the domicil, residence, nationality, place of incorporation and place of business of the parties, and

d) the place where the relationship, if any, between the parties is centered.[17]

---

15. Or at least, interest analysis domesticates the characterization problem. In order to decide whether the purpose of a rule of contract law will be furthered by applying it to a particular case, a court does need to decide wheth-er the plaintiff states a contract claim. But this is the same sort of characterization that courts must do in the ordinary domestic case.

16. Second Restatement § 145.

17. Ibid.

In keeping with the Second Restatement's generally gnomic tone, § 145 goes on to advise courts that the contacts "are to be evaluated according to their relative importance with respect to the particular issue."[18]

The Second Restatement never fully explains what it means to take a contact "into account in applying the principles of § 6," but the idea is presumably that certain of the § 145 contacts will call certain of the § 6 factors into play. In a personal injury tort case, for instance, the domicile of the victim (contact c)) will probably make the policy of the victim's state of domicile (factor b) or c)) relevant if it is a pro-recovery policy, since the state would be interested in applying its law to compensate an injured domiciliary. The location of the injury (contact a)) will probably make the policy of the state of injury (also factor b) or c)) relevant, since the state where the injury occurred usually has an interest in attaching legal consequences to conduct causing injury within its borders. If, however, the issue is one of loss-allocation, consideration of contacts a) and c) might lead the court to reason that the policy of the state of injury should get less weight than the policies of the domiciliary states, since with a loss-allocation issue a domiciliary contact is more significant than a territorial one.

That is the sort of reasoning one would expect to find in a decision applying the Second Restatement to a tort case. It is also, of course, largely what one would find in a decision applying interest analysis, and in tort cases the interest-analysis factors of § 6 tend to play a dominant role. Some courts (a minority) give substantial weight to the presumptive rules that follow § 145; in such cases the § 6 analysis will play a less prominent role. The result, however, will often be the same since the presumptive rules incorporate some of the insights of interest analysis, notably by attempting to move away from territoriality in false conflicts. Thus, loss-allocating rules like immunity and vicarious liability are either presumptively governed by domiciliary law (as § 169 provides for intra-family liability) or referred to the § 145 analysis without any presumptive rule (as § 168 provides for charitable immunity and § 174 for vicarious liability).

B. Contracts

In contract cases, the Second Restatement endorses a moderately strong form of party autonomy. Section 187 authorizes the

18. Ibid.

parties to choose any law they want to govern issues that could have been resolved by an explicit provision, and only slightly less flexibility in selecting law to govern issues that could not have been resolved by an explicit provision. The distinction drawn here is essentially that between interpretation and validity and can best be understood through that example.

Unlimited party autonomy should raise no questions with respect to interpretation. The parties could, after all, have simply written out the desired interpretive rules. Letting them choose law for interpretation instead amounts only to allowing them to incorporate those interpretive rules by reference. So too with any other issue that could have been resolved by spelling out the desired result.

The major issue that cannot be resolved by an explicit provision is validity. A contract invalid under the governing law cannot be rescued by a clause stating "This contract shall be valid and enforceable." What about one that provides that the contract shall be governed by a law under which it is valid?

In the earlier discussion of party autonomy, I suggested that allowing parties to choose governing law made sense, if it they were limited to the laws of states with some connection to the contract. This approach simply used party autonomy as a tiebreaker, or an additional factor, in choosing between states with legitimate claims to regulatory authority. The Second Restatement endorses that qualification; it requires that the state whose law is chosen "have a substantial relationship to the parties or the transaction" or that there be some "other reasonable basis" for the choice.[19] Then it adds another qualification: the choice will be invalid if "application of the law of the chosen state would be contrary to a fundamental policy of a state which has a materially greater interest than the chosen state in the determination of the particular issue" and whose law would be applied under the Second Restatement in the absence of an effective choice-of-law clause.[20]

Neither § 187 nor the commentary provides an explicit definition of "fundamental policy." In fact, the commentary proclaims it impossible: "No detailed statement can be made of the situations where a 'fundamental' policy of the state of the otherwise applicable law will be found to exist."[21] The refusal might seem simple contrariness, but there is a reasonable explanation. The comment goes on to note that, as we saw in the discussion of public policy earlier, whether a policy is sufficiently fundamental will depend not

19. Id. § 187(2)(a).
20. Id. § 187(2)(b).

21. Id. § 187, comment g.

just on its status in isolation but also on the nature and degree of contacts between the transaction and the state whose policy is in jeopardy, and also the contacts to the state whose law is chosen. In essence, the Second Restatement uses party autonomy as a factor in selecting between the laws of states with legitimate claims of authority while simultaneously trying to ensure that it is not given so much weight as to eclipse the interests of the states.

If the parties do not make an effective choice of law, § 188 tells courts to use the law of the state "which, with respect to that issue, has the most significant relationship to the transaction and the parties under the principles stated in § 6."[22] Like the torts section, § 188 then goes on to list contacts to be "taken into account in applying the principles of § 6."[23] They are:

a) the place of contracting,

b) the place of negotiation of the contract,

c) the place of performance,

d) the location of the subject matter of the contract,

e) the domicile, residence, nationality, place of incorporation and place of business of the parties.[24]

The list should not be surprising. These are the contacts that would be relevant to either interest analysis or the traditional approach, and characteristically the Second Restatement sets them out without indicating their relative significance or noting that they are drawn from very different approaches. Instead, as does § 145, it simply provides that they are to be "evaluated according to their relative importance with respect to the particular issue."

The comments to § 188, however, provide a bit more guidance: they place the Second Restatement among the modern approaches by downplaying the significance of the place of contracting. The other contacts are all described as at least sometimes significant. While the commentary does identify facts that may diminish their importance (for instance, the place of negotiation matters less if there is no one single location), it provides no clue as to how to decide cases when they point in different directions.

C. Property

In its treatment of property, the Second Restatement bears a closer resemblance to the First than it does with torts or contracts.

---

22. Id. § 188.

23. Ibid.

24. Ibid.

Like torts and contracts, property is governed by a general principle (§ 222) that directs courts to use the law of "the state which, with respect to the particular issue, has the most significant relationship to the thing and the parties under the principles of § 6."[25] The commentary that follows observes that property is an area in which § 6 factor d) (the protection of justified expectations) is of considerable importance, which in turn implies that certainty, uniformity, and predictability (factor f)) are also of unusual importance. As might be expected given this orientation, the specific rules that follow § 222 hew much closer to the First Restatement than those that follow §§ 145 and 188.

The Second Restatement's treatment of property is divided into two parts, immovables and movables. With respect to immovables, the Second Restatement almost invariably directs courts to apply the "law" (and not the "local law") of the situs.[26] The "law" of a state is the totality of its law, including its choice-of-law rules, which means that, like the First Restatement, the Second endorses the use of renvoi in the context of immovables: Its specific rules generally provide that courts should apply "the law that would be applied by the courts of the situs."[27] The reason it gives is the same as Joseph Beale's: In a case involving immovable property, the forum's object should be "to arrive at the same result a court of the situs would have arrived at upon the actual facts of the case."[28] Since in most cases the situs courts would apply their own local law, this wrinkle is of only minor practical significance.

With respect to movables, the Second Restatement departs somewhat more from the territorialism of the First, at least in theory. Its Introductory Note provides that the governing law for a controversy stemming from a single *inter vivos* transaction is the local law of the state with the most significant relationship. In these situations, the Note explains, there may be no clear line of distinction between property and contract rights, and the Second Restatement aims to have the same law decide all such questions. (In consequence, an effective choice-of-law clause will supersede the analysis of this Part if it applies to the particular issue.)

For marital property, § 257 provides that interests in movables acquired by marriage (i.e., one spouse's interest in movables owned by the other) are determined by the law of the state with the most

25. Id. § 222.

26. Id. Chapter 9, Topic 2, Introductory Note.

27. In some cases the specific rules direct courts to apply the "local law" of the situs instead. See, e.g., § 229 (method for foreclosure of a mortgage and resulting interests); § 243 (escheat of land).

28. Ibid.

significant relationship to the spouses and the property, usually the law of the state where the other spouse was domiciled at the time of marriage. Section 258 provides that interests in movables acquired during marriage are also determined by the law of the state with the most significant relationship to the spouses and the property, usually the state of spousal domicile at the time of acquisition. Section 259 provides that interests in a movable are not altered by removing it to another state.

Last, the Second Restatement treats some questions of succession to movables. Renvoi makes a reappearance here. Construction and validity of bequests of movable property, as well as intestate succession, are governed by "the law that would be applied by the courts of the state where the decedent was domiciled at the time of his death."[29]

D. Evaluation

The Second Restatement is a classic example of drafting by committee: it has elements that should make everyone happy, but nothing that ties those elements into a coherent whole. For almost any choice-of-law problem, the Second Restatement holds the correct answer. The problem is that it also holds seven or so other possible answers, depending on how the analysis is performed. As already noted, one might expect the flexibility thus created to appeal more to judges than scholars. And indeed, while the academic reviews have been scathing, the Second Restatement has fared quite well in the courts. It is currently the most popular approach to choice of law, operating in twenty-four states for torts and twenty-three for contracts.[30]

II. Better Law

A. The Approach

One more modern approach deserves mention, both because it has been adopted by a not-insignificant number of states, and because it nicely fills out the theoretical picture. It is Professor Robert Leflar's "better law" approach, developed in a series of articles and ultimately a treatise. According to the most recent

---

29. Id. §§ 260–265.

30. See Symeon C. Symeonides, *Choice of Law in the American Courts in* *2008: Twenty-second Annual Survey*, 57 Am. J. Comp. L. (2009).

survey, it is currently used by five states for torts and by two for contracts.[31]

Leflar set out to identify what he called "choice-influencing considerations," the factors that actually motivated judges to decide cases one way rather than another.[32] His perspective was positive, rather than normative; that is, he sought not to prescribe new considerations but to unearth the ones that were already at work in the cases and the leading approaches to choice of law. By making these explicit in a "manageably compact form," he hoped to allow courts to "replace with statements of real reasons the mechanical rules and circuitously devised approaches which have appeared in the language of conflicts opinions, too often as cover-ups for the real reason that underlay the decision."[33]

Leflar ultimately assembled five of these considerations: predictability of results, maintenance of interstate and international order, simplification of the judicial task, advancement of the forum's governmental interests, and, last and most controversially, application of the better rule of law. The first four factors should surprise no one; they are standard choice-of-law desiderata. In fact, § 6 of the Second Restatement contains all of them. The fact that Leflar explicitly recognizes advancement of forum interests while not mentioning foreign interests might suggest that his approach will tend to be more parochial, but in fact foreign interests come into play in the maintenance of interstate and international order. It is important for that purpose, Leflar explains, that forums defer to the laws of states with "a clearly superior concern for the facts" and avoid "across-the-board 'forum preference.' "[34] This amounts at least to an admonition not to apply the law of an uninterested forum in a false conflict, and it could be taken further.

"Better law" is the distinctive factor, and it is the one for which Leflar's approach is primarily known. But what makes one law "better" than another? One might think that "better law" will in practice mean nothing more than "forum law." Some of the cases seem to adopt this perspective. In *Milkovich v. Saari*,[35] the Minnesota Supreme Court confronted a guest statute case. Ontario residents, traveling in an Ontario-registered car, got into an accident in Minnesota. Ontario's guest statute required passengers to prove gross negligence to recover; Minnesota had no guest statute.

---

31. See id.

32. See, e.g., Robert A. Leflar, *Conflicts Law: More on Choice–Influencing Considerations*, 54 Cal. L. Rev. 1584 (1966).

33. Id. at 1585.

34. Ibid.

35. 295 Minn. 155, 203 N.W.2d 408 (1973).

The court went through Leflar's factors but found only the last two significant. After deciding that Minnesota's policy interests by themselves were not enough to justify application of Minnesota law, it reached the better law question. On this factor, the court identified Minnesota's interest, as a "justice-administering state" in seeing cases decided in a manner consistent with its "own concept of fairness and equity." It consequently refused to apply the guest statute.

Boiled down, *Milkovich* is simple forum-preference. Deciding cases consistently with the forum's concept of fairness and equity obviously means deciding them according to forum law, or at least leaning that way. Calling the forum's rule of law "better" adds nothing but insult.

It is possible, though, to try to understand "better law" in a more objective sense, and Leflar's rejection of across-the-board forum preference suggests that he had a different view. While granting that a judge might naturally feel that forum law is better, Leflar suggested that the better rule of law is the one which makes "good socio-economic sense for the time when the court speaks."

A more recent Minnesota case, *Jepson v. General Casualty Co. of Wisconsin*,[36] uses this understanding. Jepson, a Minnesota domiciliary, was a passenger injured in a car accident in Arizona. He sought benefits under an insurance policy the defendant had issued to his North Dakota business. The policy covered seven vehicles, and Jepson argued that the benefits for each vehicle should be added (or "stacked"), something permissible under Minnesota but not North Dakota law.

Jepson differs from *Milkovich* in several ways. First, it gives more weight to Leflar's first two factors. With respect to predictability, it found that the terms of the contract, which charged North Dakota rates and not the higher Minnesota rates, indicated an expectation that North Dakota law would govern. With respect to the maintenance of interstate and international order, it went beyond the idea that an uninterested forum should not apply its law in a false conflict. Instead, it focused on the fact that Jepson had obtained the benefits of lower North Dakota rates and was now forum-shopping for plaintiff-friendly law. It concluded that "[w]e interfere with the sovereignty of a sister state when we make our law available for people who seek Minnesota benefits while burdening the North Dakota insurance rate base and regulatory system."

---

36. 513 N.W.2d 467 (Minn. 1994).

When it came to the better law factor, the court essentially confessed an inability to apply it. It recited Leflar's invocation of good socio-economic sense but concluded that "[s]ometimes different laws are neither better nor worse in an objective way, just different." Indeed, it is not easy to see how a court is better placed than its local legislature to decide what law makes good sense for the times. Possibly the directive to apply the better law will militate against archaic and obsolete laws that have been rejected by those states to have recently considered the issue. (Some version of this view seems to be at work in *Milkovich*.) Ultimately, however, it tells courts to make a value judgment without telling them how.

B. Evaluation

Apart from better law, Leflar's factors do strongly resemble the Second Restatement. His illustrative applications suggest a bit more determinacy than the bare list, but, again like the Second Restatement, there does not appear to be an underlying theory that knits them together or explains how to handle cases where they point in different directions. The first factor, predictability, tends to be important in cases involving consensual transactions and insignificant otherwise. The second turns out to be essentially an admonition against applying foreign procedural law. The third, in Leflar's hands, is mostly about false conflicts, though *Jepson* does take it farther.

Better law is the most interesting factor. It is less interesting, and certainly less valuable, if it devolves into simple forum-preference, and there is a real danger of that. If it does not, and if it can be given some objective sense in terms of criteria like obsolescence and rareness, another question arises: Are the values advanced by a preference for "better law" choice-of-law values, the sort of policy-agnostic goals that a choice-of-law system should aim to promote, rather than particular policy goals like freedom of contract?[37]

It is possible that better law will advance choice-of-law values. It may be, for instance, that the law deemed better will be the one

---

37. The distinction I mean to draw is between particular policies that some states may favor and others disfavor and higher-level values that states can endorse regardless of their stance on particular policies. States will differ, for instance in how they strike a balance between freedom of contract and protection of parties with lesser bargaining power, and using choice of law to advance one of those positions seems wrong to me. Uniformity, or aggregate policy satisfaction, however, are desirable features for a choice-of-law system regardless of how we feel about freedom of contract; they are what I call choice-of-law values. States will of course differ in the weight they assign to these different values, but that is the sort of consideration that should go into crafting a choice-of-law system.

with greater current vitality, so that the better law preference actually tends to produce greater aggregate policy satisfaction in the long run. (If this is true, then better law is actually related to comparative impairment and Kramer's canons.) But it is equally possible, and perhaps more likely, that this will not happen, that the preference for better law advances substantive goals that could not reasonably be attributed to a hypothetical assembly of states bargaining about the rules that should determine the priority of their laws in various cases.[38] In that case, better law appears much like efficiency in the work of some recent scholars, an extrinsic desideratum whose appearance in the choice-of-law calculus is merely expedient. That is not necessarily a condemnation. If choice-of-law values run out, decisions must still be made somehow. But it does suggest, at least to me, that better law should be invoked only as a last resort.

C. Pervasive Problems

We have now seen all of the major approaches to choice of law, and I have said a bit about how they compare in terms of their abilities to satisfy the demands conventionally made of choice-of-law systems. We can also compare them from the perspective of the two-step model, which is one of the values of adopting that perspective. We need only ask, for each approach, what its rules of scope and priority are. Answering those questions produces the following table:

	Traditional	Interest Analysis	Second Rest.	Better Law
Scope	territoriality	State interest	reasonableness	unclear
Priority	none	multiple	Most sig. rel.	Five factors

Based on this chart, interest analysis may seem somewhat more appealing, at least relatively speaking. The traditional approach relies solely on the territorial rule of scope in order to eliminate the possibility of conflict. That is simply unworkable; even if the forum decides that territorial scope is a good idea for its laws, it cannot impose that choice on other states. The prospect of conflicts between laws must be faced, and the traditional approach has no reasoned way to do so.

(Readers, please note that the courts have not adopted this proposition. I believe, and will argue in greater detail below, that if State A follows the traditional approach, while State B follows

---

38. The fact that one law is apparently better than another regardless of how the contacts in a case are distributed strongly suggests that the values at work are not choice-of-law values.

interest analysis, a State A court cannot say that State B laws are territorial in scope. It cannot say, for instance, that a tort committed in State A between two B domiciliaries is outside the scope of State B's loss-allocating rules. In practice, however, it would do so. In fact, all approaches, to a greater or lesser degree, commit the fallacy of applying their rules of scope to the laws of states that follow different approaches. Why I believe this is a fallacy is discussed in more detail in the section on renvoi.)

The Second Restatement moves to the other extreme. It does almost nothing in terms of discerning limits to the scope of state laws. What discussion it has of the issue suggests that it presumes they extend as far as the Constitution allows.[39] When it comes to priority, the Second Restatement offers its mix of the wildly indeterminate § 6 analysis and the more specific (but non-normative) presumptive rules. In the hands of most judges, the result seems to be either largely interest analysis or largely intuition.

Interest analysis, by contrast, has something sensible to say about the scope of state laws. It is this feature that allows it to identify false conflicts, which is perhaps its greatest achievement. As far as resolving true conflicts is concerned, Currie did not get very far with rules of priority, but others have advanced the baton. Most people will find something to like among the suggestions— territorial tiebreakers, comparative impairment, Kramer's canons, etc.—and if they don't, they can always take refuge in the Second Restatement at the priority stage.

So the two-step perspective is helpful in comparing the different approaches, and in my view it shows interest analysis to good advantage. We can also gain a clearer picture of how the approaches stack up against each other by considering how they handle some of the perennial problems of choice of law.

i. Depecage

Depecage is the practice of using more than one law in deciding a single case—that is, of deciding some issues under one law and others under another. The traditional approach disfavors depecage, at least in theory. If only one state has authority to regulate a transaction, then it seems logical that that state's law should govern all issues relating to the transaction.

---

39. Section 9 of the Second Restatement imposes a weak limit on the scope of state law by providing that a state may not apply its own law to determine a particular issue "unless such application of this law would be reasonable" in light of relevant contacts. The commentary suggests that the reasonableness limit may go no further than the constitutional constraints considered in Chapter 3.

In practice, however, the traditional approach is somewhat more accommodating. When events occur in different states, for instance, the traditional approach will sometimes use the territorially appropriate law for each event rather than trying to localize the transaction within a single state. The use of the law of the state of performance, rather than that of contracting, to decide many performance-related issues is perhaps the most obvious example of this. In torts, as you may remember from Chapter 1, the First Restatement provided that for cross-border torts, the law of the place of conduct should govern some issues, such as the content of a standard of care and the existence of privilege or legal duty to act. Some status issues would also be governed by domiciliary law. For instance, under the traditional approach in antebellum America, a slave who entered a free state but did not establish domicile there would remain a slave. (The application of this rule is at the root of the famous *Dred Scott* case.)[40]

The Second Restatement endorses depecage much more enthusiastically. That is the import of its frequent invocation of the "particular issue." Second Restatement analysis is to be done separately and independently for each issue.

Of course, the Second Restatement does not tell us how to divide a case into discrete issues. The failure is unfortunate, since how to engage in depecage is just as important as whether to do so—perhaps more so, given that no approach rejects it entirely. Is each cause of action one issue? Or are the different elements, or some of them, different issues? Which ones? The Second Restatement does answer some of these questions, at least implicitly, but it does not explain how.

Title B of the Torts Chapter lists particular torts, but these are clearly not considered discrete issues, since most come with the caveat that "particular issues" may be governed by different laws. "Important Issues" are listed in Title C; they include legal cause, defenses, duty or privilege to act, immunities, damages, contribution, and vicarious liability.

Is there any principled manner on which to decide what is a single issue and what is not? I discuss interest analysis last, for this issue and others, because interest analysis captures what I believe is the correct conceptual structure of choice of law. It therefore offers the correct answer, if it is applied in a manner consistent with its underlying premises. As we will see, however, it is not always applied that way.[41]

---

40. See *Scott v. Emerson*, 15 Mo. 576 (1852).

41. The people who apply it in what I see as an incorrect manner would of

How interest analysis should treat depecage is a matter of some dispute. In THE CHOICE OF LAW PROCESS, David Cavers created five variants of a fictitious case, *Adams v. Knickerbocker Nature Society,* and drafted opinions for various professors he imagined sitting as judges. The judges were Brainerd Currie, Willis Reese (the Reporter for the Second Restatement), Harvard Dean Erwin Griswold, Chicago professor Max Rheinstein, and Cavers himself. The opinions Cavers drafted were intended to illustrate the application of the approaches championed by these different academics.

It says something significant about choice of law that the putative authors disowned a majority of the opinions upon reading them. Significant and somewhat discouraging: If Cavers couldn't get the application right, what hope do generalist judges have? Perhaps some, if Cavers' cases were extraordinarily difficult. You may judge for yourself if that is so.

Case three offers a good exploration of depecage. Its facts were as follows. The Knickerbocker Society is a New York charitable organization devoted to nature activity. Adams, a New Yorker, is a member. On a trip to Massachusetts, the Knickerbocker truck breaks down and they borrow an unregistered truck from a local. Under Massachusetts law, operators of unregistered vehicles are strictly liable for injuries they cause; under New York law they are not liable unless negligent. The Knickerbocker driver injures Adams without negligence, and he sues the charity. Massachusetts has charitable immunity; New York does not.

The case is certainly an interesting one. If it were purely domestic to either state—if the contacts were wholly New York or wholly Massachusetts—Adams would lose. He would lose if it were a Massachusetts case because charitable immunity would block the suit. And he would lose if it were a New York case because he could not show negligence. But can he prevail in the multistate case?

Cavers thought so. He thought it made sense to apply Massachusetts law on the liability question and New York law on the immunity one. On liability, New York had "no reason to assert the applicability of its negligence standard to conduct on the Massachusetts highways."[42] And on immunity, Massachusetts had no reason to interfere in the allocation of loss between two New York domiciliaries.

Currie disagreed. (This was one of the opinions Cavers got wrong; he initially drafted a "Currie" opinion agreeing with Cav-

course respond that I am simply mistaken about the underlying premises or their logical consequences.

42. DAVID CAVERS, THE CHOICE OF LAW PROCESS 40 (1965).

ers, and Currie rewrote it.) He endorsed the general idea of proceeding "on an issue-by-issue basis,"[43] but denied that these issues could be separated. Massachusetts, as he saw it, "has a policy of deterring the operation of unlicensed vehicles, [but] does not extend that policy to charities. . . ." New York "has a policy of requiring compensation for its injured residents," but not without fault. Thus, neither state's policy would be served by allowing recovery. "It is one thing to fall between two stools," he concluded. "[I]t is quite another to put together half a donkey and half a camel, and then ride to victory on the synthetic hybrid."[44]

The Currie–Cavers disagreement may seem confusing, but in fact it is relatively simple when viewed from the proper perspective. The dispute is over is the structure of the rights at issue. Cavers believes that Massachusetts law provides a general right to recover from unregistered drivers in the absence of fault but subordinates that right to a defense available to charities. Proceeding issue-by-issue, we ask whether the right is available to Adams and conclude it is: conduct and injury take place in Massachusetts, and Massachusetts tort law provides a remedy on those facts. Moving to the next issue, we conclude that the defense is not available to Knickerbocker: it is a defense for Massachusetts charities, or perhaps those performing services for Massachusetts domiciliaries, but not for out-of-state charities serving out-of-staters. Nor does New York law provide a defense. In consequence, Adams can invoke a Massachusetts tort claim and Knickerbocker has no defense.

Currie, by contrast, thinks of Massachusetts tort law as simply not extending to (any) charities. Rather than creating a right and subordinating it to a defense, it simply creates no right when the defendant is a charity. Thus, there is no claim Adams can assert under Massachusetts tort law, and it does not matter whether Knickerbocker has a defense or not.

Who is right? We have actually seen essentially this problem before in our consideration of limitations periods in Chapter 1. There, the traditional characterization of limitations periods as procedural led to depecage for foreign causes of action. Since a forum applies its own procedure, foreign causes of action would be governed by forum limitations periods. The result struck people as inappropriate. Some states legislated in reaction, and some courts responded by distinguishing between statutes of limitation, which created a (procedural) defense and statutes of repose, which extinguished the underlying (substantive) right. The test was whether

---

43. Id. at 39.   **44.** Ibid.

the limitations period was "specifically directed" to the cause of action.

Cavers suggests a similar test for depecage more generally: issues should not be analyzed separately if the rules "are closely related in purpose."[45] This is probably roughly the right idea, but thinking in terms of rights and defenses may allow us to sharpen it a little bit. The basic question we have to answer is whether Massachusetts creates a cause of action and subordinates it to a defense, in which case we face two issues, or whether it simply creates no cause of action, in which case we face only one.

This is not a question that one can answer with complete confidence, but I believe we can make a reasonable attempt. Massachusetts presumably does not believe that otherwise wrongful conduct is not wrongful or undesirable when engaged in by a charity. It has simply decided that for other reasons it will subordinate the values served by imposing liability (deterrence and compensation) to those served by protecting charities (encouragement of charitable works). That is a right subordinated to a defense, and there are therefore two issues. (Whether Massachusetts should or must extend the defense to Knickerbocker is a separate question.)

For an example of the absence of a right, we might imagine that Massachusetts imposes strict liability on drivers of unregistered vehicles in order to encourage annual inspection but exempts people who have completed certain courses in driving and mechanical engineering on the theory that they can react to and repair any breakdowns. (An unlikely law, but entertain the idea.) This legal structure can fairly be characterized as representing the view that there is nothing undesirable about such people operating unregistered vehicles, and we could reasonably conclude that there is simply no right to recover in the absence of fault. Thus, if the Knickerbocker driver had completed these courses, Adams should lose.

Of course, the existence of two issues means only that it is possible to decide each under different law, not that it is necessarily appropriate to do so. That decision should be made by whatever approach to choice of law you find most appealing. If that approach is interest analysis, or one of the approaches that incorporates policy analysis, there is one more observation to be made.

Within such approaches, it seems to me entirely possible that there is no harm in erring on the side of considering issues separately. That is, granted that there is no sure-fire way to

45. Id. at 41.

distinguish between a right subordinated to a defense and the absence of a right, it may cause no great harm to treat doubtful cases as though they presented two issues. This is so because, I suspect, a proper policy analysis of the two issues in situations that "really" present only one will lead to the conclusion that the same law should govern both.

Imagine, for instance, that we treated the hypothetical educated driver exemption above as if it were a defense. The Massachusetts strict liability cause of action is available to Adams. How about the defense? The purpose of the defense, I would say, is to allow operation of unregistered vehicles by people whose operation will not produce the harms usually associated with it. If the Knickerbocker driver has completed the required courses, he comes within that class, and the conclusion would be that the defense should be available to him. Adams would lose, just as he would if he had decided that only one issue existed. We should generally reach similar results in any case in which the state whose law provides the cause of action believes that certain otherwise undesirable conduct is benign when engaged in by certain people, because domicile will (presumably) almost never be the factor that makes it benign. That is, where there is an absence of a right, issue-by-issue analysis will conclude that the "defense" is available regardless of domicile—or in other words, that the "defense" issue should be governed by the same law that provides the cause of action.

ii. Renvoi

The traditional approach, we have seen, rejected renvoi in most circumstances but accepted it in a few exceptional cases. Joseph Beale was never able to provide a compelling explanation for this treatment, and his attempts to do so lapsed into unpersuasive distinctions or equally unsatisfying pronouncements about the nature of law. The failure is not surprising, for the theoretical commitments of the traditional approach create at least a prima facie difficulty with ignoring the other state's choice-of-law rules. The idea behind territoriality is that, for example, State A grants recovery for a tort occurring in State B because it is enforcing rights vested under the law of State B. State B, in the view of the State A court, is the only state with authority to attach legal consequences to the tort. If the courts of State B would say that no rights vested under their law, it is hard to see how State A courts can ignore that—how they can claim to be enforcing rights vested under State B law when the opinion of the State B courts is that no such rights exist.

Beale's opponents offered some arguments in favor of renvoi, but they were never able to overcome the problem of the infinite regress that wholesale acceptance would sometimes create. Neither side, in the end, had a satisfactory theoretical account of when and why renvoi should be accepted or rejected.

The Second Restatement is in this regard at least a modest improvement on the First. It too generally rejects renvoi, with similar exceptions for cases in which the goal of the forum is to reach the same results as would a court of the foreign state.[46] In its explanation of the policy analysis components of § 6 analysis, however, the Second Restatement does make the sound point that a state's choice-of-law rules are relevant to determining its interest: they can provide information about both the existence and the intensity of an interest.[47]

Interest analysis, as already noted, also tends to reject renvoi. The question of whether foreign choice-of-law rules must be heeded is essentially the question of whether interests are objective or subjective. Interest analysts who deemed them objective rejected renvoi on that ground, reasoning that State A's interests, and hence the scope of its law, were to be determined by enlightened reasoning rather than State A courts or legislatures.[48] Even interest analysts who admitted that forum interests were subjective sometimes balked when asked to respect foreign territorialist choice-of-law rules.

If I am right about how to understand interest analysis, then this hesitation is unjustifiable. The theory itself directs courts to treat foreign choice-of-law rules not merely as relevant but as binding. They are statements about the scope of foreign laws, and a court trying to ascertain scope must respect them. But even if I am wrong about how to understand interest analysis, I think the Constitution requires this respect. If we think about choice of law from the two-step perspective, the status of foreign choice-of-law rules is relatively clear. State A's choice-of-law rules set the scope of State A's law, and no other state's court has the power to contradict them. (Whether State A law should prevail in a conflict with

46. See, e.g., Second Restatement § 222, comment (e).

47. See Second Restatement, § 8, comment k ("An indication of the state interest in a given matter, and the intensity of that interest, can sometimes be obtained from an examination of that state's choice-of-law decisions."); id. § 145 comment h ("in judging a state's

interest in the application of one of its local law rules, the forum should concern itself with the question whether the courts of that state would have applied this rule in the decision of the case").

48. As noted in the preceding chapter, this is directly contrary to Currie's description of how interest analysis should operate.

State B law is a different question, and what State A law says will not bind State B courts.)

But what, you might ask, about the infinite regress? If I am saying that the Constitution requires courts to accept the renvoi, it may lead them into that hall of mirrors. Then it has turned out to be a suicide pact after all.

The answer is that the two-step perspective actually eliminates the problem of renvoi. A court operating from this perspective does not use its own choice-of-law rules to decide that some foreign law "applies" and then face the problem of whether to apply foreign choice-of-law rules. Instead, it first decides whether the relevant states' laws grant rights (claims or defenses) to the parties. This is a question of the scope of the states' laws, and in deciding it, the court will follow local choice-of-law rules in determining the scope of local law, and foreign rules in determining the scope of foreign law. (I have described above how choice-of-law rules determine scope. The traditional approach, for instance, sets territorial scope; the Second Restatement apparently provides that scope is the maximum allowed by the Constitution; interest analysis sets scope by asking whether the state is interested.) Second, the court resolves conflicts between rights by applying a rule of priority. This rule of priority will be drawn from forum law.

If we understand the conceptual structure of choice of law properly, then, the renvoi problem simply never arises. It exists only because people have mistakenly thought that forum choice-of-law rules can be used to decide the scope of foreign law and then faced the question of what to do when foreign choice-of-law rules set a different scope. (Renvoi arises, that is, when the forum's choice-of-law rules say that foreign law "applies" and foreign choice-of-law rules say it does not.) But forum law can have nothing to say about the scope of foreign law. Once we understand that, the supposed problem vanishes.[49]

iii. Complex Litigation

Complex cases, involving large numbers of claims and parties, present a fascinating and important challenge for choice of law. Deciding claims under the laws of multiple states can makes a court's job much harder and more labor-intensive. More significantly, it can pose a barrier to certification of a class action. Federal

---

49. For a much more thorough development of the argument of this section, see Kermit Roosevelt III, *Resolving* *Renvoi: The Bewitchment of Our Intelligence by Means of Language*, 80 Notre Dame L. Rev. 1821 (2005).

Rule of Civil Procedure 23(b)(3) allows certification when common issues predominate over individualized ones, but the application of different states' laws can turn what looked like a common issue (tort liability) into an individualized one (tort liability under ten, or twenty, or thirty different laws).

In response to these difficulties, judges have shown tremendous creativity in deciding choice-of-law issues in complex cases. Academics have offered various proposals designed to mitigate judicial difficulties. The federal government has also acted, in perhaps a slightly different spirit. These interventions and suggestions offer a good context in which to think about the basic nature of choice of law.

The distinctive feature of the judicial response is the willingness to go to extreme lengths to find that one law governs all claims for a particular issue.[50] There are numerous examples. *In re Air Crash Disaster Near Chicago, Illinois on May 25, 1979*[51] is one. The case featured one hundred and eighteen wrongful death actions, filed in five states and Puerto Rico by plaintiffs from ten states, three foreign countries, and Puerto Rico. Complicating matters still further, the two corporate defendants hailed from different states. The suits were transferred to the Northern District of Illinois for pretrial purposes and the Court of Appeals confronted the question of which law should govern claims for punitive damages. Astonishingly—and quite implausibly—it found that Illinois law should govern all claims on this issue.

In *In re "Agent Orange" Product Liability Litigation*, the Eastern District of New York went one better.[52] That case featured claims from more than two million Vietnam veterans for injuries allegedly caused by herbicides used during the war. The district court first decided that federal common law should govern, but the Second Circuit reversed. On remand, performing a choice-of-law analysis under the traditional approach, the Second Restatement, interest analysis, Leflar's approach, and a forum law preference, Chief Judge Weinstein concluded that each led not to the law of any particular state but to a "national consensus law" created for the occasion.

---

50. For academic analyses of this point, see, e.g., James A.R. Nafziger, *Choice of Law in Air Disaster Cases: Complex Litigation Rules and the Common Law*, 54 La. L. Rev. 1001 (1994); Larry Kramer, *Choice of Law in Complex Litigation*, 71 N.Y.U. L. Rev. 547 (1996).

51. 644 F.2d 594 (7th Cir. 1981).

52. 580 F.Supp. 690 (E.D.N.Y. 1984).

Generally speaking, academics have pushed in the same direction, suggesting either choice-of-law methods or legislation to subject all claims to a single law.[53]

The judicial and academic responses share a defect: they are trying to use a procedural device to alter substantive rights. Consolidated treatment, whether by class action or otherwise, is designed to allow more efficient processing of substantially similar claims. It is not, or not supposed to be, an end in itself or a justification for creating similarity that does not otherwise exist.[54] And therefore changing parties' rights to facilitate collective adjudication is inappropriate. Indeed, the federal Rules Enabling Act, 28 U.S.C. § 2072(b) provides that the Rules of Civil Procedure "shall not abridge, enlarge or modify any substantive right," and the Supreme Court has been relatively vigilant in enforcing this restriction in the context of class actions.[55]

Parties' rights are what a choice-of-law analysis discloses. As I have argued, saying that State A law "applies" is an unhelpful phrasing. What we mean by that, or should mean, is either that State A law creates rights (claims or defenses) pertaining to a particular transaction, or that that those rights will be given priority over conflicting rights from another state. That is, it is a statement about either the scope or the priority of State A law. In either case, it is a statement about the parties' substantive rights. Reaching a different result—Illinois law instead of Michigan, or national consensus law instead of the law of any individual state—is changing those rights.

Of course, the impulse to find one law to govern all the claims of a proposed class action is understandable. Failure to do so may prevent certification, and in recent years courts have grown more receptive to this point.[56] (Or it might not—the number of different legal rules will typically be fairly small, even if the number of applicable laws is high, and subclasses may be adequate.) But thinking of choice of law in terms of substantive rights actually discloses some possible ways of achieving unified treatment.

Consider, for instance, a products liability mass tort involving a manufacturer in State A that distributes products and causes injuries in many other states. If our analysis of State A law leads us to conclude that it offers out-of-state plaintiffs a right to recover,

53. See, e.g., Juenger, *Mass Disasters and the Conflict of Laws*, 1989 U. Ill. L. Rev. 105; Russell Weintraub, *Methods for Resolving Conflict-of-Laws Problems in Mass Tort Litigation*, 1989 U.Ill. L. Rev. 129.

54. See *Phillips Petroleum Co. v. Shutts*, 472 U.S. 797 (1985).

55. See *Amchem Products, Inc. v. Windsor*, 521 U.S. 591, 613 (1997).

56. See, e.g., *Castano v. American Tobacco Co.*, 84 F.3d 734 (5th Cir. 1996); *In re America Medical Systems, Inc.*, 75 F.3d 1069 (6th Cir. 1996).

that claim could be asserted by all plaintiffs and its analysis would present common legal issues. The plaintiffs' home state's law might be more generous or plaintiff-friendly, but the plaintiffs, if they wanted, should be able to assert their rights under State A law, rather than their home law, in order to proceed via the class action vehicle. Whether their home states had a more significant relationship, or were the location of the injury, or had the better law should not prevent this; it is a simple election of remedies.

If the plaintiffs' home laws were more defendant-friendly, a court would have to decide if those laws were intended to grant defenses to out-of-state manufacturers in such cases. (They might do so in order to encourage manufacturers to ship products into the state.) If they were, there would be a conflict between the rights created by the manufacturer's home law and that of the plaintiff. If this conflict was resolved in favor of the plaintiff's home law, the uniformity would be lost.[57] Thus, the suggestion is not a panacea. In some cases, however, it should allow class treatment when conventional views of choice of law would obscure the possibility.[58]

In contrast to judges and academics, Congress has recently been acting in ways that do not indicate a preference for certification. In 2005, it passed the Class Action Fairness Act ("CAFA"), which allows defendants to remove to federal court state-law class actions where the amount in controversy exceeds $5 million and minimal diversity exists. CAFA contains no choice-of-law provision and it may be expected that choice-of-law problems will lead to the demise of a fair number of putative class actions in federal court. Academics have responded by suggesting that CAFA offers federal courts an opportunity to develop their own choice-of-law rules.[59]

---

57. In *Rowe v. Hoffman–La Roche, Inc.*, 189 N.J. 615, 917 A.2d 767 (2007), the New Jersey Supreme Court reached this conclusion, finding that Michigan was interested in applying its more defendant-friendly law to protect a New Jersey corporation from a suit by Michigan plaintiff and ultimately selecting Michigan law. In *Barbara's Sales, Inc. v. Intel Corp.*, 227 Ill.2d 45, 316 Ill.Dec. 522, 879 N.E.2d 910 (2007), the Illinois Supreme Court likewise rejected an attempt to use the defendant's home-state law for a nationwide class, on the theory that that state had no interest in offering remedies to out-of-staters for out-of-state injuries.

58. It has been accepted by a New Jersey appellate court. See *International Union of Operating Engineers Local No.* *68 Welfare Fund v. Merck & Co.*, 384 N.J.Super. 275, 894 A.2d 1136 (App.Div. 2006), rev'd on other grounds 192 N.J. 372, 929 A.2d 1076 (2007). The viability of the approach under New Jersey law has been seriously undermined by the *Rowe* decision discussed in the previous note. Professor Weintraub has also suggested a variant of the argument, which he predicted would be received skeptically by Texas courts. See Russell Weintraub, *Choice of Law as an Impediment to Certifying a National Class Action*, 46 S.Tex. L.Rev. 893 (2005).

59. See, e.g., Samuel Issacharoff, *Settled Expectations in a World of Unsettled Law: Choice of Law after the Class Action Fairness Act*, 106 Colum. L. Rev. 1839 (2006).

The extent to which the Constitution allows federal courts to do so in state-law cases is explored in Chapter 4.

iv. Characterization

By retaining the First Restatement's structure, with different rules for different kinds of cases, the Second Restatement retained as well the characterization problems that plagued the First. The Second Restatement does not offer much more than the First did in the way of guidance. It does, in the commentary following § 122, offer a good deal of generally sensible discussion of the substance/procedure distinction. But as far as deciding whether to turn to the Torts chapter or the Contracts one goes, the Second Restatement is not much help. The Introductory note to Topic 3 in the Property Chapter admits that "it may be difficult to determine whether a given issue is essentially one of property or of contract or of tort."[60] With respect to how to make the determination, all the advice the Second Restatement has is that courts should use forum law.[61]

I do not think, in fact, that a choice-of-law theory can tell us how to characterize claims. But a proper perspective on choice of law may eliminate or at least domesticate the problem, just as it did with renvoi. In the Chapter 1, I attempted to demonstrate this process using *Levy v. Daniels' U–Drive Auto Renting Co.* as an example. My argument there was that rather than trying to characterize the plaintiff's claim as sounding either in tort or in contract and then deciding which law governs, we need only ask whether any state's law gives him a right to recover—something that does not require any "characterization" analysis specific to choice of law.

Here I will consider another example, *Haumschild v. Continental Casualty Co.*[62] The Haumschilds were a Wisconsin married couple who got into a car accident in California. The wife thereafter sued the husband. Wisconsin allowed interspousal tort suits as a matter of its purely domestic law, while California did not.

How should the case be resolved? Most modern thinking suggests that when dealing with a loss-allocating issue like immunity in a suit between co-domiciliaries, domiciliary law should govern. Currie would call the case a false conflict; New York would apply *Neumeier*'s first rule; and the Second Restatement has a specific rule, in § 169, providing for domiciliary law.

---

60. Second Restatement, Introductory Note to Chapter 9, Topic 3.

61. Second Restatement § 7. To similar effect are ERNEST LORENZEN, SELECTED ARTICLES ON CONFLICT OF LAWS 80–135 (1947) and ARTHUR ROBERTSON, CHARACTERIZATION IN THE CONFLICT OF LAWS (1940).

62. 7 Wis.2d 130, 95 N.W.2d 814 (1959).

The *Haumschild* court likewise seemed to think that domiciliary law was the sensible result. Deciding the case in 1959, it did not have much of the modern teaching available, so it used depecage and characterization to reach the desired conclusion. Mrs. Haumschild's suit presented two issues, the court reasoned: the tort claim and the issue of capacity to sue. The tort claim would be governed by the law of the place of the accident (California). Capacity to sue a spouse, as a family law issue, would also be governed by the territorially appropriate law, namely the law of marital domicile (Wisconsin).

What happens if we think about the case in terms of scope and priority? Our first question is whether the laws grant the parties claims or defenses. Does California do so? The best reading of California law is probably that it does create a tort claim for Mrs. Haumschild. Immunities, I have suggested, are generally better understood as the subordination of a claim to a defense. (To the extent that interspousal tort immunity rests on the idea that a married couple is one legal entity, it might more properly be considered the absence of a claim; however, the *Haumschild* court rejected this understanding of the immunity.) What about the defense; is it available as well? The *Haumschild* court assumed that California's interspousal immunity would govern all cases decided under California law, and hence that "applying" California law would mean that Mrs. Haumschild could not recover. But of course that is true only if "applying" California law means deciding the case as if it were wholly internal to California, something I have argued is a mistake.

In fact, California courts had confronted the *Haumschild* situation before, and they had ruled that they would treat capacity to sue as governed by domiciliary law. That is, if the *Haumschild* court had looked to California choice-of-law rules, it would have seen that California *does not* grant one out-of-state spouse immunity against the other, unless their home law so provides. Wisconsin does not offer Mr. Haumschild a defense on the immunity issue,[63] and so the case is easy. It is a false conflict: California law grants a claim and no defense opposes it.

That may seem too easy a resolution, for certainly cases will arise in which the state where the accident occurs is not so accommodating. What of them? Assume that California did not, as a matter of its choice-of-law rules, allow out-of-state spouses to sue each other under California law. Again, we need to start with an analysis of the scope of the relevant states' laws.

---

63. There might still be a conflict between California and Wisconsin law on other issues, such as the measure of damages.

Now California law will be no help to Mrs. Haumschild. It gives her a claim, but subordinates it to a defense that it grants her husband.[64] What about Wisconsin law? Wisconsin law probably does give Mrs. Haumschild a claim. Wisconsin has a policy of compensating its injured domiciliaries and deterring conduct that injures them, and those policies are implicated in this case. It does not give Mr. Haumschild a defense. We are left with the conclusion that Mrs. Haumschild has tort claims under California and Wisconsin law, and her husband has a defense under California law.

How do we decide which of these legal rights gets priority? We know that the California defense prevails over the California claim; that is simply how California law works. So what we are left with is the conflict between Mrs. Haumschild's claim under Wisconsin law and her husband's defense under California law. We need a rule of priority that will resolve it.

I will have more to say about the permissible construction of rules of priority in the next chapter. This case is still relatively easy. If Wisconsin and California were to bargain over whose law should get priority in *Haumschild* and a mirror-image case, where a California married couple had an accident in Wisconsin, it is likely that they would agree that Wisconsin law should prevail in *Haumschild* and California law in the mirror image. If they were forced to adopt rules of priority that claimed only one of a pair of mirror-image cases, their rules would agree on the appropriate outcome of *Haumschild*.

In fact, since the *Haumschild* case was brought in Wisconsin, we need only consider Wisconsin's rule of priority. If the Wisconsin legislature had to choose between *Haumschild* and its mirror-image, it is highly likely that they would choose *Haumschild*, and a court that thought so would be justified in giving priority to the rights created by Wisconsin law.

The facts of *Haumschild* provide a good opportunity for choice-of-law analysis, and I hope the analysis I have offered is appealing. The more specific lesson it offers for characterization is this. Doing choice-of-law analysis properly will require us to decide which, if any, of the potentially relevant state laws grant rights to the parties. This may be a difficult task, as *Haumschild* and *Levy* show. But it does not require any characterization analysis, and still less one specific to the field of choice of law.

64. Alert readers may wonder why it grants her husband this defense—why should California grant a Wisconsin husband this benefit? My answer is that it is constitutionally required to do so, a topic pursued in more detail in the next chapter.

Chapter 4

CONSTITUTIONAL CONSTRAINTS ON CHOICE OF LAW

Thus far we have been largely considering the choice-of-law question from the perspective of a state wondering which approach to adopt. We now turn away from the merits and demerits of the different approaches and take up the question of external constraints on choice of law. When will the Constitution forbid a court from deciding a case under its local law?[1] (The question of when federal statutory law may have this effect is considered in Chapter 5.)

There are two basic issues here. The first is when the Constitution limits a state's authority to attach legal consequences to events. What is the line beyond which a state's legislative jurisdiction simply cannot extend?[2] The second is when the Constitution prescribes a resolution to a conflict between two states' laws. When must a state's assertion of legislative jurisdiction yield to the claim of another state?

These issues fit quite naturally with the two-step model. They are the questions of what limits the Constitution places on, respectively, state rules of scope and state rules of priority. The model thus provides a useful framework within which to think about them. It will be easiest to begin by discussing the relevant constitutional provisions, then to consider the different issues to which they apply.

I. Relevant Constitutional Provisions

A. Due Process

The first relevant clause, the Due Process Clause of the Fourteenth Amendment, provides that no state shall "deprive any person of life, liberty, or property, without due process of law...."

---

1. In theory, the question is more general; it is when a court will be forbidden to apply some particular state's law. In practice, since courts generally do not strain to apply foreign law, the question is almost always about when a court can apply its own state's law, and that is how I will phrase it in this chapter.

2. A variant of this question, considered later in the chapter, is when the Constitution requires a state to assert legislative jurisdiction by granting rights to out-of-staters.

The clause works to set limits on state legislative jurisdiction; that is, it constrains a state's ability to impose obligations on individuals. (The Due Process Clause of the Fifth Amendment operates similarly with respect to federal legislative jurisdiction, but we will focus on the Fourteenth Amendment's application to state laws.)[3] As we will see in Chapter 6, it also restrains the exercise of judicial jurisdiction: it sets limits on a state's ability to adjudicate an individual's rights. Legislative jurisdiction is our focus now.

There are two different ways to understand the operation of due process in the choice-of-law context. The first, historically significant but now largely forgotten, proceeds via a straightforward application of the text. The Due Process Clause requires states attempting to restrict individual liberty to do so by means of a valid law. If there is no state law attaching particular consequences to certain acts, the state may not visit those consequences on individuals who perform the acts. Or put more plainly, if the facts of a case are not within the scope of state law, the state cannot decide the case under its law.

Thus described, due process is not so much a limit on state legislative jurisdiction as a means of enforcing pre-existing limits.[4] It patrols a line that must be drawn by other means. Those other means used to exist—territoriality served very well when it was accepted as part of the nature of law—but they no longer do. For that reason, this understanding of due process has less significance for the modern caselaw.

The other way of understanding the due process requirement is as a protector of essentially procedural values, especially notice and fairness. From this perspective, the Due Process Clause ensures that states do not assert authority over individuals in ways that create an unfair surprise. It may also—although this requirement has grown less clear over time—ensure that individuals receive something in return for being subjected to a state's regulatory authority.

---

3. For an analysis of Fifth Amendment constraints on federal legislative jurisdiction, see Lea Brilmayer & Charles Norchi, *Federal Extraterritoriality and Fifth Amendment Due Process*, 105 Harv. L. Rev. 1217 (1992).

4. This is, I have argued, the way that due process was understood in its early "substantive" incarnation in the *Lochner* era. See Kermit Roosevelt III, *Forget the Fundamentals: Fixing Substantive Due Process*, 8 U.Pa. J. Con. L. 983 (2006). The connection between the *Lochner*-era due process cases and choice of law is substantial and worth exploring: *Allgeyer v. Louisiana*, 165 U.S. 578 (1897), often cited as the birthplace of the "fundamental" right to contract is in fact a choice-of-law case about the territorial limits of legislative jurisdiction. For a more detailed analysis, see James Y. Stern, *Choice of Law, the Constitution, and* Lochner, 94 Va. L. Rev. 1509 (2008).

B. Privileges and Immunities

Where due process restricts a state's ability to impose obligations on individuals, the Privileges and Immunities Clause of Article IV addresses the issue of scope from the other side. It provides that "The Citizens of each State shall be entitled to all Privileges and Immunities of Citizens in the several States." What this clause does is to place limits on a state's ability to withhold from out-of-staters rights that it grants to its own citizens.

If taken seriously, the Privileges and Immunities Clause could have dramatic consequences for choice of law. However, it has not been taken seriously. The Supreme Court, we shall see, has ended up reading the Constitution so that it does very little in the choice of law context, and this is especially true of the Privileges and Immunities Clause.

C. Full Faith and Credit

The Full Faith and Credit Clause provides that "Full Faith and Credit shall be given in each State to the public Acts, Record, and judicial Proceedings of every other State." It requires states to respect the laws of other states, not to deem them inferior merely because they are foreign. From one perspective, it differs from due process and privileges and immunities. Both due process and privileges and immunities, as I have described them above, are concerned with the relationship between individuals and states, and in particular the scope of state laws. Due process sometimes stops states from extending their laws to individuals (to impose obligations), and privileges and immunities sometimes requires them to do so (to grant rights). The Full Faith and Credit Clause, by contrast, is concerned with the relationship between states, and in particular with the relative priority of their laws.

From another perspective, we might put privileges and immunities and full faith and credit together on one side of the line and due process on the other. The former two are both found in Article IV, the article of the Constitution concerned with interstate relations. They are both nationalizing clauses, intended to yoke the discrete states into a single nation.[5] And they both do so by forbidding discrimination: privileges and immunities forbids discrimination against sister-state citizens, and full faith and credit

---

5. See, e.g., *Magnolia Petroleum Co. v. Hunt*, 320 U.S. 430, 439 (1943) (describing nationalizing effect of full faith and credit); *Toomer v. Witsell*, 334 U.S. 385, 395 (1948) (same for privileges and immunities).

forbids discrimination against sister-state law. Due process, by contrast, is concerned with fundamental fairness in the relationship between states and individuals; it is not concerned with creating or preserving a national union.

The possibility of drawing conceptual lines in these two different ways makes structuring the discussion of this topic slightly harder, and the task is further complicated by the fact that the Supreme Court has decided that a single doctrinal test suffices for both due process and full faith and credit. The decision is unfortunate. Not only do the two clauses protect different interests, but they also operate at different steps in the choice-of-law analysis, due process at the scope stage and full faith and credit at the priority stage. But because the Court has merged the analysis, I will discuss due process and full faith and credit together under the single heading of the use of local law as a rule of decision. I will then return to full faith and credit in the context of discrimination.

D. Others

One might also expect to find some limits on state choice-of-law rules in other constitutional provisions. The Equal Protection Clause, for instance, might be thought to prohibit discrimination in the same way as the Privileges and Immunities Clause. The Dormant Commerce Clause might work to block state choice-of-law rules that burden interstate commerce.

The Court has done essentially nothing with the Equal Protection Clause. The failure to invigorate Equal Protection in the choice-of-law context is reasonable, however—certainly more reasonable than the neglect of the other clauses discussed above. The Privileges and Immunities Clause is specifically addressed to the problem of discrimination against out-of-staters. Equal protection, as it has worked out in court, is typically concerned with discrimination *among* state citizens. Equal protection cases do deal with the scope of state law, since the question they typically raise is whether the state may grant rights to some and withhold them from others, but they lack the multistate factors that would bring them under the conflict of laws umbrella.[6]

---

6. Differential treatment of locals inside and outside the state might, in theory, raise equal protection questions. Brainerd Currie argued that a state violates the Equal Protection Clause if it denies the benefit of its law to a resident outside the state on grounds that have no relation to the purpose of the law. See CURRIE, SELECTED ESSAYS, at 536–583. That meant, for Currie, that setting a territorial scope to a state's contract law was unconstitutional because it unreasonably denied that law to a resident contracting outside the state—"unreasonably" because the purposes of contract law are unrelated to the place of

The Dormant Commerce Clause has received somewhat greater attention. It has been used to limit state legislative jurisdiction when excessively broad assertions threaten commerce. Thus, in *Brown–Forman Distillers Corp. v. New York State Liquor Authority*,[7] the Court struck down a New York law requiring distillers who sold in New York to affirm that the prices they charged New York wholesalers were no higher than the lowest price they charged wholesalers outside the state. This, the Court said, was an impermissible attempt to regulate out-of-state transactions.

The clause has also been used to grant some constitutional stature to the internal affairs doctrine. In *Edgar v. MITE Corp.*,[8] the Court considered an Illinois law that purported to regulate the acquisition of corporations when ten percent of their stock was held by Illinois residents. The Court struck this down on the grounds that it unduly burdened commerce and commented in passing that "Illinois has no interest in regulating the internal affairs of foreign corporations."[9] On the other hand, faced with an Indiana anti-takeover statute that applied only to Indiana corporations, the Court upheld it against a Dormant Commerce Clause challenge.

Read for all it is worth, the *Edgar* dictum[10] could support an argument that only the state of incorporation has authority to regulate a corporation's internal affairs. ("Internal affairs" are the rights and obligations among the participants in the corporate venture.) The argument probably belongs under the Full Faith and Credit Clause, although it might also be based on due process. Briefly, it would be either that the interest of the state of incorporation is so evidently superior that its law must be given priority (a full faith and credit argument) or that the application of some other state's law would constitute an unfair surprise to parties who had structured their relationship in reliance on the law of the state of incorporation (a due process argument).

As we will see, neither due process nor full faith and credit retains enough vitality to give the argument great chances of success, though the full faith and credit version may still be plausible. The anemic nature of the Court's due process and full

contracting. The Supreme Court has never indicated any enthusiasm for this line of argument.

7. 476 U.S. 573 (1986).

8. 457 U.S. 624 (1982).

9. Id. at 645–46.

10. The remark came in the context of the Court's rejection of Illinois' attempt to justify its law on the grounds of its interest in regulating the internal affairs of Illinois corporations. The Court first rejected that characterization, pointing out that the transfer of stock to a third party is not a matter of internal affairs. It then pointed out that the statute applied to foreign-chartered corporations as well, as to whose internal affairs Illinois had no interest.

faith and credit jurisprudence is regrettable, in my view, but it is of little practical significance as far as internal affairs goes because the internal affairs doctrine is universally accepted, and should any state deviate from it, the Court might very well find a Dormant Commerce Clause problem.

II. Limits on the Use of Local Law as a Rule of Decision

The first topic we consider is the role of due process and full faith and credit in restricting a court's ability to decide a case under its own law. Barriers, we shall see, could arise either at the stage of scope or at the stage of priority. In my view, as already noted, due process is relevant to the first of those and full faith and credit to the second. This seems to have been the original, or at least the early, understanding. Over time, however, as the choice-of-law inquiry came to be framed as "what state's law applies?" the two stages were collapsed, and the Court's analysis followed suit.

A. Original Understandings

The traditional approach to choice of law probably does a relatively good job of capturing the understandings of those who drafted and ratified the original Constitution and the Fourteenth Amendment. Conflicts does not seem to have been a major topic of debate at either time, although the Full Faith and Credit and Privileges and Immunities Clauses are clearly directed to conflict of laws issues.[11] (I refer here to "conflicts" rather than "choice of law" because full faith and credit also speaks to recognition of judgments, which is a conflicts topic but not a choice of law.) The reason that conflicts topics were not contentious is probably that they seemed relatively straightforward. Given the dominant understanding of the nature of law, conflicts problems were easy.

As far as the permissible scope of state law was concerned, the nature of law, as Joseph Beale would repeat, was understood to impose fairly tight territorial boundaries on state legislative jurisdiction. These limits would have existed as a matter of general

---

11. Future Chief Justice John Marshall did, however, apparently state the vested rights theory at the Virginia ratifying convention. See Douglas Laycock, *Equal Citizens of Equal and Territorial States: The Constitutional Foundations of Choice of Law*, 92 Colum. L. Rev. 249 (1992). For early analysis of the conflicts provisions, see, e.g., 3 JOSEPH STORY, COMMENTARIES ON THE CONSTITUTION OF THE UNITED STATES § 1304 (1833) (discussing full faith and credit); id. § 1800 (discussing privileges and immunities). For a more recent treatment, see WILLIAM L. REYNOLDS & WILLIAM M. RICHMAN, THE FULL FAITH AND CREDIT CLAUSE (2005).

constitutional law, and they were made federal by the adoption of the Fourteenth Amendment's Due Process Clause.[12] As for people within the state, the Privileges and Immunities Clause of the original Constitution required states to treat out-of-staters not as aliens but as entitled to (most of) the rights of locals.[13] Thus, states were generally bound to make rights under their laws equally available to all U.S. citizens inside their borders, and not to impose burdens on persons outside.

As for priority, the question did not arise in any substantial way. Given the territorial limits to the scope of state laws, conflict between them was simply impossible. The only question a court could face was whether rights created by foreign law would be enforced at all—not whether they would be enforced in the face of contrary local rights. Full faith and credit gives a relatively clear answer to this question: foreign rights must be respected. (The lingering question is perhaps whether full faith and credit renders the public policy exception unconstitutional, something scholars have argued.)[14]

The original, or early, understanding thus gives the relevant constitutional provisions clear and distinct roles to play. It provides for quite robust constitutional supervision of state choice-of-law practice, and it does so without requiring judges to make any difficult or policy-rooted decisions. It does all this, however, only because the master principle of territoriality suppresses the possibility of conflict between state laws and sets limits to their scope for the Due Process Clause to enforce. As territoriality eroded, the original system of constitutional choice of law became destabilized and ultimately unworkable.

B. Evolution

i. Full Faith and Credit

Early cases under all three of these clauses follow the lines set out above. In due process cases, the Court limited state authority to events located inside the state's geographical boundaries. If it deemed a contract formed in State A, for instance, the Court would

---

12. For a more thorough discussion of general constitutional law and its federalization through the Due Process Clause, see Michael G. Collins, *Before Lochner—Diversity Jurisdiction and the Development of General Constitutional Law*, 74 Tul. L. Rev. 1263 (2000); Michael G. Collins, *October Term 1896—* *Embracing Due Process*, 45 Am. J. Legal Hist. 71 (2001).

13. See Story, supra, at § 1800.

14. See, e.g., Larry Kramer, *Same-Sex Marriage, Choice of Laws, and the Unconstitutional Public Policy Exception*, 106 Yale L. J. 1965 (1997).

hold it unconstitutional for State B to use its law to alter the parties' rights under the contract. *Allgeyer v. Louisiana*,[15] typically considered one of the early *Lochner*-era liberty of contract cases, is in fact a choice-of-law case in which the Court bars Louisiana from affecting rights under a New York contract. To similar effect are *New York Life Insurance Co. v. Dodge*,[16] prohibiting Missouri from altering a New York contract, and *Home Insurance Co. v. Dick*,[17] prohibiting Texas from applying a Texas law extending the time to sue beyond that provided in a Mexican contract. The Texas statute, the Court wrote in *Dick*, "may not validly affect contracts which are neither made nor are to be performed in Texas."

Similarly, with a contract formed in State A, it would be a violation of the Full Faith and Credit Clause for State B to refuse to recognize the contractual rights and obligations created under State A law. Given that due process was available as an alternate means to reach this conclusion, cases decided under full faith and credit are rarer. In *New York Life Insurance Co. v. Head*,[18] however, the Court gave a ringing endorsement to the full faith and credit rationale. Denying the power of Missouri to modify a New York contract, it wrote:

> it would be impossible to permit the statutes of Missouri to operate beyond the jurisdiction of that State and in the State of New York and there destroy freedom of contract without throwing down the constitutional barriers by which all the States are restricted within the orbits of their lawful authority and upon the preservation of which the Government under the Constitution depends. This is so obviously the necessary result of the Constitution that it has rarely been called in question and hence authorities directly dealing with it do not abound. The principle however lies at the foundation of the full faith and credit clause and the many rulings which have given effect to that clause.[19]

The independent operation of the full faith and credit clause may be seen in cases involving cross-border events. In such cases, no due process problem exists because the case has sufficient contacts with both states to make their exercise of legislative jurisdiction consistent with the territorial principle. Full faith and credit may nonetheless stand as a limit on a court's ability to decide the case under local law.

15. 165 U.S. 578 (1897).
16. 246 U.S. 357 (1918).
17. 281 U.S. 397 (1930).

18. 234 U.S. 149 (1914).
19. Id. at 161.

Bradford Electric Light Co. v. Clapper[20] arose out of an accident in New Hampshire. Leon Clapper, a Vermont resident, was employed by Bradford Electric Light, a Vermont corporation. Bradford's electric lines extended into New Hampshire. Clapper, sent there to replace fuses, died in an accident and his administrator sued Bradford under New Hampshire common law. Vermont's workers' compensation statute stated that it provided the exclusive remedy for injured employees, unless the employee or employer opted out before the accident. It also stated explicitly that it covered accidents outside the state.

After the administrator recovered under New Hampshire law in New Hampshire courts, Bradford sought Supreme Court review on full faith and credit grounds. Justice Brandeis, writing for the Court, agreed that deciding the case under New Hampshire law violated the Full Faith and Credit Clause.

Described at this level of generality, *Clapper* sounds much like *Dodge* or *Head*. But it is not simply another example of that *Lochner*-era approach to choice of law. Brandeis was in fact an opponent of the formalistic line-drawing characteristic of the *Lochner* era, and he had dissented from some of the more doctrinaire due process decisions such as *New York Life Insurance v. Dodge*. But Brandeis was not categorically opposed to constitutional limits on choice of law—he earlier wrote the unanimous opinion in *Home Insurance Co. v. Dick*. What distinguishes the Brandeis opinions from those of the more pro-*Lochner* Justices such as McReynolds (the author of *Dodge*) is their more modern and pragmatic tone. Rather than attempt to localize the contract in *Dick* on the basis of a single factor, for instance, Brandeis stressed that literally *nothing* about the contract related to Texas, and that the defendants Dick sued had never "sought favors" from Texas but "ask only to be let alone." Rather than giving talismanic significance to the place of contracting, that is, Brandeis' due process approach looks to the aggregate significance of the defendant's total contacts with the state and also incorporates a quid pro quo element.

His full faith and credit analysis is similar. A wholly traditional approach might have reasoned that the employment contract between Bradford and Clapper was formed in Vermont, that it incorporated the terms of the Vermont worker's compensation act, and that New Hampshire was bound to recognize the rights created by that contract. Instead, Brandeis starts by noting that Clapper's administrator is seeking to assert rights that "would be denied him in the State of his residence and employment" and that "the

20.   286 U.S. 145 (1932).

effectiveness of the Vermont Act would be gravely impaired" if this were allowed. He goes on to ask whether New Hampshire has an interest sufficient to justify overriding the Vermont rights. He finds that it does not: Clapper was not a New Hampshire resident; he was not continuously employed there; he had no dependent there. "The interest of New Hampshire was only casual." And because the Vermont Act was offered as a defense by Bradford, New Hampshire could not refuse to recognize it on grounds of public policy: "to refuse to give effect to a substantive defense under the applicable law of another State, as under the circumstances here presented, subjects the defendant to irremediable liability. This may not be done."

Clapper does not articulate with any precision a doctrinal test for full faith and credit claims, but it seems to stand for the proposition that a state with only a casual interest in a case may not refuse to recognize the law of a more interested state. It does not, of course, use the same concept of interest that Brainerd Currie developed, but the analysis is somewhat similar. New Hampshire has no interest, Brandeis seems to think, in interfering with the relationship between Bradford and Clapper, both of whom are Vermont domiciliaries. (This is less obvious than he supposes; New Hampshire may well have a legitimate interest in granting Clapper rights under its common law, either to deter employer negligence or to protect the interests of local medical creditors.)

Clapper is a transitional case. Its cross-border tort facts show some of the tensions within the traditional system, which the erosion of territoriality threw into progressively sharper relief. It still seems to assume, however, that the Full Faith and Credit Clause prescribes unique right answers to many or most choice-of-law questions. Without territorial limits to identify a unique state with a legitimate claim to legislative authority, however, prescribing a single right answer will require courts to adjudicate between competing claims of state interest. The *Clapper* Court was willing to do so. What we see in subsequent cases is the Court recognizing the difficulty of the task it has taken on, and eventually confessing failure. Its concession came at the same time as it was abandoning the restrictive limits of the *Lochner* jurisprudence, and for much the same reason. In both contexts, the Court came to believe that it was simply incapable, or at least substantially less capable than a legislature, of drawing the lines on which the earlier jurisprudence depended.[21]

---

21. For a brief statement of this analysis of the end of *Lochner*, see Kermit Roosevelt III, *Forget the Fundamentals: Fixing Substantive Due Process,* 8

Three years after *Clapper* came *Alaska Packers*.[22] Palma, a non-resident alien, entered into a contract in San Francisco whereby he agreed to work for Alaska Packers in Alaska during the salmon canning season. The contract stated that the Alaska Workmen's Compensation Law would govern the relationship. The Alaska law provided that it was the exclusive remedy for injuries suffered there; that is, the statute itself claimed priority against other laws.

The California Workmen's Compensation Act, as then in force and as interpreted by the California Supreme Court, provided that it extended to injuries suffered outside the state if the contract of employment was formed in California. It also stated that no other law could exempt employers from liability fixed by the Act. Thus, like the Alaska law, the California Act both defined its own scope and asserted priority against any other laws.

Palma was injured during his employment in Alaska and, upon his return to California, applied for and received compensation under the California Act. Alaska Packers argued that full faith and credit required recognition of the exclusive status of the Alaska remedy. The Supreme Court rejected the argument, and in so doing gave a clearer statement of its approach to full faith and credit.

I have already said that *Clapper* is best read to endorse a form of balancing. With some effort, though, one might also extract the traditional idea that rights created by another state's law must (almost) always be respected. This view of full faith and credit, I have suggested, is probably close to the original understanding, and it made a fair amount of sense in a world in which state legislative jurisdiction did not overlap and conflicts between state laws could not arise. But it obviously makes no sense in a world in which conflicts do arise; it would mean, as the *Alaska Packers* Court put it, that "the statute of each state must be enforced in the courts of the other, but cannot be in its own." If we read *Clapper* this way, it favored Vermont law simply because the suit was brought in New Hampshire; had Clapper's administrator sued in Vermont, full faith and credit would have compelled recognition of New Hampshire's common law rights.

Alaska Packers rejects this "rigid and literal" view of full faith and credit. Rather than stating that the California courts were

U. Pa. J. Con. L. 983 (2006). For longer, generally similar ones, see HOWARD GILLMAN, THE CONSTITUTION BESIEGED: THE RISE AND DEMISE OF *LOCHNER* ERA POLICE POWERS JURISPRUDENCE (1993); BARRY CUSHMAN,

RETHINKING THE NEW DEAL COURT (1998); G. EDWARD WHITE, THE CONSTITUTION AND THE NEW DEAL (2000).

22. *Alaska Packers Assoc. v. Industrial Acc. Comm'n*, 294 U.S. 532 (1935).

bound to recognize rights created under Alaska law, it observed that *"Prima facie*, every state is entitled to enforce in its own courts its own statutes, lawfully enacted." When would full faith and credit sweep aside this entitlement? When the objecting party could show "upon some rational basis, that of the conflicting interests involved those of the foreign state are superior to those of the forum." Thus, the *Alaska Packers* Court understands full faith and credit to mandate essentially that, when laws conflict, priority shall be given to the law of the state with the greater interest. (Only, however, when the interest is substantially greater; following the quoted sentence the Court goes on to note that in some cases each state will be allowed to enforce its own law. Thus full faith and credit does not always prescribe unique solutions under *Alaska Packers*.)

On the facts before it, the Court found that Alaska's interest was not greater. It might have been sufficient for an Alaska court to follow Alaska law without violating the Constitution—the Court reserved that question—but it was not enough to require California courts to do so.

The problem with the *Alaska Packers* approach was that it required the Court to weigh and compare the states' competing interests. What exactly this weighing amounts to depends on our understanding of what an interest is. If interests are objective, a court might be able to come up with some means of ranking them. If they are subjective, as I have argued, the task is harder, since states will be free to set their own priorities and choose, as between competing policies, which is more important to them. In either case, it is a demanding job, which thrusts the Court deeply into the intricacies of interstate relations with no real guidance from the constitutional text. And as it has in other areas, the Court decided it had bitten off more than it could chew.[23]

In *Pacific Employers Insurance Company v. Industrial Accident Commission*,[24] the Court again confronted a conflict between workers' compensation laws. (You have doubtless noticed that all of these cases present the same basic fact pattern of an employment relationship formed in one state and an injury in another.) A Massachusetts resident, employed by a Massachusetts corporation, was sent temporarily to a branch factory in California, where he suffered an injury. The California Industrial Accident Commission

---

23. A good comparison is perhaps the short-lived attempt to identify essential state functions immune from federal regulation, announced in *National League of Cities v. Usery*, 426 U.S. 833 (1976), and abandoned in *Garcia v. San Antonio Metropolitan Transit Authority*, 469 U.S. 528 (1985).

24. 306 U.S. 493 (1939).

directed the employer to pay compensation as provided for in the California workers' compensation act, and the employer resisted on the grounds that the applicable Massachusetts statute operated as the exclusive remedy. The California courts gave priority to California law.

The Supreme Court affirmed. As in *Alaska Packers*, it affirmed the judicial responsibility to enforce full faith and credit. "This Court must determine for itself how far the full faith and credit clause compels the qualification or denial of rights asserted under the laws of one state, that of the forum, by the statute of another state." But the answer to the question "how far?" then turned out to be "not very." Rather than attempting to balance interests as *Alaska Packers* had suggested, the Court noted the significance of California's interests in "prescribing for itself the legal consequences of acts within it" and treated the matter as closed. California's interests need not be compared to those of Massachusetts; if they existed at all, that was enough.

Thus, *Pacific Employers* backs away from *Alaska Packers* by suggesting that full faith and credit will compel the forum to give priority to another state's law only if the forum has *no* interest— that is, if the case does not fall within the scope of forum law. How many cases fall into this category depends on how permissive the Court is in allowing states to claim an interest, a topic we will consider in a moment. It should be clear at this point, however, that under the *Pacific Employers* approach, the full faith and credit clause will only very seldom compel the outcome of a conflict between state laws. Very few choice-of-law cases will have constitutionally prescribed answers.

You are forgiven if you thought that *Pacific Employers* would nonetheless be one. It features the same array of contacts as *Clapper*, and *Clapper* said that the interest of the place of injury (there New Hampshire, here California) was "only casual." Why is California's interest adequate when New Hampshire's was not? *Pacific Employers* does feature an attempt to distinguish *Clapper* on the grounds that California has articulated a stronger public policy than New Hampshire had, but it is not very persuasive. One might also observe that California is farther from Massachusetts than New Hampshire is from Vermont, and thus that the likelihood of the injured employee running up medical bills in the state of injury is greater. But these differences are really beside the point. The key is that the Court sees a legitimate interest in attaching legal consequences to events within a state, and under *Pacific Employers*, any interest is enough.[25]

To determine whether full faith and credit retains any force at all, we need to ask how far states can go in asserting an interest. Some interests are obviously legitimate. A state can plainly assert an interest in regulating conduct within its borders, protecting and compensating its citizens, regulating the actions of its citizens, and regulating activity that has effects within its borders.

Somewhere beyond these interests, there lie constitutional boundaries. The Supreme Court has in fact rejected some asserted interests, as we shall see in the following section, but as a general matter it does not draw the boundaries very tightly. One notable decision, *Carroll v. Lanza*,[26] suggests that states can assert an interest based on the probability that similar events will trigger interests, even if the actual events underlying a case do not. *Lanza* was yet another workers' compensation case, featuring a Missouri employee, a Missouri employer, and an injury in Arkansas. The employee sued in Arkansas and obtained the benefits of Arkansas law.

Did Arkansas have an interest sufficient to meet the *Pacific Employers* requirement? One of the standard refrains in such cases is that the state of injury has an interest in applying its law in order to ensure that medical creditors within the state can recover. On the facts of *Lanza*, however, that interest was not present. The employee did not receive medical care in Arkansas; instead he returned to Missouri and was treated there. No matter, wrote Justice Douglas: Arkansas' interests "are to be weighted not only in light of the facts of this case but by the kind of situation presented."

There may be an argument as to why state interests should be evaluated in light of the "kind of situation presented" rather than the actual facts of the case. It is certainly easier to develop and administer rules based on kinds of situations rather than case by case, and a legislature considering the question of scope might draw such an overinclusive line. But Justice Douglas did not bother to give this argument, nor did he explain how kinds of situations are to be identified. *Carroll v. Lanza* suggests that the Court is quite

---

25. The internal affairs doctrine is, in some cases, an exception to *Pacific Employers*. In *Edgar v. MITE Corp.*, discussed above in the context of the Dormant Commerce Clause, the Court stated categorically (though in dictum) that a state had "no interest" in regulating the internal affairs of foreign corpora- tions. In the context of fraternal benefit societies, the Court has been willing to constitutionalize a rule granting priority to the law of the state of formation. See, e.g., *Order of United Commercial Travelers v. Wolfe*, 331 U.S. 586 (1947).

26. 349 U.S. 408 (1955).

reluctant to police state assertions of interest. The recent cases which we will see in the next section, confirm that suggestion.

ii. Due Process

As the erosion of territoriality made the overlap of legislative jurisdiction more frequent, the full faith and credit cases had posed a question to the Court. If the full faith and credit command was not to be "always recognize rights created by sister-state law," when was a state required to give priority to foreign rights? We have seen that after toying with the *Alaska Packers* answer "when the foreign state's interest is superior," the Court settled at last on the minimalist *Pacific Employers* test: full faith and credit requires a forum state to give priority to foreign rights when the forum has no interest.

Due process presented a similar question. If the geographical boundaries of a state did not set the constitutional limits on its legislative jurisdiction, how far could it go? The answer that the Court came up with was "as long as subjecting a party to its law is neither arbitrary nor fundamentally unfair."

This is not a surprising answer; arbitrariness and fairness are familiar due process touchstones, which also play a role in the context of judicial jurisdiction. To understand how they work with legislative jurisdiction, we need to flesh out the concepts a bit, but here too the answer is unsurprising. Basically, the Court has been concerned with ensuring that parties have adequate notice that they may be subjected to a state's law.

Drawing the boundaries of legislative jurisdiction at the state line will achieve this in most cases. But as territoriality eroded, the Court became more permissive. In *Watson v. Employers Liability Assurance Corporation*,[27] a Louisiana resident was injured by a product manufactured by an Illinois subsidiary (Toni) of a Massachusetts corporation (Gillette). Louisiana had a direct action statute, which allowed individuals to sue a corporation's insurer, and pursuant to this statute Watson filed suit in Louisiana. The insurance policy, however, contained a clause forbidding suits against the insurer until after Toni had been held liable. The policy had been negotiated and issued in Massachusetts and Illinois and was valid under those state's laws, but the Louisiana court disregarded it as unenforceable under Louisiana law.

The insurer sought Supreme Court review on both full faith and credit and due process grounds. The full faith and credit issue

27. 348 U.S. 66 (1954).

was easy. Since Watson was a Louisiana resident injured in Louisiana, Louisiana obviously had a legitimate interest in granting her rights.

The due process issue was only slightly harder. True, the process of contracting had no connection to Louisiana. That might have been enough for the Court that decided *New York Life Insurance Co. v. Dodge*—a pre-New Deal Court might well have said that Louisiana could not use its law to alter the rights created by a foreign contract. (The complicating factor is that Watson was not a party to the insurance contract.) But in 1954, the Court took a different approach. The insurer could not claim to be surprised at being subjected to Louisiana law, the Court wrote, because it had offered Gillette and Toni coverage against damages on account of personal injuries that might be suffered anywhere in the United States. By covering Louisiana injuries, the company should have known that it was exposing itself to the possibility of being subjected to Louisiana law.

Should it have? Claims about foreseeability and expectations frequently have a circular or self-fulfilling characteristic. After the *Watson* decision, insurers were certainly on notice that they might be subjected to the laws of states where covered injuries were caused. Before *Watson*, however, an insurer might have relied on *Dodge* for the proposition that Louisiana law could not alter rights created under an Illinois contract. *Watson* might indeed have come as a surprise at the time.

Even afterwards, it is not entirely clear what laws an insurer is on notice about. Probably the best way to understand *Watson* is as holding that if, at the time of contracting, it is foreseeable that future events may give a state an interest, due process will not protect a party from being subjected to that state's law. (Thus, in *Watson*, the insurer should have known that an injury in Louisiana would give Louisiana an interest and justify the application of its law.)

Clay v. Sun Insurance Office, Ltd., 377 U.S. 179 (1964) confirms and amplifies this view of due process. Clay, an Illinois resident, purchased personal property insurance in Illinois. Some months later, he moved to Florida. Two years after the move, he suffered a loss when his wife burnt his clothing. He submitted a claim, which the insurer denied. The policy required Clay to file any suit challenging the denial within a year of the denial, a clause valid under Illinois law but invalid under the law of Florida, which provided a five-year filing window. Clay filed suit in federal district court in Florida more than twelve months after the denial.

123

Could Florida law operate to extend his filing period? After a fairly lengthy course of litigation involving a trip to the Supreme Court and certification of the choice-of-law question to the Florida Supreme Court, which affirmed that Florida claimed priority for its law, the federal court of appeals decided that due process barred that result. The Supreme Court took the case again and reversed.

Once again, the due process question was whether the insurer should have anticipated being subjected to Florida law. The answer was yes, said the Court: the policy placed no limits on where Clay could take his property and in fact was described as a "Floater Policy (World Wide)." Having insured property against loss in any state, the insurer should have known that it risked being subjected to the law of any state where a loss occurred.

The modern due process approach thus focuses almost exclusively on the prevention of unfair surprise. The question is whether, at the time of the relevant transaction, a party should have foreseen the possibility of being subjected to the law of some particular state. The quid pro quo element of the analysis, which did exist in the earlier cases and still persists in the due process personal jurisdiction analysis, has either shrunk near invisibility or vanished entirely. (If we look for it in *Clay* and *Watson*, the Court does mention that the defendants did business in the states to whose laws they were subjected, and that may count as receipt of benefits.)

iii. Privileges and Immunities

In privileges and immunities cases of the post-New Deal era, the Court continued to enforce the requirement that out-of-staters be granted the same rights as locals. In *Toomer v. Witsell*,[28] for instance, it invalidated a discriminatory South Carolina licensing scheme that effectively banned out-of-staters from shrimping in South Carolina waters. Privileges and immunities cases were not, however, seen as a choice-of-law cases.

From one perspective, that is unproblematic and even desirable: one of my main arguments, repeating Currie's claim, is that choice of law should not generally be thought of as raising distinctive issues requiring distinctive analysis. Thus, the fact that the Court decides privileges and immunities cases with the tools of ordinary adjudication is welcome. The problem is that since the Court does not see them as choice-of-law cases, it does not see them as relevant to choice-of-law questions more generally. The privileges and immunities cases are disconnected from the Court's

---

28. 334 U.S. 385 (1948).

choice-of-law jurisprudence. In Part III, below, I explore what might happen if they were reconnected. As far as this part is concerned, however, we need not consider privileges and immunities further.

iv. The Modern Synthesis

The preceding sections have described the evolution of the Court's jurisprudence under the Due Process and Full Faith and Credit Clauses. In each case, the erosion of territoriality created substantial challenges for the Court if it was to continue to read the clauses to impose meaningful limits on state choice of law. And in each case, the Court retreated to a more permissive stance.

In *Clay*, the Court had treated due process and full faith and credit together. This might have seemed only the characteristic breeziness of Justice Douglas, who is responsible for some of the more notably sloppy choice-of-law opinions. But in *Allstate Insurance Co. v. Hague*,[29] the Court gave the matter full consideration and reaffirmed the merger.

Ralph Hague was a Wisconsin resident who commuted to work in Minnesota. He owned an insurance policy, issued by Allstate, that provided $15,000 coverage for accidents with uninsured motorists. The policy covered each of three automobiles Hague owned.

While riding as a passenger on a motorcycle, Hague was struck by an uninsured motorist. The accident occurred in Wisconsin; Hague was killed. After the accident, his wife moved to Minnesota and remarried. She subsequently sued Allstate in Minnesota, seeking a declaration that she was entitled to "stack" the coverage on the three autos, as Minnesota law provided, and recover $45,000, rather than the $15,000 to which she was entitled under Wisconsin law. Allstate argued that Wisconsin law should control, since the contract had been delivered in Wisconsin, the accident had occurred there, and the accident had involved only Wisconsin residents. The Minnesota Supreme Court, relying in large part on the premise that Minnesota had the "better law," decided that Minnesota law should be given priority.

Allstate objected that the use of Minnesota law violated its rights under due process and full faith and credit and sought federal Supreme Court review, which was granted. The Supreme Court announced a unitary test for the two clauses. To satisfy full faith and credit and due process requirements, a state "must have a significant contact or significant aggregation of contacts, creating

---

29. 449 U.S. 302 (1981).

state interests, such that choice of its law is neither arbitrary nor fundamentally unfair." On the facts of *Allstate*, it found that test satisfied.

The outcome may surprise you. It surprised the academic community. Conflicts lore has it that a Supreme Court clerk was interviewing for teaching positions soon after *Allstate* was handed down. Asked to describe the decision, he gave a letter-perfect recitation—and was denied jobs everywhere on the grounds that what he had said was so preposterous that it couldn't be accurate. The story may not be true, but it gives a sense of the academic reaction to *Allstate*, which has generally been quite negative.

I count myself one of the detractors. It is hard to see what is gained by merging analysis under the two clauses, since they are quite different in their aims and in the interests they seek to protect. Further, as the following sections will explain, I would like to see the Court take a more aggressive role in supervising state choice-of-law practice. With that disclaimer out of the way, I will give as sympathetic a presentation of *Allstate* as I can.

Justice Brennan, writing for a plurality, canvassed the Minnesota contacts. Hague was a member of the Minnesota workforce, he noted, and had commuted to work in Minnesota; Allstate was at all times present and doing business in Minnesota; and Hague's widow had become a Minnesota resident before filing suit. This aggregation of contacts, he said, was enough.

Thinking about the case in terms of the understanding of due process and full faith and credit developed in the prior sections, Brennan's analysis actually makes some sense. The test purports to merge the analysis, but it does preserve elements to satisfy the concerns of both clauses. The requirement of contacts making the choice of law neither arbitrary nor fundamentally unfair protects the due process interest, and the requirement that the contacts create interests satisfies the *Pacific Employers* understanding of full faith and credit.

Brennan's application of the test has some problems, but it is also reasonable. Consider due process first. Allstate certainly knew that Hague might drive his covered vehicles into Minnesota, and it should have expected that if an accident occurred there, it might be subjected to Minnesota law. It is hard for Allstate to make out a claim that the application of Minnesota law created an unfair surprise. (To the extent that a quid pro quo element of due process persists, it is also relevant that Allstate did business in Minnesota and thereby benefited from Minnesota law.)

Hard, but not impossible. The best argument is probably that while Allstate was on notice that a Minnesota accident would likely subject it to Minnesota law, it did not expect that a Wisconsin accident would. If we consider the actual facts of the case, rather than the range of possibilities Allstate might have contemplated at the time it issued the policy, the application of Minnesota law is indeed surprising. (In this sense, *Allstate*'s due process analysis is a bit like the full faith and credit analysis of *Carroll v. Lanza*: because something else might have happened, in which case the application of Minnesota law would have been predictable, application is deemed not unfairly surprising even given the different things that actually did happen.)

If we think about unfair surprise as an issue of whether Allstate saw any possibility of being subjected to Minnesota law at all, rather than whether it could have anticipated that Minnesota law would be applied following an accident in Wisconsin, Brennan is right. And it is not totally clear that this understanding of unfair surprise is wrong, although I would probably choose the version that considers the actual facts of the case. What about full faith and credit?

The requirement here is that Minnesota have an interest sufficient to justify giving its law priority over Wisconsin law— which, under *Pacific Employers*, really means any interest at all. The fact that Mrs. Hague was a Minnesota resident at the time of litigation gives Minnesota a very straightforward interest: giving priority to its law will help compensate its domiciliary.

Brennan did not rely solely on Mrs. Hague's after-acquired domicile. But he is on shakier ground with the other contacts, relating to Mr. Hague's employment in Minnesota. The problem is that there is no obvious connection between his status as an employee and the particular Minnesota law at issue. The argument would be easier if, instead of stacking, *Allstate* featured some employment-related law. In that case, analyzing the scope of the law, it would be natural to say that it extended rights to all Minnesota employees, and thus that Minnesota was interested in any case involving a Minnesota employee. The policy behind stacking, however, has nothing to do with Minnesota workers.

Brennan's argument is actually that Hague's status as a member of the Minnesota workforce gives Minnesota an interest in his welfare akin to that it has for domiciliaries. Thus, he sees Minnesota as having an interest in applying any Minnesota law that will benefit Hague. This is an expansive claim. It means, if we take it seriously, that Minnesota tort law protects Minnesota workers outside the state just as it protects domiciliaries. But that is an unlikely reading of Minnesota law, and the Minnesota Supreme Court, assessing Minnesota's interests, did not mention any such general interest in the welfare of the workforce.[30]

Still, Mrs. Hague's Minnesota domicile creates an interest. If the question is whether *Allstate* is consistent with due process as understood in *Clay* and *Watson* and full faith and credit as understood in *Pacific Employers*, the answer is probably yes. The problem with *Allstate* is not so much that it distorted the existing understanding of the constitutional limits on choice of law—though merging due process and full faith and credit was certainly not helpful—but rather that it confirmed the fear that the Court was unwilling to engage in any meaningful supervision of state practice.

Subsequent cases have shown that the Court will sometimes intervene. In *Phillips Petroleum Co. v. Shutts*,[31] lessors of mineral rights brought a class action against Phillips Petroleum, the lessee, for interest allegedly due on their royalties. The class contained over twenty-eight thousand lessors residing in all 50 states and owning land located in eleven states. Phillips was a Delaware corporation with its principal place of business in Oklahoma.

The Kansas Supreme Court decided all the claims under Kansas law, something obviously helpful to class treatment and perhaps necessary. The federal Supreme Court reversed, however. A majority both endorsed the *Allstate* test and concluded that the facts of *Shutts* did not satisfy it.

Because *Allstate* combines the due process and full faith and credit analyses, the Court did not specify which clause the Kansas court ran afoul of. The answer is probably both, but the due process problem is clearer. On that issue, the problem is that for many of the claims, there was no contact at all with Kansas: if the lease related to land outside of Kansas, the lessor was not a Kansas resident, and the lease was not executed in Kansas, the connection between the state and the transaction was simply non-existent. Subjecting Phillips to Kansas law on such facts is an unfair surprise.

A total lack of contacts will also create full faith and credit problems. Full faith and credit, under the *Allstate* formulation, requires contacts creating interests, and if there are no contacts, there can be no interest. Kansas asserted a procedural interest in deciding the claims under Kansas law, on the grounds that this

30. See *Hague v. Allstate Ins. Co.*, 289 N.W.2d 43, 49 (Minn. 1978).

31. 472 U.S. 797 (1985).

would allow class treatment. But as I mentioned in the discussion of complex litigation in the preceding chapter, this is not a consideration that can properly be taken into account in deciding the scope of Kansas law. Kansas law does not reach controversies over leases with no Kansas contacts—it cannot, as a matter of due process. And if Kansas law creates no rights or obligations with respect to those leases, Kansas cannot claim that those (nonexistent) rights should be given priority over contrary rights from other states.[32] (We will see this sort of full faith and credit problem again in the discussion of *Hughes v. Fetter*, in Part IV, below.)

So *Shutts* shows that the Constitution still means something—in the most extreme case, when there are literally no contacts between a case and a state, the case cannot be decided under its law. Its aftermath shows something else: determined courts can probably get around even these constitutional limits. On remand in *Shutts*, the Kansas Supreme Court decided that there were no differences between Kansas law and the laws of the other relevant states, and therefore that class treatment was still appropriate.[33] The federal Supreme Court, hearing the case again as *Sun Oil Co. v. Wortman*,[34] expressed some skepticism about this conclusion but decided that the Kansas court had not shown so blatant a disregard for the meaning of foreign law as to raise full faith and credit concerns.[35] In another aggressive move, the Kansas court applied the Kansas limitation period to allow claims that were time-barred under the laws that created them. The Supreme Court accepted this maneuver on the grounds that limitations periods were traditionally viewed as procedural.

Thus, even the minimal restraints that due process places on state legislative jurisdiction in theory may be circumvented in practice. In the full faith and credit context, the situation is no

---

32. For the same reason, it avails nothing to argue, as the Kansas court did, that the plaintiffs have opted to pursue their remedies under Kansas law. Kansas law does not and cannot give them remedies.

33. Had the court wished to be more aggressive, it might have said that substantive uniformity authorized it to decide all the claims under Kansas law. If all relevant state laws are the same, courts will usually not perform a choice-of-law analysis. Thinking in terms of scope and priority, this makes less than perfect sense. If a state's law cannot, consistent with due process, impose obligations on a defendant, it is hard to see how its permissible scope is expanded by

the fact that some other state's identical law can. The avoidance of choice-of-law analysis in such cases is probably best understood as an application of the no-harm, no-foul rule. But since the Supreme Court had already said that Kansas law could not govern claims with no connection to Kansas, the Kansas court probably did not believe it could get away with deciding them under Kansas law.

34. 486 U.S. 717 (1988).

35. Thus, a significant point, *Wortman* indicates that gross or willful misinterpretation of sister-state violates the Full Faith and Credit Clause. Id. at 731.

better. The implication of *Allstate* seems to be that virtually any contact will create an adequate interest, so the possibility of full faith and credit maintaining independent significance is slight. And in its most recent cases the Supreme Court has indicated no enthusiasm for the project of coming up with a test that would give the full faith and credit clause some meaningful independent role.

In *Nevada v. Hall*,[36] a Nevada state official drove into California on official business and there injured a California resident. The injured resident sued Nevada in California court; Nevada defended on the grounds of sovereign immunity, which under Nevada law limited damages against the state to $25,000. California has no such limit, and the California courts awarded $1,115,000.

If full faith and credit has special force anywhere, one might think, it would be in the context of state sovereign immunity, where the state seeks respect not just for its laws but for its sovereignty—or, to use the language of the Supreme Court's sovereign immunity cases, its "dignity."[37] Federal laws, unless enacted pursuant to Congress's power to enforce the Reconstruction amendments, cannot pierce state sovereign immunity; private parties asserting such federal claims cannot hold states liable for money damages in state or federal court.[38] After *Hall*, however, sister-state tort law can overcome sovereign immunity.[39]

The fact that state law can overcome state immunity when most federal law cannot is peculiar, given that the Supremacy Clause of Article VI explicitly makes federal law superior to state law.[40] But the Supreme Court has recently confirmed that this is indeed the result it intends. In *Franchise Tax Board v. Hyatt*,[41] Nevada law once again came into conflict with California law. On his California tax return, Gilbert Hyatt claimed that he had become a Nevada resident. The California Franchise Tax Board investigated, ultimately rejecting the claim. In the course of the investigation,

36. 440 U.S. 410 (1979).

37. See, e.g., *Federal Maritime Commission v. South Carolina State Ports Authority*, 535 U.S. 743, 760 (2002) ("The preeminent purpose of state sovereign immunity is to accord the States the dignity that is consistent with their status as sovereign entities.").

38. See *Seminole Tribe v. Florida*, 517 U.S. 44 (1996).

39. For a critical assessment of the Court's interstate sovereign immunity jurisprudence, see Ann Woolhandler, *Interstate Sovereign Immunity*, 2006 Sup. Ct. Rev. 249.

40. To defend this result, one might observe that the Eleventh Amendment endorses some vision of state immunity against the federal government but says nothing about sister states. However, the Court's current understanding of state sovereign immunity flows not from anything in the text of the Constitution but rather from its view of Founding-era assumptions about state dignity. Given that source, it is indeed surprising that these assumptions yield to state but not federal law.

41. 538 U.S. 488 (2003).

Hyatt claimed, it committed various intentional torts against him. He sued in Nevada court, under Nevada law.

California law gives the Tax Board absolute immunity for conduct during its investigations; Nevada law immunizes state agencies for negligence, but not for intentional torts. The Nevada Supreme Court rejected California's claim of immunity. The Supreme Court affirmed. Full faith and credit would not stop Nevada from holding California liable in a Nevada court.

The Court's opinion in *Hyatt* is quite candid about the source of its laissez-faire approach to full faith and credit. The experiment with balancing state interests, Justice O'Connor writes, failed because the Court could not come up with rules to guide it. In *Hyatt*, the Tax Board argued that state sovereign immunity could provide a narrow and rule-bound exception to the generally permissive approach, protecting core state functions. The Court showed no interest. It had been burned once with balancing, and once too with the notion of essential state functions, which it had tried to exempt from federal interference only to give up when the essential functions proved too difficult to identify.[42] It was easily shy enough to refuse the invitation to try either route again. "Without a rudder to guide us," the Court concluded, "we decline to embark on the constitutional course of balancing coordinate States' competing sovereign interests to resolve conflicts of laws under the Full Faith and Credit Clause."

v. Summary and Evaluation

In terms of doctrine, the Court's constitutional choice of law jurisprudence is quite simple. Due process and full faith and credit alike are governed by the "neither arbitrary nor fundamentally unfair" test of *Allstate*. The test requires contacts between the state and the litigation that create an interest. The inquiry into contacts is backward-looking: it asks whether, at the time the relevant events occurred, the defendant could have anticipated being subjected to some particular state's law.

The analysis with respect to the existence of an interest is forward-looking. It asks whether, at the time of litigation, deciding the case under the state's law will promote some state interest. Given the laxity of the Court's standards for what can count as an interest, this element of the test probably retains no independent

---

42. Compare *National League of Cities v. Usery*, 426 U.S. 833 (1976) with *Garcia v. San Antonio Metropolitan Transit Authority*, 469 U.S. 528 (1985).

significance. It is hard to think of a contact that would not create a constitutionally adequate interest.[43]

The current approach does not fit quite as neatly with the two-step model as the original understanding, but we can still understand it in those terms. The *Allstate* test allows states to extend the scope of their law to all cases and parties where sufficient contacts exist to prevent unfair surprise. It allows them to claim priority for their law in all cases where they have an interest.

The test is quite permissive. It could be tightened slightly on its own terms if the due process/unfair surprise analysis were conducted with reference to the actual facts of the case, rather than different facts that might have been within the parties' contemplation. (Thus, in *Allstate* we would ask whether Allstate was unfairly surprised at being subjected to Minnesota law for a Wisconsin accident, not whether it could have anticipated Minnesota law at all when it issued the policy.)

It could also be tightened by being slightly more demanding in the assessment of whether a state has an interest. We could discount the hypothetical *Carroll v. Lanza*-style interest and demand that the state show an interest on the actual facts of the case before the court. And we could disregard after-acquired domicile, which is one of the things that makes the *Allstate* decision seem problematic.

Those changes might be attainable, but they are relatively modest tinkering around the edges. A more dramatic rethinking is probably impossible to get from the current Court. That may not be a bad thing. The Court's passivity stems from its appreciation of the difficulty of the task and a becoming judicial modesty, two considerations that should not be discounted. The current minimal constitutional constraints are not ideal, but if the Court were to embrace some clever academic theory it might well make things worse.

Academics have had unusual influence in choice of law, and the consequences do not inspire confidence. Some of their ideas have been, frankly, bad. And even a good idea, which sparkles like crystal in the cool light of the classroom, can melt to sludge in the heat of actual litigation. Still, it is worth exploring what a real constitutional jurisprudence of choice of law might look like. Even if it turns out that fully implementing this vision is a task beyond

---

43. A possible exception, as noted above, is the internal affairs doctrine, for the Court may be willing to assert that even states that have contacts with a foreign corporation (states in which it does business, for instance) do not have an interest in regulating its internal affairs.

the ability of judges, we will gain a deeper understanding of both the Constitution and choice of law.

III.   Rethinking Constitutional Choice of Law

In this section I will sketch a vision of a revitalized set of constitutional constraints on choice of law. Primarily, this will amount to taking privileges and immunities and full faith and credit seriously—as clauses that place real limits on state rules of scope and priority, respectively.

A.   Privileges and Immunities

Start with privileges and immunities. This clause is designed to ensure that states extend the benefits of their laws to the visiting citizens of other states. It is designed, that is, to prevent them from restricting the scope of state laws on the basis of domicile.

This principle has fairly dramatic consequences for choice of law. It means that Currie's selfish state version of interest analysis, however useful as an illustrative simplification, cannot be instantiated as a state's actual approach. Restricting the benefits of local law to locals is generally unconstitutional, at least within a state's borders. (The Privileges and Immunities Clause says that the citizens of each state shall be entitled to all the privileges and immunities of citizens *in* the several states. A State A resident is entitled to the benefits of State B law when he goes into B, but he cannot claim them if he stays at home in A, even though a State B resident might take some protections of State B law with him into A.)

Generally unconstitutional, but not always. The Court's privileges and immunities jurisprudence does allow discriminatory treatment if it is substantially related to an important state interest.[44] An interest in privileging locals over out-of-staters will not qualify, but in some cases an interest in deferring to the out-of-staters' home law may. Thus, in some cases, it will be acceptable for a state to limit out-of-staters to the rights afforded by their home law. The question will be whether this restriction is truly deference to the policies of the other states, or whether it is an opportunistic denial of benefits.

To start seeing the difference between deference and opportunism, we can look at an actual privileges and immunities case. In

44. See *Supreme Court of New Hampshire v. Piper,* 470 U.S. 274, 284 (1985).

133

Austin v. New Hampshire,[45] the state taxed out-of-staters on income they earned in New Hampshire at the same rate that their home states would have taxed them. New Hampshire residents pay no income tax. Discrimination, claimed the out-of-staters. Deference, New Hampshire replied. What is the right answer?

Austin is actually easy. It is pretty clearly not the case that the other states believe it is morally right to pay taxes on income and would thank New Hampshire for taxing their citizens when they cannot do it themselves. They tax their citizens because they want the revenue. Simply taxing these people advances no policy of their home states. New Hampshire could claim to be deferring if it taxed the out-of-staters and then gave the taxes to their home states. But since it kept the money, it was simply behaving opportunistically.

How does this principle play out in the choice-of-law context? Douglas Laycock offers a useful hypothetical.[46] Consider a couple, Mary, from Maryland, and Del, from Delaware. They go out driving together. As is typical in choice-of-law cases, they are not very good drivers. Each of them, in fact, manages to get into an accident while driving and injure the other. Each sues the other in Delaware. Delaware has a guest statute, intended to protect drivers from ungrateful guests, and Maryland does not.

If we follow the selfish state version of interest analysis, we will get some troubling results. Mary's suit against Del is a true conflict. Mary has a claim under Maryland law and Del has a defense under Delaware law. Following Currie's suggestion, the forum will resolve the conflict in favor of its own law, so Del wins. Del's suit against Mary, however, is a false conflict. Del has a claim under Delaware law and Mary has no defense, because the benefits of the Delaware guest statute are reserved for locals. Thus, Del wins this suit too.

Letting Del win both suits is opportunism, and that is what the privileges and immunities clause should prevent. Delaware has a prima facie obligation to offer Mary the benefits of its law, including the guest statute. It can defeat that obligation by showing that withholding those benefits will advance the policies of an out-of-stater's home state. But it cannot make that showing in *Del v. Mary*. The point can be made on an intuitive level. If you think about how Maryland, personified, would want Mary to be treated, you will probably decide it would want her to be able to invoke the

<hr>

45. 420 U.S. 656, 657 (1975).

46. See Douglas Laycock, *Equal Citizens of Equal and Territorial States: The* *Constitutional Foundations of Choice of Law*, 92 Colum. L. Rev. 249, 276 (1992).

guest statute against Del.[47] Maryland law does reflect the policy that drivers should be liable for negligently injuring their guests. But merely imposing liability on a Maryland resident for doing this outside Maryland and injuring a non-Maryland resident does not advance this policy. And we should also ask whether Maryland, personified, would like its citizens to be denied the benefits of Delaware law when they travel to Delaware. On that question, the answer is probably no.

We can also try to go beyond the intuitive level and make the point with more precision. In interest analysis, to say that some result will advance a state's policy is typically to say that its law actually directs that result: we define the scope of a state's law with reference to applications that would advance its underlying policy. So a more precise way to decide whether Delaware is deferring or behaving opportunistically would be to ask whether there is, in fact, a result under Maryland law to which it defers by denying Mary the benefit of the guest statute. The answer to this question is almost certainly no. Maryland law almost certainly does not impose liability on Mary for injuring a Delaware resident in Delaware.[48] It does not give Del a right to recover, and were the case decided under Maryland law (that is, by considering only rights and liabilities created by Maryland law), Del would not be able to state a claim. Thus Delaware does not advance any Maryland policy by holding Mary liable.

Matters are different if Mary is driving with another Maryland resident and gets into an accident in Delaware. In that case, Maryland law does impose liability on her—she has injured a Maryland resident—and if the case were decided under Maryland law, Mary would be liable. In this case, interpolation of the Delaware guest statute as a defense would interfere with Maryland's attempt to allocate loss among two of its residents. Delaware appears to be meddling, and withholding the guest statute can be justified as deference to Maryland policy. Again, the result we reach by asking whether Maryland law purports to attach legal consequences to these facts matches what I believe is the common intuition: in a suit between two Maryland residents, Maryland personified probably would want its loss-allocating rule to control.

---

47. Personifying states is a useful way to generate intuitions. If you offer it as serious analysis, people will probably object. The sophisticated thing to say is something about what the Maryland legislature would have provided if they had considered this case—would they have decided that Maryland law should deprive Mary of the benefits of the Delaware guest statute?

48. Maryland could do this, but it seems unlikely.

Significantly, a Delaware court would reach this result not by deciding the case under Delaware law while withholding some rights from the out-of-stater, but rather by granting Mary all the rights that Delaware law provides but then deciding that, in a conflict, Maryland law should prevail. Thus, in general, it will make sense to say that State A is deferring to State B policies if it does so by giving priority to State B law, rather than simply by withholding rights under State A law.

B. Full Faith and Credit

Privileges and immunities can thus play a sensible role in choice of law by constraining a state's ability to define its own interests—that is, to set the scope of its law. It can prevent a state from drawing the scope of its law so as to exclude out-of-staters for selfish reasons. Full faith and credit can play a similar role in preventing discrimination. It will do so not with the scope of a state's law but with the state's rules of priority.

Think again about Laycock's hypothetical and consider only the accident in which Del injures Mary. Laycock did not specify where the accidents took place, but it will be relevant for my purposes, so I will. Let us suppose that this accident occurs in Delaware, and suit is also brought there.

The analysis will be clearer if we think first about what rights the parties can invoke under the different states' laws, and then about what rules of priority might be used to resolve conflicts between the rights. Mary has a claim under Maryland law. She is a Maryland resident, and Maryland law is intended both to compensate her for her injuries and deter the wrongful conduct that harmed her. Del has a defense under Delaware law; he is a Delaware resident and Delaware's guest statute is intended to protect Delaware drivers. *Mary v. Del*, then, is a true conflict.

How will Delaware resolve it? Currie's first suggestion for true conflicts, recall, was simply to apply forum law. I think this is plainly a violation of the Full Faith and Credit Clause. If that clause means anything for rules of priority, it should mean that a state cannot grant priority to forum law merely because it is forum law—or to put the point the opposite way, it cannot disfavor foreign law merely because it is foreign.

How much farther does faith and credit go? The most aggressive vision of the clause is that it prescribes a unique right answer in every case, so that choice of law is actually fully constitutionalized, with no discretion left to states.[49] I would not go that far. I think that granting "full faith and credit" to another state's law simply means treating it as equal in stature to local law and subordinating it only for reasons that, in other appropriate cases, would also lead to the subordination of local law.

Thus on my view Delaware is not bound to use any particular method of resolving true conflicts. Forum-preference is off limits, but it could use almost any one of the alternative plug-ins we considered in chapter two: comparative impairment, the *Neumeier* rules, Kramer's canons, or Cavers' principles of preference. All of these possible rules of priority are constitutionally sound in my view, for each appeals to something other than the fact that local law is local and foreign law is foreign. Each turns on what Herbert Wechsler famously called "neutral principles"—rules that "in their generality and their neutrality transcend any immediate result that is involved."[50]

We can get a sense of what counts as a neutral principle by thinking about what the Constitution aims to prohibit in choice of law. It aims, I have argued, to prevent states from discriminating against the laws and citizens of other states, so any rule of priority that does not turn on the citizenship of the parties (unless it can truly be characterized as deference to another state's law, as described above) or the source of the law should be acceptable. Requiring rules that are neutral in this sense prevents opportunism. If Delaware follows the *Neumeier* rules, for instance, it will claim priority for its own law in *Mary v. Del* because the accident took place in Delaware. But this approach will bind it to other results that may not favor its law or its domiciliary. If Del is driving and injures Mary in Maryland, the *Neumeier* rules will give priority to Maryland law.[51]

So at the least, I believe, the Full Faith and Credit Clause should be read to prohibit Currie's forum-preference solution to true conflicts. That is doing something, but it is not doing much.

---

49. This is, for instance, Douglas Laycock's view. See Laycock, supra, at 296–97, 331–36.

50. Herbert Wechsler, *Toward Neutral Principles of Constitutional Law*, 73 Harv. L. Rev. 1, 19 (1959).

51. If Mary is driving and injures Del in Delaware, note that the *Neumeier* rules provide for Delaware law, a result that favors the out-of-stater. I think that outcome is correct, but having consid-

ered the Privileges and Immunities Clause, we can justify it better. Delaware law gives Del a claim, but it also gives Mary a defense, since withholding the guest statute in that case cannot be understood as deference to Maryland law or policy. We then have simply a conflict between a Delaware tort claim and the Delaware guest statute, and Delaware law is clear that in such cases the guest statute prevails.

The forum-preference solution was never very popular,[52] and Currie himself eventually offered the alternative of moderate and restrained interpretation.

If we were more ambitious, we might try to do more. We might try not just to review state rules of priority for formal neutrality, but to review their application. Suppose, for instance, that a state uses the Second Restatement to resolve true conflicts. Second Restatement analysis is so indeterminate that simply adopting this rule of priority may not in fact bind the state's courts to give foreign law priority in any individual case. What a court might do, in such circumstances, is use what I have called mirror-image cases to facilitate analysis.

Recall the *Schultz* case from Chapter 2. There, the employee of a New Jersey charity injured a New Jersey domiciliary in New York; the injured boy's parents sued for negligence in the hiring. New Jersey gave charities immunity; New York did not. The New York Court of Appeals decided that the case presented a false conflict because New York had no interest in allocating loss between two New Jersey domiciliaries. I suggested, as did a dissenting judge, that this analysis slighted New York's deterrent interest and that the case was more likely a true conflict.[53]

The dissenting judge also argued that the conflict should be resolved in favor of New York law. The New Jersey Supreme Court has made the same claim under the Second Restatement in an analogous case. Faced with a negligent supervision suit against a New Jersey charity, one of whose campers had sexually abused another at the charity's camp in Pennsylvania, it gave priority to Pennsylvania law imposing liability and subordinated New Jersey's charitable immunity.[54]

Resolving the conflict on its own seems hard, at least if we do not have the bright lines of something like *Neumeier* to guide us. Certainly it seems a close enough call that either outcome is consistent with what I have suggested as the requirement of full faith and credit, that a state have some reason to prefer local law other than the mere fact that it is local.

But consider a mirror-image case, in which a charity from the pro-liability state acts negligently and an individual, also from the pro-liability state, is injured in the pro-immunity state. If we

---

52. Michigan is the most notable exception, having adopted an explicit preference for forum law.

53. See *Schultz v. Boy Scouts of America, Inc.*, 65 N.Y.2d 189, 205, 491 N.Y.S.2d 90, 480 N.E.2d 679 (1985) (Jasen, J., dissenting).

54. See *P.V. ex re. T.V. v. Camp Jaycee*, 197 N.J. 132, 962 A.2d 453 (2008).

imagine that *Schultz* had presented these facts, so that a New York charity had caused injury to a New Yorker in New Jersey, it seems relatively clear that New York would want to claim priority for its law in that case—and, more relevantly, that it would rather claim priority in the mirror-image case than in *Schultz* itself.

The consideration of the state's relative desire with respect to the two cases is more relevant because if the cases are true mirror-images, full faith and credit should imply that the state can claim priority for its law in only one. The reason is simple. Full faith and credit requires that there be some reason behind a grant of priority to local law, other than that it is local. But whatever nondiscriminatory reason can be given in favor of local law in one of a pair of mirror-image cases can be given in favor of foreign law in the other. If New York asserted priority in the *Schultz* mirror-image case because it involved an issue of loss-allocation between two New Yorkers, for instance, the same argument would be available to support New Jersey law in *Schultz* itself. For a state to claim priority for its law in both of a pair of mirror-image cases, then, suggests a full faith and credit problem, and thinking about which of the pair the state would be more likely to claim can help us determine whether a state's claim is plausible in a single case.

I think that this line of reasoning makes some sense, and in some cases it will work well—*Schultz* is perhaps a particularly good example. It will not work well in all cases, however. The basic problem is that not all approaches are in fact susceptible to mirror-image analysis. If a state claims priority for its compensatory law in one case "because the plaintiff is a local injured within the state" it is easy to see how to construct a mirror image: ask what would happen if the local were a defendant who had injured an out-of-stater in that person's home state. (There mirror-image analysis would suggest that foreign law must be given priority, because the same argument can be given in its favor: the plaintiff was injured in his home state.) If it seems unlikely that the state would reach the opposite result in the mirror-image case, it is unlikely that it sincerely believes its law deserves priority in the actual case: it is likely that there is discrimination against foreign law.

But what if the state wants to give priority to local law "because the local interest would be more severely impaired"? Or what if the reason is "because local law is better"?[55] It is much less

55. The Minnesota Supreme Court's decision in *Allstate* obviously flunks the mirror-image test if we think about it as an ordinary balancing of interests approach. Had there been an accident involving Minnesota residents, in Minnesota, with the Wisconsin contacts being the fact that the decedent worked in

clear how to construct mirror-image cases to assess sincerity with comparative impairment or better law, even assuming that we understand "better" to mean something like "modern and popular rather than antiquated and unenforced." It is possible. We could ask why the local interest is assertedly more impaired and apply the same reasoning to other similar laws, or we could consider cases in which the local law is obsolete—if any such laws exist. But this sort of venture is probably more suited to scholars than judges. I believe it is a useful way to think about the constitutional issue, but I would not expect courts to take it up, or to produce much of an improvement if they did.

C. Conclusion

The vision of constitutional constraints I have sketched here is relatively modest. It relies on fairly minimalist readings of full faith and credit and privileges and immunities, requiring in both cases essentially that a state come up with some reason other than foreign status for disfavoring foreign citizens or foreign law. Deference to the law or policy of a sister state may be such a reason, but deference must be distinguished from opportunistic disadvantaging.

The consequences of the suggested approach are also relatively modest. Most dramatic is the privileges and immunities suggestion that an out-of-stater should be able to invoke local loss-allocating rules. But the ultimate consequence of even that is minor, since the forum will frequently be able to achieve the same result as it would achieve by withholding the right via a rule of priority subordinating its local right to foreign law as a means of deferring to foreign law or policy.

The other significant consequence is that a rule of forum-preference is an impermissible method of resolving true conflicts. This result seems a fairly straightforward consequence of any plausible understanding of full faith and credit, *Pacific Employers* notwithstanding, and it is also easy to defend on policy grounds. Forum preference is a terrible solution to true conflicts, which destroys uniformity, encourages forum shopping, exacerbates interstate tensions, and does all these things needlessly, given that perfectly adequate forum-neutral alternatives exist.

Wisconsin and the widow moved there after the accident, Minnesota courts would surely have applied Minnesota law. But the case only becomes a mirror-image on the better law approach if we add the supposition that Wisconsin law is "better." Minnesota courts might well apply Wisconsin law in that case (though it seems unlikely)—but they might also never decide that Wisconsin law is better, which means that our mirror-image analysis is not doing much to prevent discrimination against Wisconsin law.

The only remaining question is whether these suggestions are within the judicial competence. I mentioned at the outset that embracing clever academic theories might just make things worse, and that is true if the theories demand too much of judges. The inevitable result of excessively complicated theories is error or deliberate misapplication. So what I suggest here is deliberately minimalist. Judges should be capable of distinguishing between deference to foreign law and opportunistic disadvantaging of out-of-staters. They do it already in privileges and immunities cases. They should also be able to identify facially discriminatory rules of priority. That is as clear and objective an issue as one can find in choice of law. I do think that choice of law would be improved if these constitutional constraints were enforced, though I harbor no illusions about the likelihood of that occurring.

IV. The Obligation to Provide a Forum

There is one more topic conventionally considered as part of the constitutional constraints on choice of law: the question of when litigation can be either excluded from or restricted to local courts. The main case here, *Hughes v. Fetter*,[56] is usually considered very puzzling. I think to the contrary that it is a very easy case to understand, but it does show how thinking about choice of law in terms of "what law applies" can lead us astray. It is thus a useful demonstration of the analytical superiority of the two-step model.

The plaintiff in *Hughes* was the administrator of the estate of Howard Hughes, a Wisconsin resident (not the famed aviator) killed in an automobile accident in Illinois. The other driver was also a Wisconsin resident, and his insurance company, also named as a defendant, was a Wisconsin corporation. The administrator sued in Wisconsin, relying on the Illinois wrongful death statute.

The defendants responded by invoking the Wisconsin wrongful death act, which was by its terms limited to deaths "caused in this state." The trial court entered summary judgment for the defendants on the grounds that the Wisconsin statute established a policy against entertaining suits brought under the wrongful death acts of other states. Oddly, it described the judgment as "dismissing the complaint on the merits." (You may recall from Chapter 1 that the traditional public policy exception should not produce a judgment on the merits but rather a dismissal without prejudice.)

The Wisconsin Supreme Court affirmed this decision, but the federal Supreme Court reversed. Wisconsin might have had a policy

---

56. 341 U.S. 609 (1951).

against entertaining such suits, Justice Black wrote, but against that policy stood "the strong unifying principle embodied in the Full Faith and Credit Clause looking toward maximum enforcement in each state of the obligations or rights created or recognized by the statutes of sister states." Wisconsin's policy had to give way.

So far, so good: the opinion sounds very much like *Bradford Electric Light v. Clapper*, where the Court essentially weighed the competing interests and resolved the conflict in favor of the greater one. But now comes the puzzling part. *Hughes v. Fetter* comes after *Pacific Employers*, where the Court decided that a state could apply its own law as long as it had any sort of interest, and in fact in footnote ten of *Hughes*, Justice Black reaffirmed that principle. "The present case," he wrote, "is not one where Wisconsin, having entertained appellant's lawsuit, chose to apply its own instead of Illinois' statute to measure the substantive rights involved." That, he intimated, would have been perfectly permissible. (Rather than cite *Pacific Employers*, Black quoted from *Alaska Packers* the proposition that "Prima facie every state is entitled to enforce in its own courts its own statutes, lawfully enacted.")

And yet what would have happened if Wisconsin had chosen to apply its own law? Since the Wisconsin wrongful death act explicitly grants rights only for deaths caused "in this state," the result would have been the same: defendant wins on the merits. And so, it seems, Justice Black was at most insisting that the Wisconsin court offer a different reason for something it had the power to do anyway.

That is the way some people read *Hughes*, anyway. I think about it differently. *Hughes*, I think, is actually an example of the kind of full faith and credit cases that were standard on the original understanding but now arise only infrequently: cases where legislative jurisdiction does not overlap. In a world where laws are territorially limited, I've said, conflicts between them are extremely rare. The typical full faith and credit question will not be whose law prevails in a conflict, but simply whether foreign law will be recognized or not, and full faith and credit demands that it shall be recognized.

If we think about the scope of the laws at issue in *Hughes*, we can see that it presents just such a case. Illinois law granted Hughes (or his estate) a right to recover. Wisconsin law simply did not reach the event. It did not give the estate a right to recover, since its scope was limited to deaths caused within Wisconsin. But it surely did not give Fetter a defense, either: the meaning of the territorial limit was that Wisconsin law attached no consequences

142

to deaths caused outside the state, not that it protected people who caused such deaths. This is likely what the Court sought to convey by saying that Wisconsin "has no real feeling of antagonism against wrongful death suits in general." So what *Hughes* presents is a right to recover under Illinois law unopposed by any defense under Wisconsin law. The question is whether this right will be recognized, and the answer is that full faith and credit requires recognition, at least in the absence of any defense or contrary policy.[57]

What about the policy against enforcing a foreign cause of action? The Court's reasoning, which seems sensible, is that this sort of policy is forbidden by full faith and credit. If Wisconsin had contrary law—so that it did in fact provide a defense to Fetter for killing Hughes—it could give that law priority and decide against Hughes on the merits. And if it had a contrary substantive policy— if it simply had no wrongful death act because it believed such claims should not exist—it could invoke the public policy exception and dismiss without prejudice. But with neither of those justifications available, it could not simply refuse to recognize the rights created by Illinois law.

That leaves only the puzzle of footnote ten. What would have happened if the Wisconsin court had decided to apply local law? Having read the previous discussion, you may realize that there is actually something wrong with this question. The problem is that it fails to distinguish between the two senses in which law may "apply."

As noted in Chapter 2, to say that Wisconsin law applies may mean two different things. It may mean that Wisconsin law reaches this case—it attaches legal rights and obligations. Or it may mean that the court will decide the case under Wisconsin law. The danger in talking about choice of law in terms of "what law applies" is that we lose sight of this distinction. It is only when we lose sight of it that we might think it makes sense to say that the Wisconsin court could have "applied Wisconsin law" in *Hughes v. Fetter*.

In fact, the Wisconsin court could not have applied Wisconsin law (in the second sense) because Wisconsin law does not apply (in the first sense). Wisconsin law attaches no legal consequences to the facts in *Hughes*, and the court could no more decide the case under the Wisconsin wrongful death act than it could under the Sherman Antitrust Act. If we wanted to keep talking about what

---

57. This is the same situation that arose in *Phillips Petroleum*—for dispute over leases having no connection to Kansas, there were rights created by other states' laws and no opposing Kansas rights. It would have violated full faith and credit for Kansas to claim priority for its rights in such circumstances.

law applies, we could state the rule of *Hughes* as follows: if forum law does not apply, and some other state's law does apply, then the court must apply the other state's law.[58] But this is a joke, really, designed to show how unhelpful the conventional vocabulary is. A more useful way to describe it is this. A court needs some justification to refuse to enforce foreign rights. If contrary local rights exist, that will usually be an adequate justification, given the minimal requirements of full faith and credit as interpreted in *Pacific Employers*. But if no contrary local rights exist, as in *Hughes*, then foreign rights must be recognized.[59]

The converse of the *Hughes* situation arises when states try to keep litigation in their own courts. Here, too, the Supreme Court has held that the Constitution imposes limits, though the explanation is not quite as clear as in *Hughes*. In *Tennessee Coal, Iron & RR. Co. v. George*,[60] the plaintiff was a workman injured on the job in Alabama. He sued his employer under an Alabama statute allowing recovery for injuries caused by defective machinery. But he sued in Georgia, and the Alabama statute provided that all suits under it must be brought in Alabama and not elsewhere. The Georgia courts ignored that restriction and allowed the plaintiff to recover under the statute.

The Supreme Court affirmed the recovery. "There are many cases," it admitted, "where right and remedy are so united that the right cannot be enforced except in the manner and before the tribunal designated by the act." But this was not one; the Alabama restriction referred not to some specialized tribunal but to any "court of competent jurisdiction within the state of Alabama." Given that, the restriction was a venue provision, not a limitation on the cause of action, and it did not have to be respected. Courts of a sister state are bound "to give full faith and credit to all those substantial provisions of the statute which inhered in the cause of action, or which name conditions on which the right to sue depends. But venue is no part of the right...."

58. We might also say that to decide a case under a law that does not apply—as the Wisconsin act did not apply to the death of Hughes—is a due process violation. This is essentially the reasoning of the early due process cases enforcing territorial limits on state legislative jurisdiction. By the time of *Hughes*, the Supreme Court no longer believed that those limits existed as part of the nature of law, but if Wisconsin had chosen them of its own will, the Due Process Clause could be used to enforce them.

59. That is, they must be recognized to the same extent as equivalent local rights. Wisconsin could create courts of limited jurisdiction, which would not have to hear foreign claims if they would not hear equivalent Wisconsin claims, and *Hughes v. Fetter* also casts no doubt on the doctrine of *forum non conveniens*. What it prohibits is the refusal to recognize foreign rights *merely because* they are foreign.

60. 233 U.S. 354 (1914).

Thus far, the case makes sense as a statement about the reach of the Full Faith and Credit Clause: the clause commands recognition of foreign substantive rights, not procedural or venue-related restrictions that accompany them under their originating law. (Consider by way of analogy the principle that a foreign limitations period may be deemed procedural and supplanted by the forum's longer limitations period.) But the Supreme Court also seemed to suggest that it would have violated the Constitution for the Georgia court to respect the limitation and dismiss the action. That provision of Alabama law, the Court suggested, was simply ineffective and had to be considered a nullity: "a state cannot create a transitory cause of action and at the same time destroy the right to sue on that transitory cause of action in any court having jurisdiction."

Why should that be so? The best explanation is probably that the Full Faith and Credit Clause binds the state whose law creates rights as well as other states. Whether Alabama-created rights are enforceable in Georgia, that is, is not a matter of Georgia law, because the Full Faith and Credit Clause supplants any Georgia policy of non-recognition. Equally, *George* seems to say, it is not a matter of Alabama law. Again, the Full Faith and Credit Clause supplants any Alabama attempt to make its rights unenforceable in other states.

Subsequent cases have pushed *George* even farther. In *Crider v. Zurich Ins. Co.*,[61] the Court confronted a similar case involving a worker injured on the job. The worker sought compensation in an Alabama court, relying on the Georgia Worker's Compensation Act. Like the Alabama statute in *George*, the Georgia Act had a venue restriction. In *Crider*, however, the restriction designated not any Georgia court but the Georgia Compensation Board as the exclusive tribunal, apparently presenting a case in which the right and remedy were united by the specialized nature of the tribunal. Justice Douglas nonetheless ruled that an Alabama court could grant relief under the Georgia Act, apparently reasoning that Alabama could grant, as a matter of Alabama law, the relief to which the plaintiff was entitled under Georgia law.[62] *Crider* does not suggest, however, that Alabama was constitutionally required to grant this relief.

---

61. 380 U.S. 39 (1965).

62. *Crider* thus seems to embrace what is known as the "local law theory," which holds that courts purporting to enforce foreign law are in fact enforcing local law shaped to resemble that foreign law. See WALTER WHEELER COOK, THE LOGICAL AND LEGAL BASES OF THE CONFLICT OF LAWS 19–20, 239–51 (1942).

Part II
OTHER APPLICATIONS
Chapter 5
FEDERAL–STATE CONFLICTS

In the preceding chapter, we looked at federal constitutional constraints on state choice-of-law rules. But there are other ways in which state and federal law can interact in the field of conflicts. First, a federal court hearing a case must decide which issues are governed by federal law and which by state law—and then, perhaps, *which* state's law. This is the *Erie* problem, familiar from civil procedure. Second, federal law may come into conflict with state law. How to resolve these conflicts is an easy question. The Constitution gives us a rule of priority in the Supremacy Clause of Article VI: if federal and state law conflict, federal law prevails. The harder question is how to decide when such conflicts exist. This is the problem of preemption, and relatedly of the creation of federal common law. This chapter treats those problems in turn.

I. The *Erie* Doctrine

In *Erie Railroad v. Tompkins*,[1] the Supreme Court famously held that there was no general common law, and that federal courts exercising diversity jurisdiction were bound to apply the laws of the states in which they sat, as those laws had been interpreted by the state courts of last resort. Understanding what this holding meant requires a little more explanation.

The facts of *Erie* are relatively simple. Harry Tompkins, a Pennsylvania citizen, was walking along the tracks of the Erie Railroad, in Pennsylvania, when he was struck by an object projecting from one car of a passing train. The legal issue was the duty of care owed to him by the railroad. Was it liable for ordinary negligence, or would he have to show wanton or willful negligence? Had Tompkins sued in a Pennsylvania court, he would have gotten the Pennsylvania courts' view on this question: that the railroad was not liable unless wantonly negligent. Instead, he sued in federal court in New York, seeking thereby to obtain the different view of the federal courts.

---

1.   304 U.S. 64 (1938).

Erie gives us an example of forum shopping, but it is an unusual kind of forum shopping, and one which (thanks to *Erie* itself) no longer exists. Tompkins did not sue in New York in order to obtain New York law. No one disputed which law governed his claim: it was the general common law of tort. The difference of opinion between the Pennsylvania courts and the federal courts was not about which law controlled; it was about what the content of that law was.

That may sound puzzling, and to understand it, we need to take a step back. Prior to *Erie*, under the legal regime associated with *Swift v. Tyson*,[2] the conventional understanding identified several different types of law. There was federal law, embodied in federal statutes and the Constitution, and occasionally made by federal courts in their common law-making function. (Federal common law is considered in greater detail in Part III, below.) The authoritative interpreters of federal law were the federal courts. There was also state law, embodied in state statutes and constitutions, and sometimes in state-court decisions. The state courts were the authoritative interpreters of state law. And last, there was the general common law.

The general common law governed such classic common law topics as torts and contracts. It was not embodied in any writing, at least not definitively, and it was not created by any sovereign. It existed independently, and while judicial decisions were evidence of the content of general common law, no court could claim authority in its exposition. As Joseph Beale wrote, it "is accepted by all so-called common law jurisdictions but is the particular and peculiar law of none."[3] All courts deciding tort or contract cases, then, were in theory applying the same law; but no court had the last word on what the substance of that law was—whether, for instance, the railroad was liable for mere negligence, or whether Tompkins had to show wanton negligence.

The idea of binding law without a sovereign source or authoritative interpreter is odd to modern eyes. It was odd to some contemporaries, too; Justice Holmes famously derided it as "a brooding omnipresence in the sky"[4] and insisted that law "does not exist without some definite authority behind it."[5] And by the time

---

2. 41 U.S. 1 (1842).

3. 1 Beale, § 4.1 at 27. Justice Holmes described the general common law as "a transcendental body of law outside of any particular state but obligatory within it unless and until changed by statute." *Black & White Taxicab Co.*

v. Brown & Yellow Taxicab Co., 276 U.S. 518, 533 (1928) (Holmes, J., dissenting).

4. *Southern Pacific Co. v. Jensen,* 244 U.S. 205, 222 (1917) (Holmes, J., dissenting).

5. *Black & White Taxicab,* 276 U.S. at 533 (Holmes, J., dissenting).

of *Erie*, several problems with the approach had become apparent. The first was practical. The hope behind *Swift v. Tyson* was that state courts would defer to federal courts as to the content of general law. Had that happened, the unifying power of the Supreme Court would have eventually created a nationally uniform body of general common law. This would have been desirable, especially in the area of commercial law, at issue in *Swift*.

However, state courts did not defer. In consequence, what *Swift* produced was disuniformity within the states. In a case where the rule of decision would be drawn from the general common law, the federal and state courts within the state might differ on the correct interpretation of the law—again, the duty of care owed to Tompkins can serve as an example. When diversity between the parties allowed for federal jurisdiction, the availability of different rules of law in state and federal courts created serious problems of forum-shopping. Indeed, even when diversity did not exist, corporate parties could manufacture it by reincorporating under the law of a different state, as occurred in the notorious *Black & White Taxicab Co. v. Brown & Yellow Taxicab Co.*[6]

Second, the *Erie* Court had apparently become convinced that *Swift* rested upon a mistaken statutory construction. The Rules of Decision Act, § 34 of the Judiciary Act of 1789, provided that where no federal law governed, the "laws of the several States ... shall be regarded as rules of decision ... in the courts of the United States." *Swift* had read the reference to state "laws" to include only local law—state statutes and some state court decisions, such as those dealing with rights to property located within the state. The statute did not, *Swift* held, instruct federal courts to follow state courts on matters of general law. *Erie* rejected this interpretation. "[R]ecent research of a competent scholar," Justice Brandeis wrote, referring to his friend Charles Warren, "established that the construction given to it by the [*Swift*] Court was erroneous...."

Neither of these problems, by itself or in conjunction, required the overruling of *Swift*. The practical problems could have been mitigated, and it is a rare case indeed in which new scholarship will persuade the Court to abandon the interpretation of a statute it has followed, with apparent congressional approval, for almost a hundred years. But the third problem did. Its source was more theoretical. If, as Justice Holmes and other positivists insisted, there could be no law without a sovereign, the idea of general common law was simply incoherent. The rules of tort and contract had to have some

6. 276 U.S. 518 (1928).

positive source. They had to come from the states or the federal government; they had to be either state law or federal law.

They were plainly not federal. Had they been real federal law, the inconsistency of the *Swift* regime would not have existed, for the federal rules would have preempted contrary state law. But federal court interpretations of the general common law did not preempt state court interpretations; nor did they create federal question jurisdiction, which real federal law did. Moreover, the federal government simply lacked the power to make such a vast body of law—perhaps not on the facts of *Erie* itself, which concerned a railroad and a close link to interstate commerce, but more generally.

This is the constitutional basis for the *Erie* decision: the limited federal government created by the Constitution does not have the ability to make all the rules of the general common law. Thus, those rules had to be state law. And once their source was established, it was clear, as it had long been clear with respect to state statutes, that state courts had the last word on their meaning.

After *Erie*, then, all domestic law[7] emanates from some sovereign, and the courts of that sovereign—the federal government or the several states—are authoritative as to the meaning of that law. Federal courts exercising diversity jurisdiction apply state law when no federal law is on point, and as far as the content of that state law is concerned, federal courts defer to state courts.

At least, that is true for matters of substantive law. But there is no similar reason for federal courts to follow state procedural law, and of course they do not. Federal courts apply federal procedure, even when deciding substantive issues under state law. And so the *Erie* problem arises: how do we draw the line between matters of substance, decided under state law, and matters of procedure, decided under federal law?

This is, of course, an issue that arises in choice-of-law cases as well, and there are some similarities between substance/procedure characterization and *Erie* analysis. But there are also some differences, and it is important to remember that the substance/procedure line may fall in different places in the two contexts.

As far as *Erie* analysis goes, the easiest way to learn it is to walk through the major cases. The first significant post-*Erie* decision dealt with one of the topics that had proved difficult in the

---

7. International law may be a different matter, but it is outside the scope of this book.

choice-of-law context as well: limitations periods. In *Guaranty Trust v. York*,[8] the Court decided that limitations periods were substantive for *Erie* purposes, contrary to their traditional choice-of-law characterization. More generally, the Court explained, the intent of *Erie* was to insure that in diversity cases, "the outcome of the litigation in federal court should be substantially the same, so far as legal rules determine the outcome of a litigation, as it would be if tried in a State court." The *Guaranty Trust* test is typically referred to as "outcome determinativeness"—if the choice between the state and the federal rule will affect the outcome of the case, the rule is substantive and should be drawn from state law.

Of course, the test needs a little more refinement, since almost any rule can be outcome-determinative if it is ignored. Filing deadlines, for instance, are outcome-determinative if a party misses them and sees his brief rejected. The question should probably be whether the rule is outcome-determinative as of the beginning of litigation, assuming all rules governing the conduct of litigation are observed.

In 1958, the Court introduced a new wrinkle. Federal policies (procedural ones) might be at stake in the application of a federal procedural rule, and if so, state law might have to yield even if it were substantive under the outcome-determinativeness test. In *Byrd v. Blue Ridge Rural Electric Co-op.*,[9] the Court found such a federal policy in the Seventh Amendment. The plaintiff in *Byrd* sued under the South Carolina Workmen's Compensation Act, under which some issues were to be determined initially by the Industrial Commission and then, on judicial review in state court, by the judge rather than a jury.

In federal court, the Supreme Court held, those issues would go to the jury. The identity of the factfinder might be outcome determinative, or it might not; towards the end of the opinion Justice Brennan hedges on the question. But in either case, the federal policy was strong enough to prevail. *Byrd* thus introduces a balancing of interests element, also familiar from choice of law, to the analysis: even on outcome-determinative issues, a sufficiently strong federal interest will result in giving priority to federal law. In effect, *Byrd* recognizes that the substance/procedure characterization can involve not just a choice between state and federal law but a conflict between them. If both state and federal policies are at stake, both laws are presumably intended to apply, and the court must decide which law gets priority. (There is, however, a limit to

---

8. 326 U.S. 99 (1945).   9. 356 U.S. 525 (1958).

Byrd balancing: it cannot be used to alter the content of state-created rights. If a state rule is, as Justice Brennan puts it, "bound up with the definition of the rights and obligations of the parties," it must be given effect.)

Hanna v. Plumer[10] took the idea of federal priority one step further. In that case, the plaintiff served the defendant in a manner that satisfied Federal Rule of Civil Procedure 4(d)(1) but not the applicable state rule. The lower courts decided that the state rule was substantive for *Erie* purposes and dismissed the complaint. The Supreme Court reversed. The Court indicated some skepticism about the idea that the method of service was substantive, but it focused on the fact that there was a Federal Rule of Civil Procedure on point. If that rule was valid, the Court reasoned, it should control: "the court has been instructed to apply the Federal Rule, and can refuse to do so only if the Advisory Committee, this Court, and Congress erred in their prima facie judgment that the Rule in question transgresses neither the terms of the Enabling Act nor constitutional restrictions."

After *Hanna*, some cases involving the Federal Rules of Civil Procedure are easy: if the Rule is directly on point, and it is valid, it controls, regardless of the state policy it displaces. (To make things even easier, you can as a practical matter assume the Rule is valid, since the Court has never yet found one to go beyond the Enabling Act or the Constitution.) This makes some sense given the supremacy of federal law and the stipulation in the Rules Enabling Act that "[a]ll laws in conflict with such rules shall be of no further force or effect."[11] (The counterargument is that the relevant rule of priority is not the Supremacy Clause or the sentence of the Rules Enabling Act nullifying conflicting laws, but the immediately preceding sentence of the Act, which specifies that the rules "shall not abridge, enlarge, or modify any substantive right."[12] If one focused on this language, one might argue that when a substantive state law is at stake, the Rules should give way.[13])

What about cases in which the Federal Rules are not directly on point, in that they do not resolve the precise issue? All rules have gaps, and issues will arise which are not resolved by the text of a Rule alone. In federal question cases, the courts make federal common law to fill these gaps; there is no other choice. In diversity

---

10. 380 U.S. 460 (1965).

11. 28 U.S.C. § 2072(b).

12. Id.

13. For a sampling of scholarship on this issue, see John Hart Ely, *The Irre-* *pressible Myth of* Erie, 87 Harv. L. Rev. 693 (1974); Stephen B. Burbank, *The Rules Enabling Act of 1934*, 130 U. Pa. L. Rev. 1015 (1982).

cases, however, state law will sometimes provide another option. Sometimes, that is, state law that is deemed substantive for *Erie* purposes will conflict with the (procedural) common law that federal courts have created to fill a gap in one of the Federal Rules of Civil Procedure. How should that conflict be resolved?

In *Walker v. Armco Steel Corp.*,[14] the Court confronted just this question. Walker was a carpenter who brought a products liability suit under Oklahoma law against Armco Steel. (He was injured when a nail he was hammering shattered.) He filed his complaint in federal district court within the Oklahoma limitations period, but service of process was not effected until after the limitations period expired. The question was whether filing the complaint tolled the running of the limitations period, or whether service of process was required. Oklahoma law said that service was required. In a federal question case, however, a federal court would deem an action commenced, and a limitations period tolled, as of the date the complaint was filed, pursuant to Rule 3 which provides that an action "is commenced by filing a complaint with the court."[15]

The Court had actually decided this issue already, in *Ragan v. Merchants Transfer & Warehouse Co.*,[16] where it held that a Kansas statute providing that service was required to toll a limitations period should govern, rather than the federal common law rule. Walker's argument, and a reasonably plausible one, was that *Hanna* had overruled *Ragan*. But the Supreme Court said it had not. *Hanna* dealt with cases where there was an "unavoidable" and "direct collision" between a Federal Rule and state law. In *Walker*, by contrast, there was "no direct conflict."

No direct conflict between the Rule and the Oklahoma statute, perhaps. There was certainly a direct conflict between the statute and the gap-filling federal common law. And the federal common law was connected closely enough to the text of the Rule that it could fairly be called interpretation rather than common lawmaking. (The line between statutory interpretation and common lawmaking to fill gaps is never precise, but the idea that commencing an action tolls the limitation period is not much of a stretch.) What the Court did in *Walker* was essentially to adopt a moderate and restrained interpretation of the Federal Rule—just as Currie had suggested, it asked not simply whether the Rule *could* reach far enough to decide the tolling issue, but also whether it was intended to do so when the result would be to preempt a state law that was substantive for *Erie* purposes.

14. 446 U.S. 740 (1980).
15. See id. at n.11.

16. 337 U.S. 530 (1949).

The idea here, described in conflicts terms, is that when a Rule is directly on point, the questions of scope and priority have both been settled. The scope question is answered by the text of the Rule, which establishes that it reaches some issue, and the priority question is answered by the Rules Enabling Act and the Supremacy Clause. When, however, the source of the federal procedural law is a federal court—when a court is filling gaps in the Rules—the question of priority remains open. And if *Erie* analysis suggests that state law should prevail, it will.

The Court applied the *Hanna/Walker* dichotomy in several subsequent cases. In *Burlington Northern Ry. v. Woods*,[17] the Court decided that Federal Rule of Appellate Procedure 38, which gave judges discretion to impose sanctions for frivolous appeals, directly conflicted with an Alabama statute imposing a mandatory penalty of 10% of damages for appellants who unsuccessfully challenged money judgments. In *Stewart Organization, Inc. v. Ricoh Corp.*,[18] it likewise found a direct conflict between 28 U.S.C. § 1404(a), governing change of venue, and Alabama venue law. *Ricoh* clarifies the "direct collision" language by explaining that what is required is really only that the federal law "be sufficiently broad to cover the point in dispute." There is, then, no requirement of coextensiveness or serious inconsistency between the two: if a Federal Rule or a statute offers a rule of decision, it must be followed.

With statutes and Federal Rules that cover the point at issue, then, there is no possibility that state law will govern, and the Court has not suggested any receptiveness to compromise. In *Ricoh* and *Burlington Northern*, it was at least arguably possible to give effect to both federal and state law, but the Court rejected the idea. With federal common law, both possibilities exist. State law may govern in whole, or it may govern in part; the Court may fashion a sort of compromise. This last possibility was on display in one of the most recent *Erie* cases, *Gasperini v. Center for Humanities, Inc.*[19]

The plaintiff in Gasperini won a damages action in federal district court in New York. The jury awarded $450,000 in damages. The defendant moved for a new trial under Federal Rule of Civil Procedure 59, arguing, among other things, that the damages were excessive. The district court denied the motion. On appeal, the Second Circuit vacated the award, applying a New York statute

---

17. 480 U.S. 1 (1987).
18. 487 U.S. 22 (1988).
19. 518 U.S. 415 (1996). The most recent *Erie* case is *Semtek International v. Lockheed Martin Corp.*, 531 U.S. 497

(2001). As an example of *Erie* analysis, it is not very illuminating, and I consider it in the recognition of judgments chapter (Chapter 7) instead.

that empowered courts of appeal to order new trials when a jury award "deviates materially from what would be reasonable compensation." In a federal question case, by contrast, trial court review of a jury award applies a different standard and appellate review is constrained by the Seventh Amendment's re-examination clause. A federal trial judge may set aside a jury award as excessive if it "shocks the conscience," but if he does not, appellate review is restrained by the abuse of discretion standard.

So the *Gasperini* question was how to reconcile the New York statute giving the court of appeals authority to decide *de novo* whether a verdict "deviates materially" with the deferential review demanded by the Seventh Amendment, and with the federal "shocks the conscience" standard. This presents an interesting and complicated manifestation of the *Walker/Hanna* dichotomy, because it features both federal statutory (actually, constitutional) law in the form of the Seventh Amendment and federal common law in the form of the "shocks the conscience" standard.

The first question is the status of the "deviates materially" standard. This was substantive for *Erie* purposes, the Court decided—in fact, by analogizing it to a damages cap, the Court came close to suggesting that it was "bound up in the definition of rights and obligations of the parties," as *Byrd* put it. Had that been the case, federal courts would apparently be required to apply it. But the mere fact that it was substantive was enough, given that the federal law opposing it—the "shocks the conscience standard"— was judge-made. Thus, the Court reasoned, the "deviates materially" standard had to be given effect.

Round one, we could say, goes to state law; the issue falls on the *Walker* side of the *Walker/Hanna* line. But round two presents an issue on the *Hanna* side and thus goes to federal law. The "deviates materially" standard, the Court said, would not be given effect in the same manner it would be in New York courts. The Seventh Amendment did cover the point in dispute, and it had to be followed: appellate review of the trial judge's decision whether or not to set aside a verdict must be for abuse of discretion. So the end result is a split decision. The state and federal policies could both be given effect, the Court decided, by instructing the district court judge to use the "deviates materially" standard, followed by deferential appellate review.

Gasperini is a complex case, but it does make sense as an application of *Walker* and *Hanna*. It confirms the continuing vitality of the distinction between statutory (or constitutional) and judge-made federal procedural law. With judge-made law, the prior-

154

ity question remains open and must be resolved by a consideration of the respective state and federal policies—essentially *Byrd* balancing.[20]

II. *Klaxon*

The preceding section has suggested that the *Erie* problem can profitably be considered from the conflicts perspective. The basic task is familiar from choice of law, and some of the Court's thinking is also recognizable as closely analogous to various choice-of-law ideas. But choice of law arises in the *Erie* context in another way as well. A federal court exercising diversity jurisdiction will have to decide what to make of a state's choice-of-law rules: are they substantive or procedural for *Erie* purposes?

The short answer is that they are substantive. A federal court exercising diversity jurisdiction will follow the choice-of-law rules of the state in which it sits, as the Supreme Court held in *Klaxon v. Stentor Electric Mfg. Co.*[21] It is worth spending a little more time on *Klaxon*, though, because it has some serious implications for choice of law generally—or it could, if it were taken seriously.

Start with the question of *Klaxon's* source. *Erie*, we saw, is based on a constitutional principle—that the federal government lacks the power to make a general common law. (It is based on policy considerations and statutory interpretation, too, but the constitutional grounding renders those somewhat less important.) Is *Klaxon* constitutionally grounded in a similar way?

Most people think it is not, and many of them think that in fact the decision was a mistake. I think it is constitutionally grounded, at least partially, but before explaining my view I will set out the alternative. There are two reasons one might believe that federal courts are entitled to disregard state choice-of-law rules in diversity cases. First, one might think that choice of law really is procedural, and that therefore the use of a federal choice-of-law rule is simply the appropriate outcome under *Erie*. On this view, federal courts should make and follow federal choice-of-law rules, but state courts would continue to apply their own.

20. For another attempt to view *Erie* doctrine through the lens of conflicts, see Bauer, *The Erie Doctrine Revisited: How a Conflicts Perspective Can Aid the Analysis*, 74 Notre Dame L. Rev. 1235 (1999).

21. 313 U.S. 487 (1941). Note that the *Erie* and *Klaxon* rules also apply to state-law claims heard in a federal question case through the exercise of supplemental or pendent jurisdiction. *United Mine Workers of America v. Gibbs*, 383 U.S. 715, 726 (1966) (*Erie*); *Baltimore Orioles, Inc. v. Major League Baseball Players' Association*, 805 F.2d 663 (7th Cir. 1986) (*Klaxon*).

This outcome strikes me as undesirable on policy grounds. It is essentially the *Swift v. Tyson* approach, with federal law permitted as procedural rather than as the federal interpretation of a general common law, and it would present the same problems. But beyond the policy concerns, the idea that choice-of-law rules can be classed as procedural is, in my view, deeply mistaken.

For one thing, they are obviously outcome-determinative in the *York* sense. That suggests that they should be given effect in federal court. The *Klaxon* critics presumably believe that choice of law presents a case of *Byrd* balancing, where the federal procedural interest is sufficient to prevail. But this focuses on the wrong part of *Byrd*. State choice-of-law rules, I think, are "bound up with the parties' rights and obligations" in the *Byrd* sense and therefore must be heeded regardless of any countervailing federal procedural interest.

At least, I think that is true to the extent that choice-of-law rules are about scope. The main argument of this book is that it is useful to think of choice-of-law rules as doing two things: setting the scope of state law and assigning priority to one or the other of conflicting laws. The question of the scope of a state's law is the question of whether it creates rights or obligations in a particular case. There is no question more substantive than that. A federal court cannot claim to be applying state law if it disregards the views of that state as to who may claim rights under that law. If State A has adopted a territorial approach to choice of law, for instance, it has pronounced that its law attaches no legal consequences to events occurring outside its borders, just as if the statute included an express restriction to "events in this state." A federal court that decides, following its own choice-of-law rule, to "apply" State A law to an out-of-state event is not, in my view, applying State A law at all.

Klaxon in fact contains some language suggesting that the Court feels the force of this argument. Within constitutional limits, the Court wrote, a state "is free to determine whether a given matter is to be governed by the law of the forum or some other law." The scope of state law, in other words, is within the authority of the state. A federal court cannot contradict a state legislature that writes a statute so that it applies only to in-state events, and it likewise cannot contradict a legislature or state high court that makes this determination via a choice-of-law rule.

If the scope of state law is indeed a substantive matter, and not to be displaced by any judge-made federal procedural law, what follows? State law can still be preempted by federal law, as will be discussed in more detail later. And Congress does have power to legislate about choice of law. The Full Faith and Credit Clause, in addition to demanding that states grant full faith and credit to each other's laws, gives Congress the power to specify "the Effect" that state law shall have in sister states.

So the constitutional problem that existed in *Erie*—that the federal government simply lacked the power to create the law the federal courts had been applying—may not exist in *Klaxon*. The federal government might have that power. If it were exercised, however, it would not produce a *Swift v. Tyson* situation. Instead, this would be real federal law, preempting inconsistent state rules. And this is the second way in which one might think federal courts could be independent of state choice-of-law rules: they might be able to create their own choice-of-law rules which would be binding on state courts.

Upon further reflection, however, this alternative is not very persuasive either. For one thing, the Full Faith and Credit Clause gives power to Congress, not the courts, and it is at best unclear that the clause is one of the areas in which the courts have lawmaking power in the absence of congressional action.[22] For another, it is also unclear—and I think unlikely—that even the congressional power extends so far. The Full Faith and Credit Clause, we have seen, is in its original version about recognizing rights created by sister-state law, and in its modern one about resolving conflicts between state laws. It is not about the scope of state law, and giving Congress power over the scope of state law, rather than merely priority in case of a conflict, is an awfully big step to take without better textual support. Thus while I think the clause would allow Congress to provide, for instance, that all conflicts must be resolved in favor of the state within whose borders the relevant events occurred, I do not think Congress could prescribe that no state's law should extend beyond its borders.[23]

22. For an excellent study of the general issue, see Larry Kramer, *The Lawmaking Power of the Federal Courts*, 12 Pace L. Rev. 263 (1992).

23. The point requires some elaboration. I think "no effect" is an effect, and thus that Congress could provide that a state law shall have no effect in the courts of another state with respect to events outside the first state. (Other scholars disagree, arguing that Congress can require states to recognize sister-state law but cannot excuse them from the obligation, a sort of one-way ratchet.

See, e.g., Joseph William Singer, *Same Sex Marriage, Full Faith and Credit, and the Evasion of Obligation*, 1 Stan. J. C.R. & C.L. 1, 44 (2005); Larry Kramer, *Same-Sex Marriage, Conflict of Laws, and the Unconstitutional Public Policy Exception*, 106 Yale L. J. 1965 (1997). The one-way ratchet theory seems hard to maintain for the simple reason that whenever Congress resolves a conflict between two states' laws, the outcome will be that one is given no effect.) Such a federal law might bind sister-state courts, but it would still not restrict the scope of the law. State A courts would

Even if the second point is unsound, the first remains, and either one by itself is dispositive. Federal courts cannot contradict states as to the scope of their law. They certainly cannot without congressional authorization, which does not now exist, and I doubt that Congress could authorize them to do so. In that limited sense, *Klaxon* is constitutionally grounded.

The question of priority is different. Congress certainly could override a state rule of priority under the effects clause, and there are good reasons to do so. Congress is not subject to the temptation of forum-preference, so it would probably come up with a nondiscriminatory rule of priority, and perhaps even a wise one. And whatever its wisdom, having a single rule of priority, rather than a welter of competing approaches, would produce uniformity. (If states were free to follow their own rules of priority, we would simply have returned to *Swift v. Tyson*, but since Congress has the power to create real federal law on the question of priority, it could make a rule of priority that bound the states.)

However, Congress has not acted. We are thus left with the question of how to view rules of priority under *Erie*. *Klaxon* indicates that federal courts must follow state rules of priority as well—though this guidance is only implicit since *Klaxon* does not distinguish between scope and priority. That is probably right; rules of priority are outcome-determinative and thus substantive for *Erie* purposes, and the only federal law they could confront would be judge-made rules of priority. Federal courts can make these, because sometimes they must,[24] but I doubt that there is a sufficiently forceful federal procedural policy behind them to prevail in a *Byrd* balancing.

Our next question is what consequences *Klaxon* has for choice of law more generally. But before wading into that, a brief recapitulation may be useful. *Klaxon* simply says that state choice-of-law rules are substantive for *Erie* purposes, and thus that federal courts exercising diversity jurisdiction must follow the choice-of-law rules of the states in which they sit. Most scholars think that *Klaxon* is not constitutionally grounded, and many are critical of it.

I think that the scholarly analysis of *Klaxon* suffers from the failure to distinguish between the issues of scope and priority. If we make the distinction, I believe, we will see that federal courts are indeed constitutionally compelled to follow state courts on the

---

be free to give State A law effect with respect to out-of-state events, so long as no conflicting rights existed under the laws of other states.

24. As, for instance, in cases of admiralty jurisdiction. See, e.g., *Siegelman v. Cunard White Star*, 221 F.2d 189 (2d Cir.1955).

question of the scope of state law. There is no similarly clear compulsion to defer on the question of priority, but in the absence of congressional action this is probably the right result under *Erie*.

There is a serious consequence that follows from this view of *Klaxon*. The relevant question may have occurred to you already. *Klaxon* deals with the obligations of a *federal* court to follow state choice-of-law rules when applying state law, but might it also mean something for a *state* court applying another state's law?

The answer, of course, depends on our understanding of *Klaxon*. The conventional view is that *Klaxon* means nothing for state courts; it is policy-based and unique to the federal system. I think that view is wrong. On the account that I have developed, *Klaxon* is at least in part constitutionally based, and federal courts are at least to some extent constitutionally required to follow state choice-of-law rules. (They are required to do so, I believe, insofar as those rules are about the scope of state law.) So we should ask whether that limited constitutional mandate applies to state courts as well.

I think it does. The constitutional requirement I have identified comes from the very simple principle that states are authoritative as to the scope of their law. Within constitutional limits, a state is entitled to say that its law gives rights to some people but not others, in some places and not others, and federal courts cannot contradict it. This principle applies with equal force to sister states—as between two states, each is authoritative as to the scope of its law. The conclusion that follows is that each state must defer to other states' definition of the scope of their law.

If you try to put this conclusion in the conventional choice-of-law vocabulary, it will sound something like this: "When applying State B law, State A must also apply State B's choice-of-law rules, at least to some extent." That is, it will sound like the conclusion that the Constitution requires states to accept the renvoi. That conclusion is of course unacceptable, for it will lead in some cases to an infinite series of references back and forth between State A and State B law. And that is probably why conventional choice-of-law scholarship has not done much in terms of asking what *Klaxon* might mean for state courts.

If, however, you describe it in terms of scope and priority, there is a much simpler and entirely unproblematic way of putting the conclusion. It is simply this: "When ascertaining the scope of State A law, remember that this is a question of State A law." That is, if State A is a territorialist state, its law is territorially bounded. It does not matter whether the other state trying to determine the scope of State A law is not territorialist. It might be State B, which

159

follows interest analysis, or State C, which follows the Second Restatement. No matter. The scope of State A law—the question of who can claim rights under it—is a question of State A law. It does not vary depending on the law of the other state asking the question.[25]

This conclusion is of course obvious with respect to non-conflicts questions about the scope of State A law. If we are talking about who can claim rights under a State A statute on the basis of the statutory text alone (e.g., who is a "pedestrian"), everyone agrees that this is a question of State A law. It would be absurd to say that if the case is litigated in State B courts, State B law determines the answer. It would, in fact, be unconstitutional for State B courts to ignore what State A courts have said and impose instead the State B understanding of the word "pedestrian."[26]

It is somewhat astonishing, then, that this is exactly what the conventional approach to choice of law does. A territorialist State A following the traditional approach will announce not only that State A law is territorially bounded, but that the laws of State B and State C are as well—even if those states follow interest analysis or the Second Restatement. State B, following interest analysis, will extend its laws as their purpose requires—and will likely do the same thing to State A's law, despite the fact that State A courts pronounce it territorially bounded. If we think of choice-of-law as presenting the single question "what state's law applies?" there is perhaps no alternative. But if we separate the question into the distinct issues of scope and priority, we see that it is in fact possible—and, I would argue, constitutionally required—to grant each state authority with respect to the scope of its law, and not with respect to the scope of any other state's law. That is the import of *Klaxon*, properly understood.

The analysis set forth above departs substantially from current practice and current law. It suggests that there are pervasive constitutional problems with most approaches to choice of law. Put simply, whenever a state uses its own view of the appropriate scope of state law to define the scope of some other state's law, rather than just its own, it has violated the Full Faith and Credit Clause. Within the conventional understanding of choice of law, there is no

---

25. As I argued in Chapter 3, this approach actually eliminates the renvoi problem, which arises only when we suppose that State A can determine the scope of State B law.

26. Indeed, the constitutional basis here—the Full Faith and Credit Clause—applies more clearly to the in-

terstate context than to the state-federal one. See *Sun Oil Co. v. Wortman*, 486 U.S. 717, 730–31 (1988) (stating that misconstruction of sister-state law "that is clearly established and that has been brought to the court's attention" violates full faith and credit).

easy way to assimilate this insight, which is perhaps why it has been resisted. (To the extent that interest analysis and the Second Restatement consult the choice-of-law rules of other states, they are moving towards the appropriate view.) But if we distinguish between scope and priority, it becomes very easy to see how State A can defer to State B with respect to the scope of State B law but not with respect to its priority vis-à-vis A law.

III. Federal Common Law

Erie held that there was no such thing as the general common law, and hence no independent federal interpretation of that law either.[27] This did not mean, however, that there was no such thing as federal common law. One of the points on which *Erie* rests is that the federal courts lack the power to make law across the vast range of the general common law. But they do not lack that power entirely. Federal courts can make law under some circumstances. This federal common law is real federal law, which the pre-*Erie* federal interpretation of the general common law was not; it creates federal question jurisdiction and preempts contrary state law. But when is it created?

The short answer is that federal courts create federal common law when power to do so exists and a federal interest makes federal lawmaking appropriate. There are several different circumstances in which the Supreme Court has found these criteria satisfied. I have divided them into four categories, but the lines between the categories are not precise. Some circumstances could reasonably be placed in more than one category. Nevertheless, I hope the following taxonomy is useful.

A. Rights and Obligations of the Federal Government

When the rights and obligations of the United States are at issue, they are governed by federal law. Thus in *Clearfield Trust v. United States*,[28] the Supreme Court ruled that federal law would control the question of whether the United States government could recover the payment it made on a check that had been stolen and fraudulently endorsed. The basic policy explanation for this is

---

27. This independent federal interpretation is sometimes described as "federal general common law," and indeed *Erie* itself used those words. I will not; the description is misleading because it suggests a law created by the federal government, which the general common law was not.

28. 318 U.S. 363 (1943).

that it would be inconvenient for the federal government to have to navigate through a large number of inconsistent state laws rather than following a single rule.[29] For that reason, the *Clearfield Trust* rule is about the rights of the federal government, and not about rights in government-issued commercial paper more generally. Litigation between private parties about such securities will not be governed by federal law.[30]

B.   Other Federal Interests

The federal common law-making power will also be called into play when a sufficiently important federal interest is at stake. Some areas of law are so infused with a federal interest that in fact *only* the federal government has the power to make law. Those are discussed in the following section. Here, I note some instances in which, despite the presence of concurrent state lawmaking power, the Supreme Court has decided that the federal interest at stake in litigation between private parties is sufficiently great to warrant the creation of federal common law.

Typically, a sufficient federal interest will be found only when application of state law would interfere with some obvious federal purpose.[31] For instance, in *Boyle v. United Technologies Corp.*,[32] the family of a Marine pilot who died in a helicopter crash sued the manufacturer on a design defect theory. The Supreme Court held that the liability of federal contractors would be governed by federal common law, not state law, and further that a contractor was not liable if it had complied with reasonably precise specifications and warned the government of dangers known to the contractor but not the government. The ability of the federal government to obtain equipment made to its specifications is an obvious federal interest, and holding manufacturers liable for complying with federal requests would undermine it.

C.   Lack of State Power

In some areas, states simply lack authority to make law at all. Perhaps the most notable of these is foreign relations. Foreign policy is the domain of the federal government, and states cannot

---

29. A subsidiary reason is that the rights of the United States cannot exist at the mercy of state law.

30. *Bank of America v. Parnell*, 352 U.S. 29 (1956).

31. Thus, the question of whether this sort of common law is appropriate is essentially the same question asked to determine whether conflict preemption is warranted. See Part IV, below.

32. 487 U.S. 500 (1988).

enter it. Thus, if law is needed, it must be federal, and if it does not exist, courts must create it. Here, federal courts create common law because there is no alternative candidate.[33]

Much the same situation arises when there is a dispute between two states. On these questions, as the Supreme Court put it in *Hinderlider v. La Plata River & Cherry Creek Ditch Co.*, "neither the statutes nor the decisions of either State can be conclusive."[34] If the Court is called upon to apportion water from an interstate stream, as in *Hinderlider*, it will fashion federal common law by which to do so.

D.   Congressional Authorization

Another variant of necessity inspired common lawmaking occurs with federal statutes. If a statute grants federal courts jurisdiction over certain cases but sets out no substantive standards to apply, courts may interpret the vesting of jurisdiction as an implied directive to develop a body of common law rules.[35] In other cases, the federal statute may set out standards that are so broad that they cannot be applied directly but require the creation of implementing rules. The Supreme Court has approved this venture under the Sherman Antitrust Act and also the federal Employee Retirement and Income Security Act.[36]

One particularly interesting variant of this situation arises when Congress enacts a law governing multistate cases but fails to provide a choice-of-law rule. It has done so twice in recent memory, first with the Multiparty, Multiforum Trial Jurisdiction Act of 2002, and second with the Class Action Fairness Act of 2005. Each of these acts allows federal courts to exercise jurisdiction over certain multiparty cases based on minimal diversity (i.e., diversity among any, rather than all, adverse parties). Should federal courts in such cases take the congressional silence as an invitation to craft federal choice-of-law rules? Scholars hold a diversity of views.[37] My

---

33. Just as the federal interest-inspired common law corresponds to conflict preemption, necessity-inspired federal common law corresponds to field preemption.

34. 304 U.S. 92 (1938).

35. See, e.g., *Textile Workers Union of America v. Lincoln Mills of Alabama*, 353 U.S. 448 (1957).

36. See *National Society of Professional Engineers v. United States*, 435 U.S. 679, 688 (1978) (Sherman Act);

Firestone Tire & Rubber Co. v. Bruch, 489 U.S. 101, 110 (1989). One could also understand many of the vaguer constitutional provisions, such as the Equal Protection Clause, as operating in the same way. See generally Richard H. Fallon, Jr., Implementing the Constitution (2001).

37. See, e.g., Samuel Issacharoff, *Settled Expectations in a World of Unsettled Law: Choice of Law After the Class Action Fairness Act*, 106 Colum. L. Rev. 1839 (2006).

own, as already discussed, is that federal courts must follow state choice-of-law rules as to the scope of state law but may in appropriate cases reject state rules of priority.

E. The Content of Federal Common Law

Once a federal court has decided that the creation of federal common law is appropriate, it faces a further question: what will be the content of that law? If the area of law is one in which states are categorically barred from regulating, such as foreign relations, the court must simply find an appropriate substantive rule. But if state authority exists, the first question the federal court will ask is whether the federal common law should simply incorporate the otherwise-applicable state rule.

It is relatively common for federal statutes to do this. The Federal Tort Claims Act, for instance, makes the federal government liable for the torts of its agents "in accordance with the law of the place where the act or omission occurred."[38] The Supreme Court has also incorporated state law to fill gaps in federal statutes on such questions as who can qualify as "children" under the copyright laws[39] or the meaning of a demand requirement for a shareholder derivative action under the Investment Company Act.[40] Incorporation of state law has the dual benefits of preserving uniformity between state and federal law while also allowing for departure if necessary to protect federal interests. The Supreme Court has taken essentially the same route in determining the preclusive effect of judgments issued by federal courts exercising diversity jurisdiction, as we will see in more detail in Chapter 7.[41]

IV. Preemption and Supremacy

A. Preemption

When federal courts create common law, that law preempts inconsistent state law. A court deciding the issue will follow the federal rule and ignore the state one. The preemption question in such cases is relatively easy. Given that the federal courts have created federal common law on a particular issue, we know that it

---

38. 28 U.S.C. § 1346(b). Interestingly, the Supreme Court has held that the "law" referred to by the FTCA includes a state's choice of law rules; that is, it has accepted renvoi in this circumstance. See *Richards v. United States*, 369 U.S. 1 (1962).

39. *De Sylva v. Ballentine*, 351 U.S. 570 (1956).

40. *Kamen v. Kemper Financial Services, Inc.*, 500 U.S. 90 (1991).

41. See *Semtek International v. Lockheed Martin Corp.*, 531 U.S. 497 (2001).

is intended to displace state law on that issue. And we know that federal law takes priority over state law in a conflict; that principle is embodied in the Supremacy Clause of Article VI.

But preemption questions can be much harder. The hard preemption questions will not be about the relative priority of state and federal law—that issue is always resolved by the Supremacy Clause. (Note that for the purposes of the Supremacy Clause, regulations enacted by an agency with rulemaking authority also count as federal law.[42]) The hard questions will instead be about whether a conflict exists that requires the preemption of state law. This question can take two basic forms. First, it can be about the scope of federal law—whether a given federal law does in fact overlap with a state law. Second, it can be about the purpose of federal law, and in particular whether allowing a state law to operate will compromise that purpose. (If not, state and federal law may coexist.) We will see each form of the question in the discussion that follows.

Preemption is usually divided into three categories. First, **express preemption** occurs when Congress explicitly states that certain state laws are to be preempted. Such a preemption clause will typically provide that no state shall maintain any requirement not identical to the requirements of federal law, or words to that effect. A question about the scope of such preemption clauses arose when courts had to decide whether they preempted state common-law causes of action as well as state legislative or administrative acts. The courts concluded that the preemption clauses did reach common-law actions.[43] Consequently, an explicit preemption clause will generally prevent state authority, in any form, from imposing consequences not identical to those under federal law.

Congress may also include a savings clause, exempting certain state laws from the sweep of the preemption clause. The National Traffic and Motor Vehicle Safety Act of 1966,[44] for example, contains both. Its preemption clause provides that once a federal motor vehicle safety standard is in effect, no State or political subdivision "shall have any authority either to establish, or to continue in effect, with respect to any motor vehicle or item of motor vehicle equipment[,] any safety standard applicable to the same aspect of performance of such vehicle or item of equipment which is not identical to the Federal standard."[45] This clause might have been

---

42. See, e.g., *Geier v. American Honda Motor Co.*, 529 U.S. 861 (2000).

43. See, e.g., *Medtronic, Inc. v. Lohr*, 518 U.S. 470, 502–504 (1996).

44. 15 U.S.C. § 1381 et seq.

45. 15 U.S.C. § 1392(d).

read to preempt state tort claims, but the savings clause provides that compliance with a federal standard "does not exempt any person from liability under common law."[46]

Second, *field preemption* occurs when a particular area of law is reserved for federal activity alone. This may be because the federal government has created a regulatory scheme so comprehensive that any state requirements would interfere (e.g., nuclear safety)[47] or where the federal interest is so dominant that state action is per se undesirable (e.g., foreign affairs).[48] The difficult questions with respect to field preemption tend to be about the precise boundaries of the field—in what circumstances, for instance, does a state tort claim by a power-plant worker enter the prohibited realm of nuclear safety?[49]

Last comes *implied* or *conflict preemption*. This occurs when it is impossible to comply with both state and federal law,[50] or when state law "stands as an obstacle to the accomplishment and execution of the full purposes and objectives of Congress."[51] Of these two variants of conflict preemption, the latter is, unsurprisingly, more difficult to identify. There can be no "rigid formula or rule," wrote Justice Black in a seminal case, by which to identify a conflict warranting displacement of state law.[52] Courts proceed by articulating the policies and purposes behind a federal law and then deciding, as best they can, whether allowing state law to operate would interfere. In *Geier v. American Honda Motor Co.*, for instance, the Supreme Court considered the National Traffic and Motor Vehicle Safety Act discussed above. The Department of Transportation had promulgated a safety standard requiring auto manufacturers to equip some, though not all, of their vehicles with "passive restraint" systems such as airbags. Alexis Geier was injured when her Accord hit a tree and brought a design defect claim against Honda, arguing that the car should have been provided with an airbag.

Would allowing this suit to go forward stand as an obstacle to the full achievement of the federal purpose? The Supreme Court decided that it would. The intent of requiring passive restraints in

---

46. 15 U.S.C. § 1397(k).

47. See, e.g., *Pacific Gas & Electric Co. v. State Energy Resources Conservation & Dev. Comm'n*, 461 U.S. 190, 212–13 (1983) (nuclear safety);

48. See, e.g., *Zschernig v. Miller*, 389 U.S. 429 (1968) (foreign affairs).

49. See *English v. General Electric Co.*, 496 U.S. 72 (1990) (finding that wrongful discharge claim based on al-

leged retaliation against a worker who pointed out safety hazards was not preempted).

50. See, e.g., *Fidelity Fed. Sav. & Loan Ass'n v. de la Cuesta*, 458 U.S. 141 (1982).

51. *Hines v. Davidowitz*, 312 U.S. 52, 67 (1941).

52. Ibid.

only some cars was to encourage manufacturers to experiment with different approaches and to introduce passive restraints gradually. Geier's claim, if successful, would amount to a requirement that all cars have airbags, which would defeat the federal purpose. But the decision was a difficult one; the vote in *Geier* was five to four.

Preemption is not always included in conflicts courses, but it should be. It is, for one thing, as clear an example as you can find of the conflict of laws. It is also of substantial practical importance. Corporations are always looking for defenses against state tort claims, and preemption is one of the most frequent battlegrounds in that struggle.

But preemption it is also an important topic because it may teach us something about choice of law. We can think of preemption as a conflicts problem from the two step perspective. First, courts must ask whether the facts of a particular case come within the scope of the relevant federal law, whether the law is best construed as granting rights to the parties. Second, they must resolve conflicts with state law. (This second step is of course easy because of the Supremacy Clause: the rule of priority is simply that federal law prevails.)

Thinking about preemption as an example of choice of law can show us three things. First, and most obviously, the analysis that courts perform in deciding whether to invoke conflict preemption is quite similar to the analysis Brainerd Currie recommended as a means to determine the scope of state law. In each case, the court must ask what the policies behind the law are, and whether applying the law to the facts before it would promote those policies. To some extent, then, the existence of conflict preemption suggests that interest analysis is indeed feasible and appropriate for courts.[53]

Second, it shows us something about how the scope of a state's law should be determined. In deciding the scope of federal law, the Court frequently reminds us, "the purpose of Congress is the ultimate touchstone."[54] This is true regardless of whether the case is heard in state court or federal court, and if state court, regardless of which state's court. If we generalize this point to interstate choice of law, it implies that scope is subjective rather than objec-

---

53. There are, however, some differences between the two contexts. For one, the preemption analysis never turns on the domiciliary factors that play such a large role in interest analysis. This is because, for purposes of federal law, the United States is one country and not a collection of states. Determining the scope of federal law in preemption cases thus does not require courts to make judgments about people and places who are beyond the enacting state's borders. And that means that preemption analysis looks more like ordinary statutory interpretation than does interest analysis.

54. *Medtronic*, 518 U.S. at 470.

tive, to return to the terms used in Chapter 2. It is up to the state legislature, or the state courts with respect to common law causes of action. Within constitutional limits, state law reaches those cases that state lawmaking authorities say it reaches, and no others. No enlightened scholar or sister-state court can contradict a state as to the scope of its law.

Last, the fact that federal law *must* prevail in a conflict with state law should tell us something about conflicts between sister state laws. It tells us, I think, that they are substantive—that choice of law is about resolving clashes between substantive rights created by different sovereigns. It is not merely a procedural matter of choosing the appropriate law according to whatever rules the forum thinks are appropriate.

Modern choice of law decisions and modern scholarship do not always view the matter this way. Decisions sometimes give the impression that choice of law is simply procedural, as some of the scholarship on *Klaxon* argues as well. The characterization is plausible because the Supreme Court has read the Constitution to permit states to use almost any rule of priority they want. When a state "chooses" its own law, the subordination of foreign rights is real, but because of the laxity of constitutional supervision, it is of no significance. Preemption shows this with particular clarity. In a preemption case, there is only one permissible rule of priority: federal law prevails. States cannot avoid this consequence by claiming that they are simply "choosing" state law instead—something that should be permissible if choice of law is merely procedural.[55] Thus, realizing that preemption cases are choice of law cases shows us that choosing one sovereign's law means rejecting rights created by the law of another sovereign.

B. Federal Law in State Courts

The Supremacy Clause has its most obvious impact when state law conflicts with federal law. In such cases, as we have just seen, state law is displaced. Supremacy has some further ramifications, though. In particular, it affects state courts hearing federal claims.

There are basically two points at which to think about the problem of federal law in state courts. First, there is the question whether states are obliged to open their courts and provide a forum

---

55. They obviously cannot do this via a conventional choice-of-law analysis, and the Supreme Court has also rejected attempts to do it through escape devices. See, e.g., *Mondou v. New York, N.H. & H.R. Co.*, 223 U.S. 1 (1912) (rejecting argument that federal law was contrary to state public policy).

for federal claims. On this question we might start our analysis with *Hughes v. Fetter*, which addresses the same issue in the interstate context. Second, once a state court decides that it will hear a federal claim, there arises what has been called a reverse-*Erie* situation. The state court applies federal law as a rule of decision, but it may also apply state procedure; how do the two interact? The two questions are sequential, but also to some degree complementary, and we will consider each in turn.

Start with *Hughes v. Fetter*. The best way to think about that case, I suggested in Chapter 4, was as standing for approximately the following proposition. When foreign law gives a plaintiff a claim, and local law does not give the defendant a defense, a state must recognize the foreign claim, unless the claim is contrary to public policy or barred by some neutral procedural restriction. That is the analysis when the foreign law comes from a sister state. But what happens when the foreign law is federal?

Things are different in that case, because while sister state law must be treated *equally*, federal law is hierarchically superior. States cannot erect substantive state-law defenses to federal claims, and they cannot have substantive state policies contrary to federal policies. One way of putting this is that federal law is supreme. Another, somewhat gentler formulation is that federal law and policy are not foreign; they are local law and policy in every state.

The Supreme Court uses both formulations. In *Testa v. Katt*,[56] for instance, the Rhode Island Supreme Court refused to enforce a federal cause of action allowing for treble damages on the grounds that it was a foreign penal law. Penal, perhaps, said the U.S. Supreme Court, but foreign, no. Federal laws cannot be treated "as though they were laws emanating from a foreign sovereign. . . . [T]he Constitution and the laws passed pursuant to it are the supreme laws of the land . . . the policy of the federal Act is the prevailing policy in every state."

In short, the substantive justification that *Hughes v. Fetter* allows for the refusal to recognize rights created by sister state law is simply not available for federal law. With rights created by federal law, local substantive law and policy *cannot* be to the contrary. So if we translate *Hughes v. Fetter* to the federal-state context, we get the proposition that federal rights must be recognized, as far as local substantive law is concerned. Local procedural law is different. States can create courts of limited jurisdiction, and those courts are not required to hear federal or sister-state claims if they would not hear analogous claims under local law. (A Wisconsin

---

56. 330 U.S. 386 (1947).

traffic court, for instance, would not have been required to hear the wrongful death claim at issue in *Hughes*, and it would not be required to hear a federal claim either.)

In the terms the Supreme Court uses, the rule is that state courts cannot refuse to hear federal claims without a "valid excuse."[57] A valid excuse will be something like a jurisdictional limitation that affects local claims as well as federal. The procedural justifications for limited jurisdiction do not stand contrary to federal law or policy, and they are therefore not affected by the supremacy of federal law. Contrary substantive state law or policy, by contrast, will never constitute a valid excuse. Roughly, the result is that state courts must hear federal claims if they would hear analogous local claims. Procedural restrictions on a state court's jurisdiction can sometimes justify a refusal to hear a federal claim (though they would not justify a decision on the merits against the federal claimant); contrary substantive law or policy cannot.

What about the situation that arises when a state court has agreed, or been compelled, to hear a federal claim? The analogy to *Erie* is useful. Just as there are no substantive federal interests at stake when a federal court exercises diversity jurisdiction, there are no substantive state interests at stake when a state court is presented with a federal claim. The reason for the absence of substantive interests is different, of course. There are no federal substantive interests at stake in a diversity case because federal law does not attach consequences to the underlying facts—if it did, the case would be a federal question case. By contrast, there are no state substantive interests at stake when a federal claim is presented not because state law does not reach the facts, but because any contrary state substantive interests are preempted. Still, the upshot is much the same in the *Erie* and reverse-*Erie* contexts. In the former, federal courts apply state substantive law but federal procedure; in the latter, state courts apply federal substantive law but state procedure.

Where substantive and procedural law overlap, however, an asymmetry arises because of the Supremacy Clause. In the *Erie* analysis, the Supremacy Clause means that a federal procedural rule will trump contrary state law, even if that law is substantive. In reverse-*Erie*, it means that state procedural laws that undermine federal substantive interests will be invalidated. In both cases, then, state law will be displaced if it conflicts with federal law. The question is how to decide when such a conflict occurs. The mere fact that state procedural law makes the federal claimant lose is not

57. *Howlett v. Rose*, 496 U.S. 356 (1990).

enough. If he fails to meet the filing deadline for a brief, for instance, the fact that his underlying claim is federal will not save him.[58] What is required is an adverse impact not on the particular plaintiff but on the federal interest underlying his claim.

In *Dice v. Akron, Canton & Youngstown Railroad*,[59] the plaintiff Dice brought a Federal Employers' Liability Act claim for injuries sustained on the job. The employer defended in part by asserting that the Dice had signed a document releasing it from liability in exchange for $924.63. Dice said he was told that the document was merely a receipt for back wages. The Ohio courts held that the validity of the release was to be determined by Ohio law, and further that the question was to be decided by the judge, rather than the jury.

The Supreme Court reversed on both issues. The first was easier, for the potential interference with federal rights was plainly intolerable. "Manifestly," the Court wrote, "the federal rights affording relief to injured railroad employees under a federally declared standard could be defeated if States were permitted to have the final say as to what defenses could and could not be properly interposed to suits under the Act." (That sounds a bit like conflict preemption analysis, but one could simplify it by turning to characterization. A substantive state-law defense, which the release was, can never stand against a federal right.)

The allocation of the issue to the judge presented a harder question, for the division of labor between judge and jury is at least arguably procedural. Labels aside, the Court decided that the right to a jury determination was too important to be taken away. It was "part and parcel of the remedy afforded railroad workers under the act" and "a goodly portion of the relief which Congress has afforded them." This analysis again looks mostly like conflict preemption. The Court invoked substance/procedure characterization only to reject it as a justification for following Ohio law. It pronounced the jury right "too substantial a part of the rights accorded by the Act to permit it to be classified as a mere 'local rule of procedure' for denial ..." Conflict preemption is probably the right way to think about the reverse-*Erie* case: courts should ask whether allowing the state procedural rule to operate will stand as an obstacle to the full achievement of the congressional purpose.

---

58. Limitations periods are a different matter; in at least some cases the Court has held that states must hear the claims of plaintiffs who file within the federal period even if they are time-barred under the analogous state limit.

See, e.g., *Engel v. Davenport*, 271 U.S. 33 (1926).

59. 342 U.S. 359 (1952).

Chapter 6

JUDICIAL JURISDICTION

The question of legislative jurisdiction, we have seen, is when a state's lawmaking bodies can extend its law to reach particular persons or events: when does the state have authority to attach legal consequences to those events? The question of judicial jurisdiction is related. It is about when a state's courts can issue judgments that bind particular persons: when do they have the authority to decide the rights and obligations of those persons? Limits on the authority in both cases come from the Constitution, in particular the Due Process Clause, though it is also true that in each case states may decline to exercise the full extent of jurisdiction permitted by the Constitution.

Legislative and judicial jurisdiction are thus both necessary elements for the full exercise of state power. For State A courts to adjudicate a party's rights under State A law, both legislative and judicial jurisdiction must exist. (Note, however, that either may exist on its own. A State A court might have jurisdiction over a person but be unable to apply State A law, or a State B court might apply State A law when State A courts lacked judicial jurisdiction.) Judicial jurisdiction may be further subdivided into personal and subject-matter jurisdiction, where the former relates to the relationship between a person and a state[1] and the latter to a court's power to decide a case at all. Here we will be considering personal jurisdiction.

With both legislative and judicial jurisdiction, the analysis can be largely boiled down to the same question: do the contacts between the person and the state meet the constitutional threshold? We have seen already how the Supreme Court's approach to legislative jurisdiction moved from an initial stage of fairly rigid territoriality to the much less constraining *Allstate* standard. Judicial jurisdiction will display a similar progress, though the endpoint is not quite as nugatory as *Allstate*. The focus in the two contexts is also slightly different. With respect to legislative jurisdiction, the key concept is unfair surprise. With judicial jurisdiction, we shall

---

1. Sometimes courts will assert judicial jurisdiction based on the contacts between the state and a piece of property that is the subject of a dispute. In that case the jurisdiction is not over persons (*in personam*) but over things (*in rem* or *quasi in rem*), and it binds the parties only insofar as their rights to the property are concerned.

see, the quid pro quo element plays a larger role through the concept of purposeful availment.

That the two doctrines have relaxed in tandem is not surprising, since in both cases the driving force was the decline of territoriality. It is, however, a little bit disappointing. The problems typically attributed to broad legislative jurisdiction (forum-shopping, unpredictability, disuniformity, etc.) could be mitigated by tighter constraints on judicial jurisdiction. A plaintiff who picks State A courts typically hopes for State A law; if he could sue the defendant only in State B, where State B law would be applied, it would not matter that State A courts would apply State A law. Conversely, giving the plaintiff a broad choice of forum would not matter if constraints on legislative jurisdiction were tight enough that both State A and State B courts would be compelled to apply the same law. Many scholars have thus suggested that the Supreme Court would do well to craft a more demanding test for at least one of these exercises of state power.[2]

As we will see, it has not. The overarching due process test for the exercise of personal jurisdiction requires that an individual have "minimum contacts" with the state that make the exercise of jurisdiction consistent with "traditional notions of fair play and substantial justice."[3] The main question for this chapter will be what sort of contacts satisfy this test in different contexts. First, though, it is worth taking a brief look at the approach to judicial jurisdiction during the territorialist era.

I. Territoriality

The classic territorialist case is *Pennoyer v. Neff*.[4] The facts are somewhat complicated, but the upshot is quite simple. First, the upshot: under *Pennoyer*, judicial jurisdiction is based on presence within the state, presence either of the defendant or of relevant property. Now for the facts. Neff, living in Oregon, incurred a debt to Mitchell. When he failed to pay, Mitchell sued him in an Oregon state court. By the time of suit, Neff had left Oregon and resided in California. Unable to locate Neff, Mitchell attempted to serve him

---

2. For a sample of some of the scholarship on this topic, see, e.g., Harold G. Maier & Thomas R. McCoy, *A Unifying Theory for Judicial Jurisdiction and Choice of Law*, 39 Am. J. Comp. L. 249 (1991).

3. *International Shoe Co. v. Washington*, 326 U.S. 310, 316 (1945). The exercise of jurisdiction also requires constitutionally adequate notice, and the question of what constitutes proper notice has given rise to its own line of Supreme Court cases. See, e.g., *Mullane v. Central Hanover Bank & Trust Co.*, 339 U.S. 306 (1950).

4. 95 U.S. 714 (1877).

by publishing a notice in an Oregon newspaper. Whether Neff ever knew of the suit is unclear, but in any case, he failed to appear and Mitchell won a default judgment.

To satisfy that judgment, Mitchell had the sheriff seize and sell Neff's Oregon property. At the sheriff's sale, Mitchell bought the property himself and subsequently sold it to Pennoyer. Neff then returned to Oregon and sued Pennoyer in federal court there to recover the property, arguing that the Oregon state court judgment against him was invalid.

The federal Supreme Court agreed. The Oregon judgment was not entitled to recognition in federal court, it said, because the requirements for the exercise of jurisdiction over the person of a non-resident[5] (jurisdiction *in personam*) had not been met. Neff had not been served with process within Oregon; he had not consented to jurisdiction; and he had not appeared to defend the suit. The fact that Neff owned property within Oregon might have given the state the power to adjudicate rights to that property, even if his dispute with Mitchell did not relate to the property.[6] But for that kind of an action (a suit *"quasi in rem"*), the court would have had to have attached the property and made it the subject of the action before its judgment. Since it did not, the judgment was, or purported to be, against Neff *in personam*. And since the territorial basis for jurisdiction *in personam* was lacking, the judgment was not entitled to recognition in federal court.

To that point, as an analysis of when a state-court judgment is entitled to recognition under the Full Faith and Credit Clause or its federal implementing statute,[7] *Pennoyer* broke little or no new ground. Where it innovated was in its next pronouncement: that the restrictions on jurisdiction *in personam* were embodied in the Due Process Clause. This dictum was significant because it converted restrictions on the enforceability of judgments (which might never be an issue in many cases) into restrictions on the ability to maintain a suit at all (which could always be raised as a defense). It

---

5. States can assert general jurisdiction over their domiciliaries, as we will see later in this chapter. From a strict territorialist perspective, this does not make perfect sense, but one might say that domiciliaries consent to jurisdiction, or alternatively that they are in some sense always legally present in their state of domicile.

6. In *Shaffer v. Heitner*, 433 U.S. 186 (1977), discussed later in this chapter, the Supreme Court rejected the practice of using the presence in the forum of a defendant's unrelated property as a basis for jurisdiction.

7. The Full Faith and Credit Clause prescribes recognition of state judgments in sister-state courts; the implementing statute expands the obligation to all courts "within the United States," thus bringing federal courts within its ambit as well. Act of May 26, 1790, 1 Stat. 122.

was taken up by subsequent courts and eventually flowered into a robust jurisprudence of territorial constraints on judicial jurisdiction.

II. Evolution of Specific Jurisdiction

The theory developed in post-*Pennoyer* cases was that the Due Process Clause barred state courts from exercising *in personam* jurisdiction over non-resident defendants without in-state service, voluntary appearance, or consent. For actions *in rem*, the court would similarly have to exercise authority over the property before the entry of judgment, typically by attachment or seizure. It could then adjudicate rights to that property, either with respect to all persons (a pure *in rem* action) or as between the parties to the suit (an action *quasi in rem*).

What these bases for jurisdiction have in common is that in all of them the forum has *de facto* power over the defendant or the property, based largely on presence within the forum at the time jurisdiction is asserted. The requirement of *de facto* power proved increasingly problematic as the nation modernized. Nonresident motorists, for instance, might drive into a state, cause an accident, and depart; or corporations might manufacture products that made their way into a state and caused injury there.

The *Pennoyer* regime had some resources to deal with such problems. States might, for instance, enact laws providing that anyone who used their roads thereby consented to jurisdiction for cases arising from accidents thereon.[8] Or corporations might be allowed to do business in a state only if they maintained an agent there to receive service of process, or be deemed present if they conducted enough business.

But these resources grew increasingly fictive, and eventually they proved insufficient. In *International Shoe Co. v. Washington*,[9] the Supreme Court broke with the *Pennoyer* framework. International Shoe had salesmen operating in Washington State, but no Washington office or agent to receive process. The state sued the corporation to recover taxes on sales commissions. The Court rejected the concept of presence as a prerequisite for jurisdiction, stating instead that "due process requires only that to subject a defendant to a judgment *in personam*, if he be not present within the territory of the forum, he have certain minimum contacts with

---

8. *Hess v. Pawloski*, 274 U.S. 352 (1927) upheld such a statute.

9. 326 U.S. 310 (1945).

it such that the maintenance of the suit does not offend 'traditional notions of fair play and substantial justice.' ''

What do those rather vague terms mean? The test, the Court continued, "cannot be made simply mechanical or quantitative." It depended on the "quality and nature of the activity" and also upon the extent to which the obligations the state sought to impose were connected to the activity within the state and the benefits thereby obtained. In *International Shoe* itself, the Court found the test satisfied. The corporation had carried on "systematic and continuous" activity within Washington, producing a "large volume of interstate business" during which it had received the benefits of Washington law, and the obligations Washington sought to impose "arose out of those very activities."

Subsequent cases clarified the minimum contacts standard further, or tried to. In *McGee v. International Life Ins. Co.*,[10] the Court allowed California to exercise jurisdiction over International Life, a Texas company, in a suit to recover on a life insurance policy. The contract had initially been issued by a different company, whose obligations International Life assumed. International Life mailed the initial offer to continue coverage to the insured in California but did no other business there.

International Life's contacts with California were extremely slender. They were, however, all directly connected to the obligations California sought to impose, and the company had received a benefit from them. It was enough, the Court said, "that the suit was based on a contract which had substantial connection with California."

That sounds a bit like language from a case dealing with the constitutional limits on legislative, rather than judicial jurisdiction. Indeed, the Court paid substantial attention to California's "manifest interest in providing effective means of redress for its residents"—a point more responsive to a Full Faith and Credit argument about choice of law than a Due Process one about personal jurisdiction. *McGee* may in retrospect mark the broadest reach of state-court personal jurisdiction. In *Hanson v. Denckla*,[11] the Court found for the first time in a post-*International Shoe* case that a state had gone too far.

In *Hanson*, Florida attempted to exercise jurisdiction over a Delaware bank that served as trustee for a Florida decedent. The contacts were insufficient, the Court said: the trustee had no office in Florida and did not do business there; the trust assets were not

10. 355 U.S. 220 (1957).   11. 357 U.S. 235 (1958).

in Florida, and the case did not arise out of any act done there (the trust agreement was executed in Delaware while the settlor was domiciled in Pennsylvania). The settlor had moved to Florida, true, and while there had sent instructions to and received income from Delaware. But the bank had done nothing to associate itself with Florida. In *Hanson*'s most influential phrase, the Court stated that "it is essential in each case that there be some act by which the defendant purposefully avails itself of the privilege of conducting activities within the forum State, thus invoking the benefits and protections of its laws."

Fair play and substantial justice, after *Hanson*, turned crucially on the concept of purposeful availment, a sort of quid pro quo element. Defendants who purposefully acted within a state and thereby obtained benefits from its laws could be held accountable in its courts for the consequences of those acts. But purpose admits of degrees—in the criminal context, for instance, there are several different gradations of *mens rea*. Subsequent cases wrestled with the question of what degree was required for personal jurisdiction.

In *World-Wide Volkswagen v. Woodson*,[12] New York residents bought a Volkswagen in New York. They subsequently decided to move to Arizona. En route, they got into an accident in Oklahoma and suffered injuries. They brought a design defect suit against multiple defendants, including World–Wide Volkswagen, a regional distributor.

World–Wide operated in New York, New Jersey, and Connecticut, and was incorporated in New York. It had no contacts with Oklahoma apart from the fact that the car at issue had been driven into the state. The Oklahoma Supreme Court reasoned that cars were highly mobile and thus the possibility of an accident in other states was foreseeable. That, it held, was enough to meet the minimum contacts test. (What about the quid pro quo element? The Oklahoma court decided that this was satisfied because the mobility of the cars was essential to their value; thus, their foreseeable use in Oklahoma conferred a benefit on their seller.)

That analysis would not be unreasonable under the Due Process Clause if it were legislative jurisdiction at issue. It would look a good deal like *Allstate* or *Clay*, discussed in Chapter 4, where the mobility of cars or personal property is used to defeat claims of unfair surprise. But for judicial jurisdiction, unfair surprise is not the only issue, and mere foreseeability is not enough. (If it were, the exercise of personal jurisdiction in *Hanson* would have looked almost identical to the exercise of legislative jurisdiction in *Clay*.)

12. 444 U.S. 286 (1980).

The Supreme Court held that Oklahoma could not exercise personal jurisdiction over World–Wide. Merely selling goods with knowledge that the purchaser may take them into a particular state does not count as purposeful availment of the privilege of conducting activities within that state.

Asahi Metal Industry Co. v. Superior Court brought one more refinement of the *World-Wide Volkswagen* test. *World-Wide Volkswagen* had dealt with goods sold in one state and brought into another by the unilateral action of the consumer. It had held that the seller's knowledge that this might occur was not enough to meet the demand of purposeful availment, in part presumably because the benefit to the seller from the movement of goods was indirect and unclear. But what if the goods were moved not by the consumer but by an intermediate seller? Then their ultimate sale in the forum would benefit the defendant more directly.

In *World-Wide Volkswagen*, the Court had indicated that a corporation that "delivers its products into the stream of commerce with the expectation that they will be purchased by consumers in the forum state" would be subject to suit in its courts. But what if the state of mind was not expectation, but rather mere awareness?

That was the issue in *Asahi*. A California resident was injured when his motorcycle's rear tire exploded on a California highway. He sued the Taiwanese manufacturer of the tire tube. The manufacturer cross-claimed against Asahi, the Japanese manufacturer of the tube's valve assembly. Asahi shipped valves from Japan to Taiwan and knew that some of them would end up in tubes sold in California. The California Supreme Court upheld California's exercise of jurisdiction, but the U.S. Supreme Court reversed.

The opinion, unfortunately, was fragmented. Four Justices believed that introducing a product into the stream of commerce with awareness that it might end up in the forum, but without any purposeful direction of the product there, was not enough to meet the requirement of purposeful availment. The defendant's action, a plurality wrote, must "be more purposefully directed at the forum State than the mere act of placing a product in the stream of commerce." Four other Justices rejected this view, however, and the ninth (Stevens) refused to break the tie in either direction.

The issue that proved decisive in *Asahi*, then, was a different one. Eight Justices agreed that even if Asahi's contacts with California satisfied the minimum contacts test, California's exercise of jurisdiction was unreasonable. Thus, *Asahi* drew a more general reasonableness standard from *International Shoe*'s invocation of "fair play and substantial justice," a standard which could in some cases supersede the minimum contacts analysis.

To determine whether the exercise of jurisdiction was reasonable, the Court balanced several factors. The burden on the defendant is weighed against the interests of the forum in exercising jurisdiction and the interest of the plaintiff in obtaining relief. Also relevant are "the interstate judicial system's interest in obtaining the most efficient resolution of controversies; and the shared interest of the several States in furthering fundamental substantive social policies." On the facts of *Asahi*, this calculus indicated that the exercise of jurisdiction was unreasonable. The burden on Asahi was severe, and the interests of the plaintiff and the forum were slight, given that the dispute at that point was between Asahi and the Taiwanese manufacturer. The international context also weighed against jurisdiction, as a decision by a California court might undermine the interests of foreign countries and even come close to the federal interest in foreign relations.

Minimum contacts analysis may look slightly different in cases involving consensual transactions rather than torts, for in such cases there is typically evidence of the parties' shared intent or understanding. In *Burger King Corp. v. Rudzewicz*,[13] Burger King sued a franchisee for breach of contract. The franchise was located in Michigan, but the contract provided that the franchise relationship was established in Miami, where Burger King's principal offices were located, and governed by Florida law. The Florida jurisdictional statute provided that the state could exercise jurisdiction over any person who breached a contract in the state of Florida by failing to perform acts required by the contract to be performed there. (Burger King alleged that Rudzewicz had failed to send required payments to Miami.) The Supreme Court held that this statute did not exceed the limits of the Due Process Clause.

Rudzewicz's contacts with Florida were quite minor. His partner had attended a training course there, but he had never visited and did not maintain any offices there. By signing a contract that had a substantial connection to Florida, however, he had reached out beyond Michigan and associated himself with Florida. The Court gave weight to the fact that the contract recited that it was formed in Florida and selected Florida law as evidence that Rudzewicz had "purposefully invoked the benefits and protections" of Florida's law, making it reasonable for Florida to exercise jurisdiction over him.

13.   471 U.S. 462 (1985).

The *Burger King* contract did not contain a clause providing that all suits had to be brought in Florida—in fact, it contained a clause saying that they did not need to be. But such forum selection clauses are common, and they are generally enforceable. The leading case, *Carnival Cruise Lines, Inc. v. Shute*,[14] enforced a choice of forum clause requiring a Washington resident to bring suit in Florida for an injury suffered on a cruise from Mexico to California.

III. General Jurisdiction

One of the key factors in the cases we have seen so far has been the connection between the defendant's contacts with the forum state and the injury the plaintiff seeks to redress. The general principle is that an exercise of jurisdiction is much more likely to be upheld if the plaintiff's claim arises from the defendant's contacts with the jurisdiction rather than some unrelated act. This should strike you as reasonable: it makes sense to assert jurisdiction over an out-of-state motorist for an accident occurring in the forum state, but it would make much less sense to use that motorist's drive through the forum as a basis for jurisdiction over an unrelated contract claim.

The exercise of jurisdiction for claims arising out of particular contacts with the forum is what Arthur von Mehren and Donald Trautman called "specific jurisdiction."[15] They distinguished it from "general jurisdiction," which is the forum's power to determine the rights and obligations of an individual with respect to any claim whatsoever. Most of the cases we have seen so far have dealt with specific jurisdiction, but the idea of general jurisdiction is there too. General jurisdiction in fact could be considered the earlier concept. All of the bases of jurisdiction that *Pennoyer* considers are general in that in none of them does the nature of the claim play any role. *International Shoe* shifts the focus to specific contacts whose significance varies depending on their relation to the claim. But *International Shoe* did note the distinction between causes of action arising out of contacts with the forum and unrelated claims, and it reaffirmed the principle that a sufficient volume of contacts could create jurisdiction for unrelated claims. General jurisdiction based on domicile, which had been suggested in *Pennoyer*, was explicitly endorsed by the Supreme Court in 1940.[16] And later cases confirmed that it existed even for non-residents. *Heli-*

---

14. 499 U.S. 585 (1991).
15. Arthur Von Mehren & Donald Trautman, *Jurisdiction to Adjudicate: A Suggested Analysis*, 79 Harv. L. Rev. 1121 (1966).

16. *Milliken v. Meyer*, 311 U.S. 457 (1940).

copteros Nacionales de Colombia, S.A. v. Hall endorses the concept of general jurisdiction, while declining to find it in the specific case.[17]

Helicopteros was a suit brought by the estates of four Americans who died in a helicopter crash in Peru. They sued the Colombian transportation company, Helicol, in Texas. Helicol had fairly substantial contacts with Texas: it purchased parts and helicopters, amounting to 80% of its fleet, from Texas, and sent its pilots there for training. Additionally, the transportation contract had been negotiated in Texas. But these contacts were not related to the wrongful death claim, and, the Supreme Court said, they did not add up to a sufficient connection for the exercise of general jurisdiction.

One of the notable things about *Helicopteros* is what it does not decide. The Court did not set out any concrete standard for when contacts would be enough to support general jurisdiction. Nor did it consider whether the Texas suit could go forward as an exercise of specific jurisdiction. It simply pronounced that the contacts between Helicol and Texas were not related to the suit. It did this, a footnote explained, because the plaintiffs had not argued for specific jurisdiction. But what if they had? Then the Court would have had to answer a question that it has not yet: what is the test that distinguishes a related contact from an unrelated one?

The spectrum of possibilities is broad. At one extreme, a contact could count as related if it is a "but-for" cause of the injury complained of. This position is almost certainly too extreme, since many remote occurrences (the defendant's birth, for instance) qualify as but-for causes. Exercising jurisdiction over a person because he was born in the forum, on the theory that the natal contact is "related to" some subsequent tort, is absurd. At the other end, some courts suggest that related contacts are only those that actually constitute an element of the cause of action.[18] In between is the idea of proximate cause, which demands some undefined degree of relevance or connection beyond but-for causation. Lower courts have adopted all of these various possibilities, and the difference of opinion awaits Supreme Court resolution.[19]

17. 466 U.S. 408 (1984).

18. See Lea Brilmayer, *How Contacts Count: Due Process Limitations on State Court Jurisdiction*, 1980 Sup. Ct. Rev. 77.

19. See generally Note, *Specific Personal Jurisdiction and the "Arise from or Relate to" Requirement ... What Does it Mean?*, 50 Wash. & Lee L. Rev. 1265 (1993).

IV. Attachment Jurisdiction

International Shoe and its progeny supplemented the tradition-al *Pennoyer* approach based on presence and power. In some cases, of course, the two would overlap. With respect to general jurisdiction based on domicile, for instance, a *Pennoyer* analysis would lead to the same result as application of the minimum contacts test. But sometimes they would not. *International Shoe* clearly allowed for the exercise of jurisdiction when *Pennoyer* would not have. What about the reverse situation—an exercise of jurisdiction permissible under the traditional approach but not consistent with the *International Shoe* standard? The Court has taken two somewhat different approaches to this question, one in *in personam* cases and another when jurisdiction is asserted *in rem*.

With respect to *in rem* cases, the new learning has upset the old. Traditionally, jurisdiction over suits about rights to property could be exercised based merely on the presence of the property in the forum, and pre-judgment attachment. A suit *in rem* would decide rights to the property as among all possible claimants. A suit *quasi in rem* would decide rights only as between the parties to the suit. *Quasi in rem* jurisdiction was further subdivided into type 1 suits, where the dispute between the parties was about rights to the property, and type 2 suits, where the dispute was unrelated and the property features merely as a resource to satisfy a judgment.

In *Shaffer v. Heitner*,[20] the Court rejected type 2 *quasi in rem* actions. Heitner, a shareholder of Greyhound Corporation, sued its officers and directors for violation of fiduciary duties relating to an antitrust judgment against Greyhound. He filed suit in Delaware and invoked a Delaware statute allowing Delaware courts to estab-lish jurisdiction by sequestering defendants' in-state property. (In this case, the property was the directors' Greyhound stock—under Delaware law, all stock in Delaware corporations is deemed to be located in Delaware.)

The Delaware Supreme Court upheld the exercise of jurisdiction on this basis, noting simply that the action was *quasi in rem*, but the U.S. Supreme Court reversed. Even a suit *quasi in rem*, the Court observed, affected the interests of a nonresident defendant, and it too should be subjected to the *International Shoe* standard of fairness and substantial justice. That standard left most traditional actions *in rem* unaffected, but *quasi in rem* type 2 actions—where the property that served as the basis for jurisdiction was unrelated to the cause of action—did not meet it. The Court declined to give decisive, or even substantial, weight to the historical pedigree of

20. 433 U.S. 186 (1977).

quasi in rem type 2 actions. "Traditional notions of fair play and substantial justice," it said, "can be as readily offended by the perpetuation of ancient forms that are no longer justified as by the adoption of new procedures that are inconsistent with the basic values of our constitutional heritage."

V. Transient Jurisdiction

In contrast to the upheaval of jurisdiction *in rem,* it seems that the conceptual revolution started by *International Shoe* has broadened the scope of permissible *in personam* jurisdiction but not undermined the traditional justifications. In that context, *Burnham v. Superior Court*[21] suggests the continuing vitality of traditional bases for jurisdiction by approving the continuing practice of one of the more controversial traditional bases: transient, or "tag," jurisdiction.

Dennis Burnham got married in West Virginia and subsequently moved with his wife Francie to New Jersey, where their two children were born. Later they separated and Francie decided to move to California. The Burnhams agreed that Francie would file for divorce there on grounds of irreconcilable differences and take custody of the children.

After Francie left, Dennis apparently changed his mind, for he filed for divorce in New Jersey on the grounds of desertion. He did not attempt to serve Francie. When she learned of his suit, she demanded unsuccessfully that he adhere to their agreement and then filed suit herself in California. Some months later Dennis visited California on business and also went to see the children. As he returned them to Francie's house, he was served with a California summons. He made a special appearance in California court to quash the summons.

Burnham presented an example of an exercise of jurisdiction that was clearly acceptable under *Pennoyer,* for Dennis had been served with process while in the forum. Its status was less clear under *International Shoe,* so the case afforded the Court an opportunity to explore the relation between the two approaches. Writing for a plurality, Justice Scalia argued that the historical pedigree of service within the forum as a means of establishing jurisdiction immunized it from challenge as a violation of due process. He distinguished *Shaffer*'s sharply contrasting language in a somewhat

21. 495 U.S. 604 (1990).

unpersuasive fashion, and he later expressed the view that *Shaffer* was simply wrong.[22]

Four other Justices concurred to state that while tradition was an important factor in the due process analysis, it was not dispositive. They argued that an independent inquiry into fairness was necessary. On the facts of *Burnham*, they found no unfairness. Whether an exercise of *in personam* jurisdiction that would pass muster under *Pennoyer* can ever be arbitrary enough to violate the Due Process Clause thus remains an open question, though if transient jurisdiction survives it is not easy to think of what would not.

VI. Internet Jurisdiction

Particularly vexing problems applying the minimum contacts analysis can arise with respect to internet activities. It is obviously difficult to locate such activities for the purpose of deciding whether a defendant has acted within a state, and it is also difficult to decide what sort of conduct counts as "directed towards" or "reaching out to" a state in order to meet the requirement of purposeful availment. No single test has emerged from the lower courts. The trend, however, appears to be moving away from treating the Internet as a sui generis problem and towards applying the tests of *International Shoe* and its progeny.

In a notable early case, a district court based its analysis on the "level of interactivity and commercial nature of the exchange of information that occurs on the Web site."[23] Interactivity seems like a poor criterion, however, since technological advances are likely to lead to progressively increasing interactivity. More recent cases have tended to rest their conclusions on real-world activity, such as delivering a product.[24] When internet activity forms the basis for

---

22. *Shaffer* had said that "all assertions of state court jurisdiction must be evaluated according to the standards set forth in *International Shoe* and its progeny." But by "all," Scalia argued, it actually meant all exercises of jurisdiction over defendants not present in the forum. When not burdened by the need to hold onto the votes of other Justices, he was more candid: *Shaffer* and other cases that determined fundamental fairness by balancing rather than historical analysis "were in my view wrongly decided." *Pacific Mutual Life Ins. Co. v.*

Haslip, 499 U.S. 1, 36 (1991) (Scalia, J., concurring).

23. *Zippo Mfg. Co. v. Zippo Dot Com, Inc.*, 952 F.Supp. 1119, 1124 (W.D. Pa. 1997).

24. See, e.g., *Boschetto v. Hansing*, 539 F.3d 1011 (9th Cir. 2008) (California lacks personal jurisdiction over Wisconsin car dealership based on single sale over EBay); *Attaway v. Omega*, 903 N.E.2d 73 (Ind. Ct. App. 2009) (Indiana has jurisdiction over EBay buyers who picked up a car in Indiana).

jurisdiction, courts tend to rely on effects intentionally caused in the forum.[25]

In this respect, the treatment of judicial jurisdiction based on internet activities mirrors the pattern in internet scholarship more generally. The first wave of such scholarship viewed the Internet as literally a new place, an attitude well-captured in John Perry Barlow's breathless "Declaration of Independence of Cyberspace." Issued from Davos, Switzerland, in February 1996, the Declaration began with these words: "Governments of the Industrial World, you weary giants of flesh and steel, I come from Cyberspace, the new home of Mind. On behalf of the future, I ask you of the past to leave us alone."[26] In a similar vein, David Post and David Johnson argued that internet choice of law was simply impossible: "events on the Net are everywhere but nowhere in particular, are engaged in by online personae who are both 'real' . . . and 'intangible' . . . and concern 'things' . . . that are not necessarily separated from one another by any physical boundaries. . . ."[27]

A second wave of scholarship treated these claims skeptically, pointing to the continued significance of geographical factors such as the location of end-users.[28] Based on the way the cases are coming out, it appears likely that the Internet will be assimilated into conventional choice of law in the same way as other technologies that made territorial analysis more complicated. The idea of cyberlaw may end up sounding like the law of the telephone, or, as Judge Frank Easterbrook once put it, the law of the horse.[29]

VII.   Declining Jurisdiction:
Forum non conveniens

Even if jurisdiction exists, a court may decline to exercise it. Federal courts, for instance, will sometimes abstain from hearing claims out of deference to state interests.[30] And all courts may

---

25. See, e.g., *Dudnikov v. Chalk & Vermilion*, 514 F.3d 1063 (10th Cir. 2008) (Colorado has personal jurisdiction over copyright owner who sent a notice of copyright infringement to EBay alleging infringement by Colorado seller).

26. The Declaration is widely available on the Internet, for instance at http://homes.eff.org/?barlow/Declaration-Final.html.

27. David Johnson & David Post, *Law and Borders—The Rise of Law in Cyberspace*, 48 Stan. L. Rev. 1367, 1379 (1996).

28. See generally JACK GOLDSMITH & TIM WU, WHO CONTROLS THE INTERNET: ILLUSIONS OF A BORDERLESS WORLD (2006).

29. See Frank H. Easterbrook, *Cyberspace and the Law of the Horse*, 1996 U. Chi. Legal F. 207; but see Lawrence Lessig, *The Law of the Horse: What Cyberlaw Might Teach*, 113 Harv. L. Rev. 501 (1999).

30. I do not cover the topic of abstention in this book, although it does present the general conflicts question of how to reconcile overlapping authorities. For a survey, see, e.g., Leonard Bird-

dismiss a case if the plaintiff's chosen forum is inconvenient. The doctrine of *forum non conveniens* starts from the premise that a plaintiff's choice of forum should rarely be disturbed, but it recognizes that if the plaintiff's choice of forum places burdens on the forum or the defendant that are out of proportion with the plaintiff's convenience, dismissal may be appropriate.

The proportionality determination requires courts to balance " 'private interest factors' affecting the convenience of the litigants and ... 'public interest factors' affecting the convenience of the forum."[31] Private interest factors include the ease of access to sources of proof, the ability to compel the attendance of witnesses, the cost of witness attendance, and "all other practical problems that make trial of a case easy, expeditious, and inexpensive."[32] Public interest factors include the administrative burdens of court congestion, the local interest in having local controversies decided at home, the interest in having a court apply law with which it is familiar, the avoidance of unnecessary choice-of-law problems, and the unfairness of burdening residents of an unrelated forum with jury duty.[33]

The Court's leading pronouncement on the subject, *Piper Aircraft v. Reyno*,[34] established the rule that plaintiffs may not defeat a *forum non conveniens* motion merely on the ground that the alternative forum would decide the case under less favorable substantive law. It also noted that a plaintiff's choice of forum is entitled to more weight when the plaintiff has chosen his home court, since that choice is more likely to be based on convenience than forum-shopping. Beyond that it offered little guidance in how to balance the private and public interest factors. Since appellate review of district court balancing is for clear abuse of discretion, district courts enjoy considerable leeway in making their decisions.

In state courts, *forum non conveniens* dismissals may be controlled or limited by statute. In federal courts, true *forum non conveniens* is available only when the alternate forum is a foreign country. As far as the choice between different federal courts is concerned, the governing rule is 28 U.S.C. § 1404(a), which allows transfer of civil actions "[f]or the convenience of parties and witnesses, in the interest of justice." The Supreme Court has held

song, *Comity and Our Federalism in the Twenty–First Century: The Abstention Doctrines Will Always Be With Us—Get Over It!*, 36 Creighton L. Rev. 375 (2003).

31. *Piper Aircraft v. Reyno*, 454 U.S. 235 (1981).

32. *Gulf Oil Corp. v. Gilbert*, 330 U.S. 501, 508 (1947).

33. *Id.*

34. 454 U.S. 235 (1981).

that following a § 1404(a) transfer, the transferee court should apply the same law as the transferor court would have, reasoning that a litigant should not "get a change of law as a bonus for a change of venue."[35] Since plaintiffs, as well as defendants, can seek transfers under § 1404(a), the possibility exists that a diversity plaintiff could file in one district based on choice-of-law considerations and then transfer to another for convenience. The rather notorious example is *Ferens v. John Deere Co.*,[36] where an individual injured in Pennsylvania sued in Mississippi to get the benefit of a longer limitations period and then transferred the case back to Pennsylvania.

The result in *Ferens* is certainly odd, but it is a consequence of characterization more than of the idea that the transferee court should apply the same law as the transferor. The reason that filing in Mississippi allowed the plaintiff to get the Mississippi limitations period was that while the limitations period is substantive for *Erie* analysis (so that the federal court did what a Mississippi court would do), Mississippi deemed it procedural for choice-of-law purposes (so that a Mississippi court would use the Mississippi limitations period, rather than that of Pennsylvania, whose law created the cause of action). The point that a change of venue should not work a change of law seems sound.

35. *Van Dusen v. Barrack*, 376 U.S. 612 (1964).

36. 494 U.S. 516 (1990).

Chapter 7

RECOGNITION OF JUDGMENTS

I. Introduction

Issues of interstate recognition of judgments arise when a judgment is issued in one state and enforcement is sought in another. (I will follow the convention of calling the issuing state F–1, for "forum one," and the state of enforcement F–2, for "forum two.") The topic is controlled by the Full Faith and Credit Clause of the Constitution. That clause is part of Article IV, which, as noted in Chapter 4, is generally concerned with interstate relations. The overarching aim of Article IV is to take the states, which in the absence of the Constitution would relate to each other as independent sovereigns, and weld them into a single nation. The effect of most of the provisions of Article IV is to prevent states from treating other states, and also their laws and citizens, as utterly foreign. More precisely, the clauses tend to operate by requiring states to supply some nondiscriminatory reason for not granting sister-state laws or citizens the same respect as locals.

How substantial a reason is required varies from clause to clause. The Privileges and Immunities Clause, we have seen, is relatively demanding. It imposes something like intermediate scrutiny on discrimination against out-of-staters. The Full Faith and Credit Clause, as regards sister-state law, is now relatively nugatory. As the Court has framed the issue, a state may apply its own law, rather than the contrary law of a sister state, whenever it has contacts with the case that create a local interest. Since, I have suggested, the question of whether a state has an interest is just the question of whether a case falls within the scope of its law, this amounts to the rule that a state can apply its own law whenever that law applies. Or in the slightly clearer terms I have introduced, a state can give priority to its own law whenever it conflicts with sister-state law. (What it cannot do is refuse to recognize sister-state law when there is no conflict; that is the *Hughes v. Fetter* situation.)[1]

As regards sister-state *judgments*, however, the Full Faith and Credit Clause is significantly more demanding. Unless the judgment is itself nonfinal or in some way defective (a qualifier we will explore later), the rule requires recognition in F–2 basically without

---

1. See Chapter 4, Part IV.

exception. To some extent, we can still describe the recognition of judgment regime as analogous to the recognition of law regime. In both cases, we could say, the sister-state law or judgment must be recognized unless contrary local rights exist. The difference is that while contrary local rights will frequently exist with regard to sister-state law, they will almost never exist with regard to sister-state judgments. (Thus, under a choice-of-law regime in which rights do not conflict, such as territoriality, the treatment of sister-state laws will more closely resemble that of judgments.) The significant remaining difference is that with respect to sister-state law, even in the territorialist regime, the public policy exception allowed a state to close its courthouse doors and refuse to hear a foreign cause of action contrary to a fundamental local policy. There is no such public policy exception to recognition of judgments.

But what does it mean to recognize a judgment? Briefly, it means to give it some sort of preclusive effect—to treat it as the final resolution of at least some issues between at least some parties. Those issues may not be relitigated by those parties. We will examine later what this preclusive effect typically consists of. The first question is where the preclusion rules come from.

The text of the Constitution requires F–2 states to give F–1 sister-state judgments "Full Faith and Credit." This suggests three possibilities.[2] First, the reference to "Full Faith and Credit" might invoke a set of federal preclusion rules. That would make some sense. The clauses of Article IV are mostly aimed at building a national union out of the discrete sovereignties of the states, and establishing a uniform standard for the force of F–1 sister-state judgments would be a reasonable means to that end.

On the other hand, the fact that laws, as well as judgments, are entitled to full faith and credit suggests a different possibility. Giving full faith and credit to a sister-state law simply means allowing that law to operate according to its own terms. So a second possibility is to take the Full Faith and Credit Clause to suggest that F–1 sister-state judgments should be given the same effect in F–2 as they have in their home states. On this approach, the relevant preclusion rules would be those of F–1, the state where the judgment was issued.

Last, we could describe one of the overarching themes of Article IV as nondiscrimination. The Privileges and Immunities Clause, for instance, tells states to treat out-of-staters in many cases like locals. So it would also make some sense to suppose that

2. See Lea Brilmayer, CONFLICT OF LAWS 301–03 (1995).

a state may comply with the demands of full faith and credit by giving an F–1 sister-state judgment the same effect as a local F–2 judgment. In this case, the relevant preclusion rules would be those of F–2, the state where enforcement was sought.

Each possibility has some points in its favor. Under the Full Faith and Credit Clause, the choice is given to Congress, for the Clause provides that Congress may "by general laws prescribe the manner in which such acts, records, and proceedings shall be proved, and the effect thereof." Congress has chosen the second of the three options. Its Full Faith and Credit statute, which was first enacted in 1790 and has persisted essentially unchanged, provides that records and judicial proceedings of any court within the United States (thus including federal courts) "shall have the same full faith and credit in every court within the United States ... as they have by law or usage" in the issuing courts.[3]

That settles the question of where preclusion rules come from: to determine the effect of an F–1 judgment, you consult F–1 preclusion rules. But what is their content? Preclusion rules vary from state to state (otherwise the question of their source would be unnecessary), but generally speaking they contain two different principles. Historically these have been called *res judicata* and *collateral estoppel*. The Second Restatement of Judgments replaced those labels with the slightly more transparent *claim preclusion* and *issue preclusion*, which I will use for the remainder of the discussion.

Claim preclusion deals with attempts by plaintiffs, and also sometimes defendants, to (re)assert claims that were or should have been decided in an initial suit. The general idea is that a lawsuit, which is expensive and inconvenient for everyone, should be a once-and-for-all event: the plaintiff should assert every possible cause of action, and the defendant every possible defense or counterclaim, and they should all be decided at once. Thus, claim preclusion will not only prevent a plaintiff from suing the same defendant again on the *same* cause of action; it will prevent him from asserting a *different* cause of action if it is deemed part of the same claim. Defendants may likewise see counterclaims that could have been asserted in the initial action barred if they are withheld and instead presented in a subsequent suit.

One difference between state preclusion rules is how tightly a "claim" is defined. Thus, causes of action that would be barred under some states' definitions of claim might be permitted under the definitions of other states. Federal courts increasingly rely on

---

3. 28 U.S.C. § 1738.

the definition provided by § 24 of the Restatement, Second, of Judgments, which states that a valid final judgment extinguishes all causes of action arising from the same "transaction, or series of connected transactions."[4] To use a simple example, if you sustain multiple injuries in a single accident, the causes of action for those injuries obviously arise from the same transaction. If you have one accident in January and then, coincidentally, another accident with the same person in March, the injuries arise from different transactions.

Issue preclusion operates more narrowly, in one sense, but more broadly in another. Under issue preclusion, particular issues that were actually litigated and necessarily determined in one litigation are deemed conclusively decided for the purposes of other litigation. This rule is narrower because it operates with respect to particular issues, rather than all possible causes of action, but it is broader because it will apply in *any* subsequent suit between the parties, not just a suit on the same claim. It may even apply in suits that are not between the same parties. Increasingly, a party against whom an issue has been determined may be bound by that determination in a subsequent suit by someone other than the initial plaintiff. (This used to be called offensive non-mutual collateral estoppels—offensive, because it is being used by a plaintiff, and non-mutual because the defendant could not use a favorable determination against subsequent plaintiffs who were not parties to the original suit.)

For instance, if five passengers are injured in a bus accident and they bring consecutive suits against the company, the first might lose on the grounds that the driver was not negligent. This judgment would not bar the second suit, since the second plaintiff was not a party to the first proceeding. But if the second plaintiff wins and prevails on the negligence issue, the defendant can be bound by that finding for suits three, four, and five.

The general value that preclusion doctrines serve is finality. Finality is not, of course, just an end in itself; it is backed by practical concerns. It is relatively easy to see how an endless course of litigation, in which every decision remained always open to challenge, would be tremendously inefficient and would produce great uncertainty. (Somewhat similar justifications stand behind the doctrine of *stare decisis*, which can be understood as a species of preclusion.) Against finality there traditionally stands the value of

---

4. See generally John F. Wagner, *Proper Test to Determine Identity of Claims for Purposes of Claim Preclusion by Res Judicata Under Federal Law,* 82 A.L.R. Fed 829 (1987). The term "transaction" is itself obviously in need of definition. The Restatement advises courts to proceed pragmatically.

correctness, but correctness is actually not necessarily enhanced by indefinite relitigation. An appeal to the value of correctness supports re-examination of issues only when there is some reason to think that the later proceeding will be better than the earlier one.

In the interstate context, some other issues arise. F–2 states may have interests in limiting or refusing to recognize F–1 sister-state judgments that they do not have with local F–2 judgments. Generally speaking, however, appeal to those interests is unavailing. In the interstate context, just as in the local, the general rule is that a judgment is entitled to preclusive effect if it is final, valid, and on the merits. We will examine those criteria individually in subsequent sections. We start with a look at justifications that do not allow an F–2 state to refuse recognition to an F–1 sister-state judgment: error, public policy, and forum interests.

II. Error, Public Policy, and Forum Interests

In the early nineteen hundreds, several states, including Mississippi, banned futures contracts where the parties did not intend to take delivery of the underlying commodity, on the theory that such contracts were a form of gambling. Mississippi not only held these contracts unenforceable; it criminalized their making. Two Mississippi residents nonetheless entered into such a contract with respect to cotton futures, and one then sought to recover on it via arbitration in Mississippi. He received an arbitral award and sought to enforce it in Mississippi. The Mississippi court, its attention called to the criminal nature of the contract, refused enforcement. The claimant then went to Missouri, managed to obtain personal jurisdiction over the other party to the futures contract by serving him there, and sought enforcement of the arbitral award in a Missouri court. The defendant offered evidence that the underlying transaction was criminal under Mississippi law, but the Missouri court rejected it and rendered a judgment enforcing the award.

The claimant then sought to enforce the Missouri judgment in Mississippi. The Mississippi Supreme Court, understandably annoyed at this course of events, decided that the Missouri judgment was not entitled to full faith and credit, as it concerned a transaction wholly domestic to Mississippi and contrary to Mississippi law and policy. But in *Fauntleroy v. Lum*, the federal Supreme Court reversed.[5] The Missouri court might have made a mistake. And it might have made that mistake with respect to Mississippi law, endorsing a transaction that Mississippi was well within its author-

5. 210 U.S. 230 (1908).

ity to ban. But the judgment, once issued, was still entitled to recognition under the Full Faith and Credit Clause.

Fauntleroy is a classic case because of how extreme its facts are. The Missouri court gets the decision wrong, and it gets it wrong under Mississippi law, with respect to a purely Mississippi transaction. Indeed, by rejecting the evidence of Mississippi law the defendant proffered, the Missouri court probably violated the Full Faith and Credit Clause with respect to that law.[6] If F–2 interests are ever enough to outweigh the demand of Full Faith and Credit with respect to judgments, *Fauntleroy* would appear to be such a case. The lesson of *Fauntleroy* is thus that F–2 interests cannot outweigh Full Faith and Credit. Judgments based on error, even with respect to F–2 law, F–2 facts, and F–2 domiciliaries, even with respect to fundamental F–2 policies, and even errors of constitutional magnitude, still get full faith and credit.[7]

While we are listing the things the Missouri court did wrong, what about that Mississippi judgment holding the arbitral award unenforceable? Under the Full Faith and Credit Clause, that judgment should have precluded subsequent attempts at enforcement.[8] So the Missouri court appears to have violated the Full Faith and Credit Clause not merely by disregarding Mississippi law called to its attention, but also by disregarding a Mississippi judgment. Can a judgment whose issuance is a violation of the Full Faith and Credit Clause possibly be entitled to full faith and credit?

The answer is yes, by virtue of what is called the last-in-time rule. A court presented with a suit precluded by an earlier judgment should refuse to allow relitigation of concluded matters. But if it does not—if it proceeds nonetheless to render a judgment, contrary to its full faith and credit obligations—then that improperly issued judgment is the one to which full faith and credit is owed. The Full Faith and Credit Clause protects the first judgment until the second one is issued, but once that happens it switches allegiance immediately and protects the second. Of course, it protects

---

6. See *Sun Oil v. Wortman*, 486 U.S. 717, 731 (1988) (noting that refusal to follow clear law that has been called to the court's attention violates full faith and credit).

7. Marriages, which may be embodied in judicial records, are an exception to this rule. Traditional choice-of-law doctrine generally, and the federal Defense of Marriage Act, with respect to same-sex marriage, allow states to refuse to recognize marriages celebrated in other states that are contrary to local policy.

8. This is not entirely clear. The Court's opinion suggests that the plaintiff voluntarily dismissed the suit once the issue of illegality was raised, in which case there might have been no judgment on the merits warranting preclusive effect. For illustrative purposes, however, we may suppose that there was indeed a final judgment against enforcement.

that second judgment only against subsequent collateral attack. The remedy for the Missouri court's errors was direct appeal, with the possibility of ultimate review by the federal Supreme Court as to issues of federal law.

So F–2 interests and policies by themselves will not justify a state in refusing recognition to a sister-state judgment. But what if those interests and policies take the form of law? I said in the introduction that the full faith and credit analyses for law and judgments could to some extent be harmonized if we thought of enforcement of judgments as a situation where one state's law creates rights and there are no contrary rights under F–2 law. In most cases that will be true—if a prevailing party seeks to enforce judgment from F–1, it is unlikely that the other party can identify rights under F–2 law that entitle him to resist. But he might be able to—there could be rights that are in some way inconsistent or in conflict with the judgment. What happens then?

The answer is not entirely clear. *Yarborough v. Yarborough*,[9] another classic case, suggests that the Full Faith and Credit Clause still prevails. But, as we will see, it is not clear that *Yarborough* features real F–2 rights.

Mr. and Mrs. Yarborough lived with their daughter Sadie in Georgia. In 1927 they divorced. A Georgia court entered a divorce decree, awarded custody of Sadie to Mrs. Yarborough, and ordered Mr. Yarborough to pay $1,750 to her grandfather for her maintenance.[10] Under Georgia law, this was a final judgment, which entirely terminated Mr. Yarborough's support obligations and could not be modified.

Sadie subsequently went to South Carolina to live with her grandfather. In 1930, at 16, she filed suit in South Carolina, alleging that she was now ready for college and required additional support. Mr. Yarborough objected that the Georgia judgment precluded the suit. The South Carolina courts rejected his argument on the grounds that, under South Carolina law, support decrees could be modified. They ordered him to pay $50 a month towards Sadie's education.

What South Carolina did, from one perspective, was to give the Georgia judgment the preclusive effect it would have had if it had been issued by a South Carolina court, F–2. I have noted earlier that this is not an unreasonable understanding of full faith and credit. It prevents discrimination against foreign judgments, and

9. 290 U.S. 202 (1933).

10. This is probably roughly equivalent to $20,000 in 2009 dollars.

such discrimination is the core concern of the Full Faith and Credit Clause. But I have also said that it is not the understanding Congress has adopted. Judgments are entitled to the preclusive effect they would have in the issuing state, F–1. In Georgia, the judgment was final and would have precluded any new suit for maintenance. South Carolina had to give it that effect as well.[11]

But we could also think of *Yarborough* from a slightly different perspective. Certainly, Sadie might have argued, the Georgia judgment terminated support obligations that existed in 1927, under Georgia law or otherwise. But what she wants to enforce are rights created after 1927, under South Carolina law. The Georgia judgment can extinguish all rights that exist at the time it is issued, but how can it prevent South Carolina from granting her new rights?

In fact, it is not clear that Georgia could do that under all circumstances. The majority opinion expressly reserves the question. As far as the facts of *Yarborough* are concerned, an attempt by South Carolina to give Sadie new rights to support from her father would founder on the Due Process Clause. Mr. Yarborough resided in Georgia and, the Court said, South Carolina could not reach out to impose obligations on him. Had he moved to South Carolina the matter might have been different.

It seems likely, in fact, that South Carolina could attach legal consequences to events subsequent to the Georgia judgment. If Mr. Yarborough came within its legislative jurisdiction—if, in particular, he moved to South Carolina—the state would probably be able to impose an obligation of continuing support based on the continuing parent-child relationship. Thus, contrary rights probably can be created to the extent that they derive from post-judgment events.

So a judgment can free a defendant from all claims existing at the time the judgment issues, or at least those that could have been asserted,[12] but not from those that derive from subsequent events. A further question presents itself. What if the "subsequent" event from which the claims derive is the judgment itself? Could F–2 pass a law saying that anyone required to pay X dollars under a sister-state judgment enforced in F–2 immediately acquires a cause of action for X dollars against the prevailing party? Such "clawback" statutes do exist on the international stage.[13] They represent an

---

11. At least, South Carolina could not give it any *less* effect. Whether F–2 can give an F–1 judgment *more* preclusive effect than it would have under F–1 law is an open question. Compare *Hart v. American Airlines, Inc.*, 61 Misc.2d 41, 304 N.Y.S.2d 810 (N.Y. Sup. Ct. 1969) (giving greater effect permissible) with *Columbia Casualty Co. v. Playtex FP*, 584 A.2d 1214 (Del. 1991) (impermissible).

12. See Part III.B.

13. For discussion of clawback statutes, see, e.g., Joseph P. Griffin, *United States Antitrust Laws and Transnation-*

extreme failure of comity, and have never, to my knowledge, been tried in the interstate context. Technically, a clawback statute is consistent with recognition of a sister-state judgment, but it would probably be deemed unconstitutional because of its patent hostility towards the policy of full faith and credit.

III. Limits on Full Faith and Credit

To qualify for full faith and credit, a judgment must be final, valid, and on the merits. And even if it does qualify, there are some limits to the force it will have. In the preceding section, we just saw one such limit: in at least some cases, F–2 can probably create new rights or obligations that seem to undermine the effect of an F–1 judgment. In the remainder of this section we will look at others.

A. Procedural Rules, Limits on F–2 Jurisdiction

Even when deciding a case under foreign internal law, we saw in Chapter 1, the forum will follow its own procedural rules. And the adherence to forum procedure can have quite substantial (or, one might say, substantive) consequences, depending on where the line between substance and procedure is drawn. Similarly, an F–2 court enforcing an F–1 judgment will still follow F–2 procedure. And as in the choice-of-law context, forum procedure can have significant consequences.

In particular, as in the choice-of-law context, a shorter local F–2 limitations period may bar enforcement of an F–1 sister-state judgment that is still live according to the F–1 limitations period. Doing so, the Court reasoned in *M'Elmoyle v. Cohen*,[14] does not amount to a refusal to recognize the rights embodied in the judgment but simply a foreclosure of the remedy. (As in the choice-of-law context, F–2 can also subject F–1 judgments to the F–1 limitations period, though it cannot otherwise treat them less hospitably than F–2 judgments.[15]) F–1 may, however, evade the consequences of this rule if it provides procedures for the revival of judgments. A judgment "revived" under F–1 law counts as a new judgment as far as an F–2 limitations period is concerned.[16]

al Business Transactions: An Introduction, 21 Int'l Law 307, 327 (1987) (discussing clawback statutes aimed at United States antitrust law judgments). Similar measures have recently been proposed in the U.S. to counter foreign defamation judgments.

14. 38 U.S. (13 Pet.) 312, 326–27 (1839).

15. See *Watkins v. Conway*, 385 U.S. 188 (1966).

16. See *Union Nat'l Bank v. Lamb*, 337 U.S. 38 (1949).

It is also the case, on a similar rationale, that F–2 can create courts of limited jurisdiction that do not have the authority to enforce foreign judgments. A judgment creditor wielding an F–1 judgment cannot demand that an F–2 traffic court enforce it. But this means of avoiding enforcement will not work for courts of general jurisdiction, or for any courts that can enforce similar F–2 judgments.[17] (In fact, the defendant in *Fauntleroy* argued, to no avail, that Mississippi courts lacked jurisdiction to enforce the Missouri judgment.)

B. Limits on F–1 Jurisdiction

Claim preclusion bars a plaintiff or defendant from (re)asserting causes of action if they are part of the same claim and were or could have been asserted in the first action. The corollary (technically, the contrapositive) of this rule is that if a cause of action could *not* have been asserted, it is not barred. If the F–1 litigation takes place in a court of limited jurisdiction, for instance, claims that could not have been presented are not barred for subsequent litigation. At least, they are not barred by claim preclusion. If F–1 wants to set conditions on the use of a specialized tribunal, it can do so. It can tell potential claimants, that is, that they may seek certain remedies at the price of surrendering whatever other claims they may have.

The nonpreclusion rule has emerged most clearly in a series of workers' compensation cases. In the most recent, *Thomas v. Washington Gas Light Co.*, a District of Columbia resident was injured on the job in Virginia. He qualified for compensation under both the D.C. and the Virginia workers' compensation plans. He first sought and obtained benefits from the Virginia Industrial Commission. Some years later he went to the D.C. system. The employer objected on the grounds that the Virginia award by its terms excluded any other recovery "at common law or otherwise" and that this determination was entitled to full faith and credit. The Fourth Circuit accepted this argument, but the Supreme Court reversed.

The main question for the Court was how to deal with two earlier workers' compensation cases. In *Magnolia Petroleum Co. v. Hunt*, the Court had treated workers' compensation awards essentially the same as ordinary judgments and held that an award in

17. See *Kenney v. Supreme Lodge of the World, Loyal Order of Moose*, 252 U.S. 411 (1920).

one state barred subsequent attempt to recover in other states.[18] But in *Industrial Commission of Wisconsin v. McCartin*,[19] the Court changed its mind. Workers' compensation awards were special; they were rendered by tribunals that had the power only to grant particular remedies; and workers' compensation statutes ought not, in the absence of "unmistakable language," be construed to prevent supplemental recovery in other states.

The *Thomas* Court was unable to come together on a majority opinion. A four-Justice plurality, in an opinion written by Stevens, found something wrong with *McCartin*. By focusing on the language of the F–1 workers' compensation statute, they reasoned, *McCartin* had adopted a rule allowing F–1 to directly specify the effect its judgment would have in F–2. (It could, for instance, write a statute saying "Awards from this tribunal preclude subsequent suits in other states.") That was impermissible, the Stevens plurality thought, for the Full Faith and Credit Clause required that an F–1 judgment be given in F–2 the effect it would have in F–1—not whatever effect the F–1 legislature said it should have in F–2. That is, F–1 could control the effect of its judgments in F–2 *indirectly* (by adopting particular preclusion rules to govern their effects in F–1) but it could not do so *directly* (by stipulating the effects they should have in F–2, regardless of what their effects were in F–1). But these four Justices also thought *Magnolia* was wrong. Workers' compensation claims were different, as noted above—in particular, the Stevens plurality observed, the Virginia Industrial Commission was restricted by statute to considering claims under Virginia law. States had no legitimate interest in precluding supplemental recovery, and the Full Faith and Credit Clause should not preclude successive awards.

Three other Justices concurred, in an opinion written by Justice White. Where the Stevens four-Justice plurality implicitly rejected *McCartin* and openly called for the overruling of *Magnolia*,[20] the White three would overrule neither. They doubted *McCartin*'s reasoning but would follow it on the grounds that it was easily limited to workers' compensation awards, while the principles of the Stevens plurality opinion were not. Two Justices, the unlikely pair of William Rehnquist and Thurgood Marshall, dissented on the grounds that *McCartin* should be overruled and *Magnolia* applied to preclude the D.C. recovery.

---

18. 320 U.S. 430 (1943).
19. 330 U.S. 622 (1947).

20. The four-Justice plurality did not explicitly state what they thought should happen to *McCartin*.

What to make of all these opinions is not entirely clear. The Stevens plurality's argument for distinguishing workers' compensation claims from ordinary judgments is basically that the specialized tribunals lack authority to consider claims under other states' laws. And if they cannot consider those claims, their decisions should not bar them either, under the standard principles that claims that could not be asserted are not precluded.

The White concurrence challenges that distinction on the grounds that in an ordinary case, a court of general jurisdiction may find itself foreclosed by binding authority from considering claims under other states' laws as well. A court in the territorialist State A, for instance, may hear the tort suit of a resident of interest analysis State B, injured in State A. Binding authority will require the State A court to give the plaintiff whatever remedy he has under State A law. It cannot award a remedy under State B law. So why is it in any different position than the Virginia Industrial Commission?

There is, in fact, an answer to this argument. A territorialist State A court does have the power to hear claims under State B law, and it will do so for cases with State B events. When it decides the tort suit under State A law and ignores the law of State B, it is saying that State A law attaches legal consequences and State B law does not.[21] It is rejecting any claim of entitlement to recover under State B law on the facts presented, and right or wrong, that decision is entitled to recognition. A worker's compensation tribunal, by contrast, has the power to hear and decide only certain claims. If it lacks the power to hear claims, its judgment should not bar them under ordinary preclusion rules.

But rather than siding with the Stevens plurality, I would follow *McCartin*. It is true that F–1 cannot directly specify the effect its judgments will have in F–2. But it can, when creating its specialized tribunals, condition access to them on waiver of other remedies. And the "unmistakable language" test set out in *McCartin* should be understood as a means of determining whether the state has set waiver of other remedies as a precondition to the use of its workers' compensation system.[22] The relevant language thus would (or should) be not "Awards from this tribunal preclude suits

---

21. It is wrong on that point, as I argued in Chapter 3, because the scope of State B law is set by the choice-of-law rules of State B, not State A. But that is what it is saying.

22. Requiring "unmistakable language" sets a presumption against waiv-

er. That would make sense if non-waiver were the intent of most states, which may or may not be true. My main point is that the possibility of foreclosing other remedies should be conceptualized in terms of waiver and not preclusion.

in other states" but rather "Claimants who receive awards from this tribunal agree in return to surrender their rights to any other relief," and if a state adopts the former, it should be understood as an imprecise version of the latter.

Distinguishing between waiver and preclusion can help us make sense not only of the workers' compensation cases but also of some other puzzling full faith and credit decisions. In *Matsushita Electrical Industrial Co. v. Epstein*,[23] the Supreme Court considered the effect of a settlement reached in a state-law class action suit brought against Matsushita in Delaware court. Simultaneously with that suit, some members of the class were pursuing a federal class action suit against Matsushita in federal district court in California. The claims they asserted there, under S.E.C. rules, were within the exclusive jurisdiction of the federal courts.

The Delaware suit was settled while the federal plaintiffs, having been denied class status in district court, had an appeal pending before the Ninth Circuit. As part of the settlement, the Delaware class agreed to release all claims against Matsushita. Should that settlement bar the Ninth Circuit appeal? The Ninth Circuit said no, on the grounds that the Delaware court lacked jurisdiction to hear the federal claims and therefore could not bar them. The Supreme Court reversed, on the grounds that this was the result that would obtain under Delaware preclusion law. It did not try to answer the Ninth Circuit's argument that judgments do not preclude claims that could not have been asserted. However, this difficulty disappears if we understand dismissal of the federal suit not as enforcement of the *judgment* but as enforcement of the *settlement agreement*. That is, it is a matter of waiver rather than preclusion.

C. Invalidity of F–1 Judgment

Enforcement of an F–1 judgment may be resisted on the grounds that it is not valid. The most common ground of invalidity is probably lack of jurisdiction, although other grounds, such as fraud, exist. The possibility of challenging F–1 jurisdiction in F–2, however, is somewhat less than one might at first suppose, especially for personal (as opposed to subject-matter) jurisdiction. If the party resisting enforcement has appeared in F–1 and litigated the issue of jurisdiction, he will be prevented from disputing it in F–2 by issue preclusion. Even if he did not litigate it in F–1, he will be held to have waived the issue (of personal jurisdiction, at least) if he

23.   516 U.S. 367 (1996).

contested the merits. The only way to preserve the issue of personal jurisdiction for litigation in F–2 is to refuse to appear in F–1 and suffer a default judgment.

Subject-matter jurisdiction cannot be waived, and the cases have been somewhat more permissive on the question of relitigation. The classic case of *Durfee v. Duke* announces a rule that, at least when the issue has been litigated, F–1 subject matter jurisdiction cannot be contested in a later proceeding. (It dealt with the question of title to bottom land in the Missouri river, and the jurisdiction of F–1 (Nebraska) depended on whether the land was in Missouri or Nebraska.) When the issue has not been litigated, some cases have found the jurisdictional issue nonetheless foreclosed.[24] Others have allowed relitigation, depending apparently on the strength of the policy behind the jurisdiction-ousting rule.[25] The Second Restatement of Conflicts suggests that the availability of relitigation should be subject to a balancing test that weighs "the policy underlying the rules of res judicata against the policy prohibiting a court from exceeding the powers conferred upon it."[26] The Restatement does not suggest that reexamination should be categorically barred if jurisdiction was litigated in the first case but identifies this as a factor supporting finality. Other factors, including the strength of the policy denying jurisdiction and the obviousness of the jurisdictional defect, support relitigation.

One notable limit on jurisdiction is what is sometimes known as the land taboo, the rule that courts in one state lack power to affect interests in land located in another state. A court that violates the land taboo has exceeded its jurisdiction in a very obvious way, and this may entitle individuals to avoid its judgment in subsequent litigation. In *Clarke v. Clarke*,[27] for instance, a South Carolina court purported to adjudicate rights to Connecticut real estate, on the theory that it had been converted into personalty by the owner's will. In a subsequent Connecticut case, the court denied that the transformation had occurred and ignored the South Carolina judgment.

The Supreme Court sided with Connecticut. The conversion to personalty might have occurred according to South Carolina law, the Court admitted, but Connecticut law controlled the status of

---

24. See, e.g., *Chicot County Drainage Dist. v. Baxter State Bank*, 308 U.S. 371 (1940). *Chicot* is a somewhat unusual case because its jurisdictional question was entangled with a retroactivity issue.

25. See, e.g, *Kalb v. Feuerstein*, 308 U.S. 433 (1940); *United States v. United States Fidelity & Guar. Co.*, 309 U.S. 506 (1940).

26. Restatement, Second, of Conflict of Laws § 97, comment d.

27. 178 U.S. 186 (1900).

the property, and under Connecticut law it remained realty. Likewise, in *Fall v. Eastin*,[28] the Supreme Court held that a Nebraska court need not recognize a deed to Nebraska land executed by a Washington commissioner (rather than the landowner) pursuant to a Washington divorce decree. Interestingly, the *Fall* Court appeared to concede that the Washington court, having jurisdiction over both parties, could order one to convey the land to the other. What the court could not do was purport to convey the land by its own action or through its commissioner. *Fall* suggests a relatively simple way around the land taboo, at least in cases where the court has jurisdiction over both parties. If such a court can order conveyance and enforce the order through contempt sanctions, the lack of direct power over the land seems of little moment.

D. F–1 Judgment not on Merits

A judgment that is not on the merits will not have claim preclusive effect, although its resolution of particular issues will have issue preclusive effect. A judgment is not on the merits if it does not decide the ultimate issue in dispute. Examples of non-merits grounds include dismissal on the grounds that the forum limitations period has expired, for want of jurisdiction, pursuant to *forum non conveniens*, or on the grounds that the cause of action is contrary to forum policy.

E. Lack of Finality in F–1

A judgment is not entitled to preclusive effect under full faith and credit until it is final. This rule is relatively straightforward with respect to judgments that are on the path to finality but have not yet reached it. Interlocutory orders in cases where no judgment has issued, for instance, are typically not final. Judgments as to which appeal is pending may or may not be final; that is a matter to be determined by F–1 law, in keeping with the general full faith and credit principle that judgments are entitled to the preclusive effect they have in F–1, the rendering state.[29]

The operation of the rule becomes somewhat more complicated with judgments that will *never* be final because they are always subject to modification. Child or spousal support orders tend to remain open in this way. Consequently, the Supreme Court has

28. 215 U.S. 1 (1909).

29. See *Paine v. Schenectady Ins. Co.*, 11 R.I. 411 (1876) (giving preclusive effect to N.Y. judgment during pendency of appeal because N.Y. law deemed it final, though Rhode Island law would not).

never held that full faith and credit requires enforcement of such orders, even though a claimant might have, in addition to the modifiable claim for future payments, a fully matured claim for the failure to make past payments. (If the distinct past-payment claim is reduced to judgment, however, that judgment is final and must be recognized.[30])

This does not mean that sister-states *cannot* recognize and enforce such orders. They can, although the Supreme Court has held that enforcement, at least as to past obligations, requires that the defendant be given a chance to litigate the question of modification.[31] In *Worthley v. Worthley*,[32] for instance, the California Supreme Court, considering an attempt to enforce a New Jersey support decree, decided that California courts with proper jurisdiction should try such actions while allowing the defendant to assert any defenses that would be available in a suit in the rendering state. The issue of interstate conflicts with respect to support orders has now been resolved by the adoption of the Uniform Interstate Family Support Act, now in force in all fifty states and the District of Columbia. For further details, consult Chapter 8.

F. Equitable Decrees

Equitable decrees are almost always non-final in the sense of being subject to modification. Perhaps for this reason, or perhaps because enforcement of an equitable decree was considered a remedial issue within the authority of F–2, questions long persisted about whether they were entitled to recognition under the Full Faith and Credit Clause. In 1998, in *Baker v. General Motors*,[33] the Supreme Court stated explicitly that they are. It also clarified that there was no "roving 'public policy' exception to the full faith and credit due judgments." Apart from these two useful pointers, however, *Baker* is a mess.

The groundwork for the case was laid in the late 1980s, when GM's relationship with one of its employees, an engineer named Ronald Elwell, started to sour. In 1991, Elwell appeared as a witness in a products liability suit against GM. He also sued the company in Michigan state court, asserting wrongful discharge and other claims; GM counterclaimed on the theory that his testimony against it breached various duties. The GM–Elwell suit settled in 1992, and as part of the settlement, Elwell agreed to a permanent

---

30. *Lynde v. Lynde*, 181 U.S. 183 (1901).

31. *Griffin v. Griffin*, 327 U.S. 220, 233–34 (1946).

32. 44 Cal.2d 465, 283 P.2d 19 (1955).

33. 522 U.S. 222 (1998).

injunction that forbade him from testifying in GM-related litigation without GM's prior written consent. The settlement agreement provided that testimony pursuant to court order would not constitute a violation.

In rather brazen reliance on this provision, Elwell then began marketing himself as a witness against GM, arranging in each case for the plaintiffs to subpoena his testimony. Michigan courts refused to hear his testimony, but courts in other states did allow it. The Bakers were plaintiffs who filed a wrongful death suit against GM in Missouri state court. Pursuant to Elwell's ordinary practice, they subpoenaed him. The district court allowed his testimony, on the theory that the contrary injunction was against Missouri public policy and in any case was modifiable. The Eighth Circuit reversed, expressing skepticism about the existence of a public policy exception and noting that Michigan courts had declined to modify the injunction.

The Supreme Court reversed the Eighth Circuit. All the Justices agreed that the Michigan injunction should not prevent Elwell from complying with a Missouri subpoena. (Your own intuition is probably to the same effect.) But even with nine votes for that result, the majority opinion was able to gather only five votes for its rationale. The majority opinion, written by Justice Ginsburg, began with the two useful points noted above. The Full Faith and Credit Clause does apply to equitable decrees, and public policy does not provide an excuse for failure to recognize them. But then what would allow Elwell to testify in this case?

The Ginsburg majority invoked a number of the limits on full faith and credit we have seen already. Enforcement, it noted, was different from recognition or preclusion, and enforcement measures did not travel with sister-state judgments. Orders purporting to accomplish an official act within another state, it said, had been denied enforcement, and also those that interfered with F–2 litigation over which F–1 had no authority. So the Michigan injunction could not "dictate to a court in another jurisdiction that evidence . . . shall be inadmissible."

How all these principles come together to produce the desired result is not entirely clear. The distinction between recognition and enforcement does exist, but it is hard to see how it justifies a failure to enforce entirely, rather than enforcement according to Missouri mechanisms for enforcing injunctions. The disregard of orders purporting to accomplish an official act turns out, on inspection of the citations, to be just the land taboo. Interfering with F–2 litigation over which F–1 has no authority sounds bad, but the only example Ginsburg produces is the anti-suit injunction, which is typically based precisely on the existence of F–1 authority. There is, or before *Baker* was, no Supreme Court decision excluding anti-suit injunctions from full faith and credit, and there is no obvious reason why they should be excluded.

Two concurrences attempted to reach the same result on narrower grounds. Justice Scalia, writing for himself, suggested that the case could be decided on the grounds that GM needed to turn its Michigan judgment into a Missouri judgment before it could be enforced there. Justice Kennedy, for himself and Justices O'Connor and Thomas, would have focused on the fact that the Bakers were not parties to the Michigan suit and therefore could not be bound by the judgment.

There is, certainly, something unappealing about the idea that GM can buy Elwell's silence as it tried to. But none of the opinions, except perhaps the Kennedy concurrence, does a very good job of explaining why full faith and credit should not require a Missouri court to bar his testimony. I have two suggestions for more useful ways to think about the problem.

The first is to recognize that a settlement agreement is in the nature of a contract.[34] A Michigan contract can be against Missouri public policy, and if so it may not be recognized there, even if it is valid in Michigan.[35] In *Baker,* the agreement comes in the form of a judgment, but should that matter? One might argue yes—after all, states must enforce judgments even if they would not recognize the underlying cause of action, and even if the judgment is egregiously wrong. But one might also argue no—the parties to a Michigan contract that is against Missouri public policy could get a Michigan declaratory judgment that the contract is valid, but if, say, performance in Missouri is illegal, Missouri will not lose the ability to enforce its criminal laws.

So contracts and judgments are different in some ways, and that difference might be relevant. But they are similar in some ways too, most notably that they do not bind nonparties. Preclusion, essentially, is about extinguishing parties' rights or foreclosing certain of their arguments. It does not purport to extinguish the rights of nonparties. The problem with the Michigan injunction was that it aspired to do just that. Testifying against GM was in part

34. For a thorough analysis of this issue, see Polly J. Price, *Full Faith and Credit and the Equity Conflict,* 84 Va. L. Rev. 747 (1998).

35. In fact, the Michigan injunction in *Baker* seems contrary to any sensible state's policy, and its poor drafting is what caused all the trouble in the first place. GM would have done much better to have Elwell agree not to accept fees for his testimony.

Elwell's right it was something he could volunteer to do, and for which he was paid. But obtaining his testimony was the Bakers' right.[36] As the Supreme Court once put it, "the public ... has a right to every man's evidence."[37] Neither the settlement agreement nor the injunction could extinguish their right, and neither could be enforced against them.[38]

The injunction could, of course, have been enforced against Elwell. GM could have tried that; Elwell would have pointed to the Missouri subpoena; and GM might have raised the issue of good faith and fair dealing. But all that is about the GM–Elwell relationship. The Bakers' right to subpoena Elwell was not at issue in the GM–Elwell suit. Elwell had no power to release it, and the Michigan court had no power to extinguish it, as the settlement agreement recognized. In *Baker*, GM was trying to use the injunction to control things it could not, because in drafting the settlement it had failed to control the things it should have, such as Elwell's orchestrating a subpoena or accepting payment for his testimony.

IV. Diversity Judgments

The Supreme Court has recently addressed one other interesting preclusion issue. We know that F–1 preclusion law determines the effect of an F–1 judgment in F–2. So New York law, for instance, determines the effect of a New York judgment in New Jersey. It does not matter what law is being used to decide the case. The judgment may be based on New York law or New Jersey law; it is still New York preclusion law that determines its effect.

At least, that is true if the judgment comes from a New York state court. What about federal courts? Well, one might think, obviously the federal system is a different jurisdiction, and therefore federal preclusion rules govern the effect of a federal judgment. That is true, and obviously so, when the court is exercising federal question jurisdiction and deciding issues under federal law. But

---

36. Justice Ginsburg's opinion engages this point only with the observation that the Bakers' right to Elwell's testimony is not a constitutional right. But why it would need to be of constitutional stature to survive a judgment that did not bind them is not at all clear.

37. *United States v. Bryan*, 339 U.S. 323, 331 (1950).

38. For a somewhat absurd but perhaps useful analogy, imagine that as part of the Elwell–GM settlement, Elwell "agreed" not to go to jail, and an injunction to that effect was issued in Michigan. Can Elwell now rob Missouri banks with impunity? Of course not, because whether he goes to jail for that is not within his power to determine, and the Michigan injunction cannot bind Missouri authorities not to prosecute. Likewise, testimony given under compulsion of a subpoena is not within Elwell's power to withhold, and the Michigan injunction cannot bind the Missouri court not to issue the subpoena.

what about when the federal court is exercising diversity jurisdiction and deciding issues under *state* law?

The analysis for state courts, I've said, does not depend on whether they are using their own law or the law of a sister state. Should it for federal courts? This question was presented in *Semtek International Inc. v. Lockheed Martin Corp.*[39] The appropriate answer depends on how we think of federal courts exercising diversity jurisdiction. If we think of them as distinctively federal courts that have performed a choice-of-law analysis leading them to state law rather than federal law, then they seem federal, just as a New York court retains its New York character even when using New Jersey law. From that perspective, the answer is probably that federal rules should govern. But if we think of them as an attempt to mimic the courts of the state in which they sit while avoiding localist bias, then the answer may well be that the preclusion rules should come from that state.

Of the two perspectives, the second one is more consistent with the aims of diversity jurisdiction, and of *Erie*. Federal diversity jurisdiction is designed to provide a neutral decisionmaker, but apart from that the *Erie* goal is *not* to differ in meaningful ways from state courts. A state court using another state's law, by contrast, has no such goal, except perhaps in certain renvoi situations.

So it would make good sense for the preclusive effects of a federal court exercising diversity jurisdiction in New York to be determined by New York law. There is, however, a problem with allowing states to have the last word on the effect of federal judgments. It seems inconsistent with federal supremacy as a general matter, and in specific cases it might threaten federal interests. The solution, which the Court chose in *Semtek*, is to hold that the relevant preclusion rules are federal, but that they are drawn to mirror the laws of the state in which the court sits, absent exceptional circumstances. This achieves the desired uniformity between the state and federal courts within a state, while also effectively reserving a federal veto power should the state rule somehow conflict with federal interests.

39.   531 U.S. 497 (2001).

Chapter 8

FAMILY LAW

I. Introduction

It should be no surprise that family law is one of the areas in which knotty conflicts problems arise. They tend to raise questions of status—when must one state recognize marriages or divorces performed by another?—but there are also preclusion and jurisdictional matters in the mix. Perhaps surprisingly, marriage is in some ways the simplest of the issues, and this chapter starts with the basic marriage rule before moving on to divorce and child custody and support.

II. Marriage

The traditional rule for marriage, which still generally controls, is quite simple. Subject to some exceptions, the validity of a marriage is determined by the law of the place of celebration.[1] (Like other traditional rules, this one has a Latin name: *lex loci celebrationis*.) The basic exception is public policy. The public policy of two other states must be considered.[2]

First, a marriage will be invalid if it is contrary to the fundamental policy of the state with the most significant relationship to the marriage when celebrated. The reference to the most significant relationship is the indeterminate language of the Second Restatement, but it generally means the domicile of the parties, if they share a domicile and intend to maintain it after marriage, or the domicile of one party if the spouses intend to reside there. In these circumstances, in theory, the marriage will be held invalid in all states. (In practice, however, courts are somewhat more lenient—

---

1. The Second Restatement, typically, provides that the validity of a marriage is governed by the law of the state with the most significant relationship to a particular issue. See Restatement, Second, of Conflict of Laws § 283[1]. But it goes on to note that a marriage valid where celebrated will be recognized everywhere unless contrary to the strong public policy of another state which had the most significant relationship at the time of marriage, thus adopting a form of the standard rule and exception. See *id.* § 283[2].

2. Thus, there may be three relevant states: the state of celebration, the state with the most significant relationship at the time of celebration, and the state where recognition is sought. Of course, it is possible for one state to fill more than one of these categories, if, for instance, the question is about recognition in the state with the most significant relationship at the time of celebration.

they may sanction marriages that the state with the most significant relationship would not approve, if the marriage is not contrary to their own public policy.[3])

Second, a marriage will not be recognized if it is deeply contrary to the public policy of the state where recognition is sought.[4] Thus, recognition may be withheld even if the marriage is valid where celebrated and the state of celebration has the most significant relationship at the time.[5] This withholding of recognition by a particular state whose public policy is offended does not, however, mean that the marriage has been invalidated or dissolved as a general matter—other states will recognize it unless it is contrary to their own public policy.

The operation of this rule and its exceptions is complicated by a few other factors. First, validity must be distinguished from incidents. "Incidents" are the rights that attend the marital relationship, such as intestate succession and decisionmaking in medical emergencies. It is possible for a state to recognize a marriage as valid while not granting the couple all the incidents that would obtain under the law of the place of celebration. (If that law grants a husband some degree of authority over his wife that offends forum policy, for instance, the forum need not allow it.) Conversely, a state can refuse to recognize the marriage as valid while granting some incidents. (A state may, for instance, allow distribution of an intestate decedent's property to multiple wives even though it would not recognize the polygamous marriage.[6]) Put generally, it is the incidents that are usually at issue, and a state may grant some and withhold others.

---

3. See, e.g., *McPeek v. McCardle*, 888 N.E.2d 171 (Ind. 2008).

4. This traditional rule has been codified by many states with regard to same-sex marriage. See generally Andrew Koppelman, *Recognition and Enforcement of Same–Sex Marriage*, 153 U.Pa. L. Rev. 2143 (2005). At the federal level, Congress has authorized states to refuse recognition to same-sex unions formed in other states with the Defense of Marriage Act (DOMA), 28 U.S.C. § 1738C. DOMA is rather clearly unnecessary given the traditional public policy exception. Some scholars have also argued that it is unconstitutional. See, e.g., Andrew Koppelman, *Dumb and DOMA: Why the Defense of Marriage Act is Unconstitutional*, 83 Iowa Law Review

1 (1997); Larry Kramer, *Same-Sex Marriage, Conflict of Laws, and the Unconstitutional Public Policy Exception*, 106 Yale Law Journal 1965 (1997). I tend to disagree—lifting an obligation to recognize marriages that some states find deeply offensive, even if the obligation is imaginary, seems like a very reasonable use of Congress's power under the Full Faith and Credit Clause. DOMA has thus far survived all challenges. See, e.g., *Wilson v. Ake*, 354 F.Supp.2d 1298 (M.D. Fla. 2005).

5. See, e.g., *Cook v. Cook*, 209 Ariz. 487, 104 P.3d 857 (App. 2005) (noting that Arizona does not recognize foreign marriages between first cousins).

6. See *In re Dalip Singh Bir's Estate*, 83 Cal.App.2d 256, 188 P.2d 499 (1948).

Thus, to decide how a particular validity case will come out, it is important to focus on the precise incident at issue. Some will be more offensive to forum policy than others. Allowing the parties to a marriage contrary to forum policy to cohabit will typically be more offensive than allowing one to inherit from the other by intestate succession. It is also relevant in practice, though less acknowledged in decisions, that the duration of a marriage will have some weight. For instance, if a 16 year-old and an 18 year-old leave their home state, where the age of consent is 18, get married in a neighboring state where it is 16, and return home, a court would be relatively likely to invalidate the marriage after six weeks and less likely after twenty years. It may also matter who brings the challenge—in this hypothetical, the 16 year-old is probably in the best position to seek invalidation, while someone seeking to challenge intestate succession, should one of the spouses die, is in a weaker position.

III. Divorce

With marriage, the major conflicts question is when one state will recognize a marriage celebrated in another. There is typically no issue as to whether the state of celebration has the power to marry the would-be spouses, and in particular no problem of what to do when one party is present but the other is not. Divorce presents both these issues. On the other hand, the rule for recognition of divorce is somewhat simpler than that of marriage. A divorce decree is a judgment for the purposes of full faith and credit (which a marriage is not), and it must be recognized in other states ... subject to the usual qualifications about validity.

A. Ex Parte Divorce

The early divorce cases need to be understood against the backdrop of their times, and in particular the limited grounds for divorce that existed in most states in the early 20th century. Most states at this time allowed divorce only for fault-based causes, like adultery or cruelty. In practice, this meant that spouses frequently had to cooperate in seeking a divorce, possibly by stipulating to fictitious grounds. A divorce based on such grounds was, of course, a judgment procured by fraud, which frequently led to further complications down the road.

In consequence, the prospect of making use of the laws of one of the few states to adopt a more permissive divorce regime, notably Florida and Nevada, was tempting, particularly for those whose spouses would not cooperate. The practice of ex parte migratory divorce, where only one spouse was present in the divorcing juris-diction, raised an obvious conflicts question. The spouse who re-mains at home enjoys a marital relationship protected by his or her home law, and the one who travels is seeking to dissolve it under the law of another state. Whose law will prevail? The answer turns out to be a bit of a compromise, though largely a victory for the divorcing state. It comes through two Supreme Court decisions, both involving the same parties.

O.B. Williams married Carrie Wyke in North Carolina in 1916. Lillie Hendrix married Thomas Hendrix in 1920, also in North Carolina. The two couples lived in the same town in North Carolina until May 1940, when O.B. Williams and Lillie Hendrix went to Las Vegas. On June 26, they filed for divorce from their North Carolina spouses. Neither North Carolina spouse appeared, nor were they served in Nevada. (Thomas Hendrix was served by mailing the summons and complaint to his last post office address and by publication in a Las Vegas paper; Carrie Williams received a copy of the summons and complaint from a North Carolina sheriff.)

The divorces were granted on the grounds of extreme cruelty, the Nevada court noting in each case that the plaintiff was a bona fide Nevada resident and had been for the statutorily-required six weeks. Hendrix and Williams married each other in Nevada in October 1940 and returned to North Carolina. There they lived together until they were prosecuted for bigamous cohabitation.

The Nevada divorces and remarriage provided an obvious de-fense, if they were entitled to recognition in North Carolina courts. But the courts said they were not; North Carolina was not obligat-ed to recognize the Nevada divorces since the North Carolina spouses had not been served in Nevada and had not appeared. Williams and Hendrix were convicted and sentenced to jail. In the first *Williams v. North Carolina*, the Supreme Court overturned the conviction.[7] Divorce decrees, the Court said, are not like *in personam* judgments against the defendant spouse, and they do not require the exercise of personal jurisdiction over that spouse. It is enough that the spouse seeking the divorce is domiciled in the divorcing state. Domicile creates a relationship between an individ-ual and a state that allows that state to alter the individual's marital status, even if the state lacks personal jurisdiction over the other spouse, as long as the form and manner of substituted service meet the constitutional requirements.[8]

---

7. 317 U.S. 287 (1942) (*Williams I*).

8. *Williams I* overruled an earlier Supreme Court decision, *Haddock v.*

So the divorce decree was entitled to full faith and credit, just like any other judgment. But just like any other judgment, it could also be attacked on the grounds that the issuing court lacked jurisdiction. North Carolina did not leave Hendrix and Williams alone after the first Supreme Court decision; instead, it obtained another conviction on the theory that the Nevada divorce decrees were invalid since the plaintiffs had not properly established Nevada domicile. In the second *Williams v. North Carolina,* the Supreme Court affirmed the conviction.[9] The divorce decree, it stated "is a conclusive adjudication of everything except the jurisdictional facts upon which it is founded, and domicile is a jurisdictional fact."

As we saw in the judgments chapter, the Court has never fully explained when relitigation of jurisdiction is permitted, but since neither the North Carolina spouses nor the state of North Carolina had an opportunity to be heard in the Nevada divorce proceedings, it is fairly easy to conclude that the issue should be open to re-examination at their instigation. The harder question, which *Williams II* left open, is how much respect was owed the Nevada court's determination that the plaintiffs had established domicile. In the criminal trial, the jury was charged that the burden was on Williams and Hendrix to "satisfy" the jury "from all the evidence" that their Nevada domicile was bona fide, and that the Nevada decree's recitation of domicile was prima facie evidence warranting but not compelling that conclusion. This passed muster; *Williams II* pronounced that the Nevada finding had been given "appropriate weight."

So ex parte divorce is possible, though the decree may be re-examined for jurisdictional defects to the same extent as any other judgment rendered in the absence of one party. There are also other protections for the absent spouse, namely limits on what a court awarding an ex parte divorce can do. In *Estin v. Estin,*[10] a New York couple separated. A New York court awarded the wife $180 a month as permanent alimony. The husband subsequently procured a Nevada divorce in a proceeding in which the wife did not appear. He then stopped paying alimony and, when the wife sued in New York, defended on the grounds that as the Nevada decree had dissolved the marriage, it had also freed him from its consequences.

Haddock, 201 U.S. 562 (1906), which had proceeded on the theory that a court needed jurisdiction over the marriage, conceptualized as a thing (the "*marital res*"), and that when spouses separated, the *marital res* remained with the inno-cent spouse. Under the *Haddock* approach, an ex parte divorce could be obtained only by the innocent spouse.

9.   325 U.S. 226 (1945) (*Williams II*).

10.   334 U.S. 541 (1948).

Not so, said the Supreme Court. Nevada did have power to terminate the marital relationship, based on the husband's domicile, and New York had to recognize the Nevada decree. But Nevada did not have the power to erase the wife's rights under the New York support decree. The husband's Nevada domicile did not give that state the power to terminate his obligations without personal jurisdiction over his creditors, and the fact that the obligation derived from the marriage did not mean that terminating the marriage would necessarily make it vanish. (Under New York law, in fact, a support decree can survive divorce, as the New York Court of Appeals stated this one had.)

Estin illustrates the concept of "divisible divorce." A state may have the power to dissolve the marital relationship without undoing all of its incidents and consequences. Whether a particular right will survive an ex parte divorce will generally be answered under the law of the state where the spouse asserting the right is domiciled, not the law of the divorcing state. This is not merely because the wife in *Estin* had obtained a New York judgment. A later case, *Vanderbilt v. Vanderbilt*,[11] held that a support obligation need not be reduced to judgment to persist. It is because a divorcing state without personal jurisdiction over one spouse cannot terminate that spouse's rights. The divorcing state can act on the marriage, but not on the absent spouse.

Acting on the marriage may, however, prevent *future* rights from vesting. In *Simons v. Miami Beach First Nat'l Bank*,[12] the husband of a New York couple moved to Florida and obtained an ex parte divorce. His wife had earlier obtained a New York separation decree, and her rights under that decree survived, pursuant to *Estin*. Then the husband died, and his wife sought dower rights to his Florida property under Florida law. The Florida courts rejected her claim, and the Supreme Court affirmed. The New York decree, Justice Brennan wrote, required support payments but did not preserve the wife's ability to assert the rights of a spouse.

Application of the concept of divisible divorce to child custody proved difficult. In *May v. Anderson*,[13] the Supreme Court suggested that custody rights of an absent spouse were protected in a manner similar to property rights. A concurrence by Justice Frankfurter noted that while the Full Faith and Credit Clause did not require recognition of an ex parte custody decree, the Due Process Clause did not forbid recognition, and courts should proceed with a focus on the welfare of the children. This led to substantial confu-

---

11. 354 U.S. 416 (1957). **13.** 345 U.S. 528 (1953).
12. 381 U.S. 81 (1965).

sion, largely resolved by the Uniform Child Custody Jurisdiction and Enforcement Act, discussed later in this chapter.

B.   Bilateral Divorce

A bilateral divorce is one in which the divorcing court has personal jurisdiction over both spouses. Such a divorce is less subject to challenge than an ex parte one. For one thing, subsequent re-examination of the jurisdiction of the divorcing court is precluded by the appearance of both parties. In *Sherrer v. Sherrer*,[14] a couple married in New Jersey and later moved to Massachusetts, where they lived for some years and raised two children. In March 1944, Margaret Sherrer told her husband Edward that she wanted to take the children to Florida for a month. (In fact, she had already decided to stay there.)

She and the children arrived in Florida on April 4, 1944. A week later, they were joined by a Henry Phelps, who had known Margaret in New Jersey, though the extent of their prior relationship is uncertain. In July, ninety-three days after arriving in Florida, Margaret filed for divorce (Florida law requires ninety days bona fide residency). Edward, having been served by mail, hired a Florida lawyer and opposed the divorce on the grounds that Margaret did not meet the residency requirement. In November, Edward came to Florida and the Sherrers entered into a settlement agreement providing that he would have custody of the children during the school year and she would have custody during the summer. The court entered a divorce decree on November 29. On December 1, 1944, Margaret married Phelps.

In February, 1945, they returned to Massachusetts, because, according to Phelps, his father was ill and required care. They remained there after the father recovered because Edward took the opportunity to serve Phelps with papers in an alienation of affections action and, again according to Phelps, he wanted to stay in-state while the action was pending. Edward had moved out of the family house, and Margaret and Phelps moved in. In June 1945, Edward filed a petition in Massachusetts seeking a decree that Margaret had deserted him. Such a decree would be issued to a husband and would allow him to convey realty free of dower rights; thus, it required the continued existence of a marriage. To meet that requirement, Edward argued that because Margaret's Florida domicile was fraudulent, the Florida divorce decree was rendered without jurisdiction and was void. The Massachusetts courts ruled

---

14.   334 U.S 343 (1948).

that they were not precluded from re-examining the jurisdictional issue and agreed with Edward.

The Supreme Court reversed. Edward had had his day in court on the jurisdictional issue, it said. Where jurisdiction had actually been contested, relitigation would be permitted only to the extent allowed under the preclusion law of the rendering jurisdiction. Florida law would not allow relitigation, so Edward was precluded.

Sherrer is straightforward in one sense; it is an application of the standard full faith and credit rule that the effect of an F–1 judgment in F–2 is determined by F–1 preclusion law. But as noted in the judgments chapter, the law is unclear on what the prerequisite for application of this rule to jurisdictional issues is. At one extreme, if the party objecting in the second proceeding never had the opportunity to contest jurisdiction in the first, as in ex parte divorces, the rule is clear that some re-examination is permitted. At the other end of the spectrum, if there has been a full and fair contest on the issue, re-examination should presumably not be permitted, or rather permitted only to the extent it is under F–1 law. *Sherrer* presents a case in which the defendant spouse did appear and did contest jurisdiction in his pleadings, but the case was settled without a real resolution of that dispute. Thus, it indicates that preclusion will kick in well before the "full and fair contest" end of the range of possibilities.

The Court went further in *Johnson v. Muelberger*,[15] holding that a husband's mere appearance in a Florida divorce proceeding precluded his daughter from later challenging the resulting divorce. The husband had the opportunity to contest jurisdiction and had chosen not to. Under Florida law, the Court noted, the daughter was precluded, so preclusion was what full faith and credit required. Why the daughter, obviously a non-party, was precluded under Florida law is not clear. What is clear is that jurisdiction is almost never subject to relitigation after a sister-state bilateral divorce.

This rule does not hold with respect to foreign-country divorces, which are not shielded by the Full Faith and Credit Clause. Some foreign countries, including Mexico, allow divorce on grounds more lenient than U.S. states and without any significant residency requirement. Ex parte foreign divorces procured under such standards are unlikely to be recognized. Bilateral divorces have a greater chance, though recognition is far from uniform.[16] (To call

15. 340 U.S. 581 (1951).

16. Compare *Rosenstiel v. Rosenstiel*, 16 N.Y.2d 64, 262 N.Y.S.2d 86, 209

these divorces "bilateral" is a stretch in some cases; typically one spouse is physically present for a matter of days and the other appears through a local attorney.)

C. Same–Sex Divorce

As far as recognition of divorces goes, it makes no difference if the marriage being dissolved in F–1 is one that F–2 would recognize or not. In either case, the F–1 divorce decree is a judgment that must be granted full faith and credit. (Remember *Baker*'s admonition that there is no roving public policy exception to the full faith and credit due judgments.) But a different question has come up with respect to granting a divorce in the context of same-sex marriage: what about the public policy of F–1? If the marriage sought to be dissolved is contrary to F–1 public policy and would not be recognized, as is currently true of same-sex marriage in most states, will F–1 grant a divorce?

The question appears not to have arisen before same-sex marriage became legal in some states, and it has not yet been addressed by many courts. In *Rosengarten v. Downes*,[17] a Connecticut appellate court held that Connecticut courts did not have jurisdiction to dissolve same-sex marriages or civil unions. (The plaintiff was a Connecticut resident seeking ex parte dissolution of his Vermont civil union with a partner then residing in New York.) The court reasoned that jurisdiction could exist only if Connecticut recognized the validity of the union; otherwise "there is no *res* to address and dissolve."

The *Rosengarten* court evidently viewed the issues of recognition and dissolution as inseparable. All of its analysis is devoted to the question of whether Connecticut should recognize foreign same-sex unions as a general matter; it does not consider the possibility that dissolving a civil union or marriage between parties who wish to divorce need not commit the court to recognizing such a relationship between parties who wish to stay married. The traditional and well-established distinction between marital status and incidents suggests that such a distinction could be made.[18] In *Alons v. Iowa*

N.E.2d 709 (1965) (New York recognizes Mexican divorce) with *Meeker v. Meeker*, 52 N.J. 59, 243 A.2d 801 (N.J. 1968) (New Jersey does not).

17. 71 Conn.App. 372, 802 A.2d 170 (2002), appeal granted 261 Conn. 936, 806 A.2d 1066 (2002), appeal dismissed as moot (Conn. S. Ct. 2002). For another Connecticut case reaching the same con-

clusion about a Massachusetts marriage, see *Lane v. Albanese*, 2005 WL 896129 (Conn. Super. Ct. 2005).

18. See, e.g., Herma Hill Kay, *Same-Sex Divorce in the Conflict of Laws*, 15 King's College L.J. 63, 71 (2005). In 2005, Connecticut approved civil unions for same-sex couples and authorized its Superior Courts to dissolve such unions,

District Court, an Iowa lower court did so, agreeing to dissolve a Vermont civil union between two Iowa domiciliaries regardless of whether Iowa would recognize the union.[19]

IV. Child Custody and Adoption

A. Custody

Because child custody orders are modifiable, the question of their interstate recognition has proved troublesome over the years. The Supreme Court's decision that custody determinations made in the course of an ex parte divorce could, but need not, be recognized in other states did not help.[20] The Uniform Child Custody Jurisdiction Act (UCCJA), now replaced by the Uniform Child Custody Jurisdiction and Enforcement Act (UCCJEA), attempted to restore stability.[21]

The UCCJEA attempts to allocate jurisdiction to a single state for both initial and continuing custody determinations. A state (I will call it State X) may make an initial custody determination if it meets one of the following criteria.[22] First, State X is the child's home state, or has been during the six months prior to the determination and a parent or person acting as parent continues to live there. ("Home state" is defined as the place where the child lived for the prior six months, or from birth if less than six months old.) Second, no other state meets the first test, or a court of a state that does has declined to exercise jurisdiction on the ground that

---

presumably thus also granting them authority to dissolve foreign civil unions. What should happen with a foreign same-sex marriage is less clear.

19. 698 N.W.2d 858 (Iowa 2005). In 2009, the issue was mooted as to Iowa when the Iowa Supreme Court recognized a right to same-sex marriage under the Iowa Constitution. See *Varnum v. Brien*, 763 N.W.2d 862 (2009). New York courts have also entertained divorce actions to dissolve foreign same-sex marriages. See, e.g., *Beth R. v. Donna M.*, 19 Misc.3d 724, 853 N.Y.S.2d 501 (N.Y. Sup. Ct. 2008). However, this is a consequence not of a distinction between incidents and validity but rather of wholesale recognition of such marriages. See *Martinez v. County of Monroe*, 50 A.D.3d 189, 850 N.Y.S.2d 740 (N.Y. App. Div., 4th Dep., 2008); *Lewis v. New York State Dep't of Civil Service*, 60 A.D.3d

216, 872 N.Y.S.2d 578 (N.Y. App. Div., 3d Dep. 2009).

20. *May v. Anderson*, 345 U.S. 528 (1953). For commentary, see, e.g., Geoffrey C. Hazard, May v. Anderson: *Preamble to Family Law Chaos*, 45 Va. L. Rev. 379 (1959).

21. The UCCJA allowed for the possibility of concurrent jurisdiction in multiple states and produced conflict between states. In 1980, Congress intervened with the Parental Kidnapping Prevention Act (PKPA), 28 U.S.C. § 1738A, which invoked the Full Faith and Credit clause to limit states' ability to modify custody determinations. The UCCJEA revised the UCCJA to comply with the PKPA. The UCCJEA has been adopted by the vast majority of states and appears to be on the way to uniform adoption.

22. UCCJEA § 201.

State X is a more appropriate forum and the child and at least one parent or person acting as parent have a significant connection to State X and substantial relevant evidence concerning care and relationships is available in State X. Third, courts of all states meeting the first two tests have declined to exercise jurisdiction on the ground that State X is a more appropriate forum. Fourth, no other state meets any of the preceding three tests.

Once a State X court makes an initial custody determination, it retains exclusive jurisdiction until either it determines that neither the child nor any parent or person acting as a parent retain a significant connection with State X and relevant evidence is no longer available, or any court determines that neither the child nor any parent or person acting as parent reside in State X.[23] Modification is permitted by a State Y court only if that court meets one of the tests for initial jurisdiction, and then only if the State X court has determined that it no longer has exclusive jurisdiction, or that State Y would be a more convenient forum, or any court determines that neither the child nor any parent nor person acting as parent reside in State X.[24]

Conflicts problems with respect to support decrees have likewise been addressed by the Uniform Interstate Family Support Act (UIFSA), adopted in all fifty states and the District of Columbia. The UIFSA provides that a state that issues a spousal support order maintains continuing exclusive jurisdiction to modify it throughout its duration. Child-support orders, by contrast, may be modified by other states if, at the time of the modification request, the obligor, obligee, or child have left the issuing state.

B. Adoption

Historically, adoptions performed in one state were routinely recognized as valid in others. (Like divorces, adoption decrees count as judgments for full faith and credit purposes.) But just as in the context of divorce, surprising new problems arose with same-sex relationships. When same-sex couples in New York and Washington D.C. adopted Virginia-born children and requested new birth certificates containing the names of both adoptive parents, the state registrar refused on the grounds that Virginia certificates contained spaces for the names only of a mother and a father and Virginia law did not allow same-sex couples to adopt. The adoptive parents sued. The trial court upheld the registrar's decision, but in *Davenport v.*

---

23. UCCJEA § 202.   **24.** UCCJEA § 203.

Little–Bowser,[25] the Virginia Supreme Court reversed, noting that issuing revised birth certificates did not amount to an endorsement of same-sex marriage.

In Oklahoma, the legislature took a further step, amending its adoption statute to provide for nonrecognition of foreign adoptions by same-sex couples. This law was held unconstitutional as a violation of the Full Faith and Credit Clause in *Finstuen v. Crutcher*.[26] That seems pretty clearly the correct result, and so same-sex adoption should not give rise to enduring conflicts issues.

25. 269 Va. 546, 611 S.E.2d 366 (2005).

26. 496 F.3d 1139 (10th Cir. 2007).

Chapter 9

INTERNATIONAL CONFLICTS

I. Introduction

As a theoretical matter, a conflicts problem set in the international context differs little, if at all, from an interstate one. A state dealing with the laws or judgments of a foreign nation is less constrained in some ways, for it does not face the obligations imposed in the domestic case by the Full Faith and Credit Clause.[1] It is more constrained in other ways, for it may not enter into the federal realm of foreign affairs.[2] Conceptually, however, the analysis is essentially the same, and a court choosing between the laws of an American state and a foreign country will generally apply, as appropriate, one of the choice-of-law methodologies we have seen already.

With respect to federal law, the Supreme Court's approach has been somewhat different. Its analysis of the operation of federal statutes in the international arena usually does not work in terms of explicit choice of law at all, but rather casts the issue as one of statutory construction. (That is what Brainerd Currie suggested, of course, but you can decide for yourself whether the Court's approach reflects an incorporation of his insights.) With respect to the scope of the Constitution, too, the Court does not seem to view the question as one on which choice of law theory could shed light. The following sections consider federal statutes and the Constitution in turn, and the chapter concludes with a brief examination of the recognition of foreign country judgments.[3]

1. Due Process limits do exist. See, e.g., *Gerling Global Reinsurance Corp. of Am. v. Gallagher*, 267 F.3d 1228 (11th Cir. 2001) (striking down Florida law requiring insurers doing business in Florida to provide information about and pay claims of Holocaust victims on the grounds that it regulates transactions with insufficient contacts with Florida).

2. See, e.g., *Crosby v. National Foreign Trade Council*, 530 U.S. 363 (2000) (finding that Massachusetts law forbidding state entities from buying from companies doing business with Burma was preempted by federal foreign affairs power); *Zschernig v. Miller*, 389 U.S.

429 (1968) (finding that Oregon law that blocked inheritance of East German citizen was preempted by federal foreign affairs power).

3. Much of the substance of this chapter is a somewhat condensed and simplified version of Kermit Roosevelt III, *Guantanamo and the Conflict of Laws: Rasul and Beyond*, 153 U. Pa. L. Rev. 2017 (2005). That article in turn benefited from Larry Kramer's analysis of federal statutory extraterritoriality, in *Vestiges of Beale: Extraterritorial Application of American Law*, 1991 Sup. Ct. Rev. 179, and Gerald Neuman's discussion of the scope of the Constitution, in STRANGERS TO THE CONSTITUTION: IMMI-

220

II. Extraterritorial Application of Federal Statutes

How far do federal statutes reach? As is typically the case in conflicts, the judicial approach to this question progressed from an initial relatively strong territorialism to a more flexible analysis. What is unusual about the case of federal law is that territorialism made a recent return and still casts a substantial shadow over the doctrine.

The first stage should be familiar from the earlier discussions of choice of law methodology generally and constitutional constraints more specifically. In the late nineteenth and early twentieth century, at the same time as it was enforcing territorial limits on state law in domestic cases, the Supreme Court gave ringing endorsements to territorialism in the international context. In 1883 the Court declared the proposition "[t]hat the laws of a country have no extraterritorial force" to be "an axiom of international jurisprudence."[4]

The rigidity of the territorialist rule should not be overstated; exceptions existed for lands subject to no sovereign and even for application of a state's law to its own citizens.[5] By 1909, in *American Banana Co. v. United Fruit Co.*, Justice Holmes was characterizing territoriality as a presumption to be applied "in case of doubt," though also "the general and almost universal rule."[6] Even as a presumption, however, and even as it grew progressively riddled with exceptions and escape devices, territoriality proved a poor fit in an increasingly interconnected world. Gradually it gave ground as the twentieth century moved on.[7] In personal jurisdiction, *Pennoyer* yielded to *International Shoe*; in domestic conflicts the "choice of law revolution" swept from the law reviews into the state courts, though not entirely and not without resistance.[8]

For a time, the jurisprudence with respect to federal statutory law seemed to be keeping pace. Justice Holmes' analysis of the

GRANTS, BORDERS, AND FUNDAMENTAL LAW (1991).

4. *Canada Southern Ry. Co. v. Gebhard*, 109 U.S. 527, 536 (1883).

5. See *American Banana Co. v. United Fruit Co.*, 213 U.S. 347, 355–56 (1909).

6. *American Banana*, 213 U.S. at 357, 356.

7. See Kramer, supra note 3 at 192–93 (discussing roughly contemporaneous erosion of territoriality in international law, personal jurisdiction, and conflict of laws).

8. For an exhaustive description and assessment of the "revolution," see Harold L. Korn, *The Choice-of-Law Revolution: A Critique*, 83 Colum. L. Rev. 772 (1983).

scope of federal law in *American Banana* was, in the words of Larry Kramer, "pure conflict of laws," citing familiar conflicts cases such as *Milliken v. Pratt* and even a leading conflicts treatise by the English author A.V. Dicey.[9] And when Judge Learned Hand took the fateful step, in *Alcoa Steamship*, of extending the Sherman Act's prohibitions to conduct abroad affecting commerce within the United States, he commented that limitations on the extraterritorial scope of federal statutes "generally correspond to those fixed by the 'Conflict of Laws.' "[10] In the middle of the twentieth century, the Supreme Court analyzed the scope of the maritime regulations in the Jones Act with sophistication sufficient to win praise from Brainerd Currie.[11]

But then things changed. In 1991, in an apparent attempt to restore uniformity to what had become a somewhat disordered field, the Supreme Court rediscovered Holmes' presumption against extraterritoriality and embraced it in *EEOC v. Arabian American Oil Co.* ("*Aramco*").[12] The plaintiff in *Aramco*, one Boureslan, was a naturalized American citizen claiming employment discrimination on the grounds of race, religion, and national origin. The defendant was Aramco, a Delaware corporation. The allegations of the complaint fell easily within the scope of Title VII ... except that Boureslan's employment, and the alleged wrongful conduct, took place in Saudi Arabia.

Could discrimination by an American employer against an American employee abroad create liability under Title VII? The Court's opinion started promisingly enough for fans of interest analysis: it characterized the question of the scope of Title VII as "a matter of statutory construction" and described its task as divining "whether Congress intended the protection of Title VII to apply to United States citizens employed by American employers outside of the United States." (That Congress had such power was unquestioned.[13]) Then the process of statutory construction ran into the

9. See Kramer, supra note 3, at 186–87

10. *United States v. Aluminum Co. of America*, 148 F.2d 416, 443–44 (2d Cir. 1945). See also *Timberlane Lumber Co. v. Bank of America,* 549 F.2d 597, 613–15 (9th Cir. 1976) ("to determine whether American authority should be asserted in a given case as a matter of international comity and fairness ... [w]e believe that the field of conflict of laws presents the proper approach").

11. The cases are *Romero v. International Terminal Operating Co.*, 358 U.S. 354 (1959); *Lauritzen v. Larsen*, 345 U.S. 571 (1953). For Currie's evaluation, see Currie, SELECTED ESSAYS ON THE CONFLICT OF LAWS 361–75 (1963).

12. 499 U.S. 244 (1991).

13. Are there any limits on the scope of federal legislative jurisdiction? International law suggests there are. Section 402 of the Restatement, Third, of Foreign Relations Law sets out these limited bases for national legislative jurisdiction, which it calls "jurisdiction to prescribe." A state may regulate:

presumption against extraterritoriality and came to an abrupt halt. Boureslan had some arguments in favor of extraterritorial scope, the Court said, and they were plausible. (The EEOC agreed with him, but the Court gave that fact no weight.) But they were insufficient to overcome the presumption.

Why the Court chose to resurrect the presumption against extraterritoriality in such a robust form is not easy to understand. What seems most likely is that the Court picked up the language from earlier cases (its primary citation for the presumption is *Foley Bros. v. Filardo*,[14] from 1949) without paying much attention to the fact that it was facing a choice-of-law issue and consequently did not investigate whether choice of law had progressed in the intervening forty-two years.[15] Only that sort of inattention can explain why it repeated one of *Foley*'s main arguments against extraterritorial application: that if Title VII gave rights to Boureslan, it must also furnish rights in other circumstances, to foreigners working for Americans (as *Foley* claimed), or to Americans working for foreigners (as *Aramco* claimed). "We see no way of distinguishing" those cases, the *Aramco* Court wrote.

The distinction, however, is simple. Unless Saudi Arabian law intends to authorize U.S. employers to discriminate against their

(1)(a) conduct that, wholly or in substantial part, takes place within its territory;

(b) the status of persons, or interests in things, present within its territory;

(c) conduct outside its territory that has or is intended to have substantial effect within its territory;

(2) the activities, interests, status, or relations of its nationals outside as well as inside its territory;

(3) certain conduct outside of its territory by person not its nationals that is directed against the security of the state or against a limited class of other state interests.

The Fifth Amendment's Due Process Clause may also play a role in international conflicts similar to the one the Fourteenth Amendment Due Process Clause does in the domestic arena. See Lea Brilmayer & Charles Norchi, *Federal Extraterritoriality and Fifth Amendment Due Process*, 105 Harv. L. Rev. 1217 (1992).

14. 336 U.S. 281 (1949).

15. For some reason, the Court seems especially vulnerable to this misstep in the conflicts arena. In 1996, it relied on *New York Life Ins. Co. v. Head*, 234 U.S. 149 (1914), one of the strictest early cases enforcing constitutional limits on legislative jurisdiction, for the proposition that extraterritorial application of state legislation violated the Constitution. See *BMW of North America, Inc. v. Gore*, 517 U.S. 559, 571 n16 (1996) (" '[I]t would be impossible to permit the statutes of Missouri to operate beyond the jurisdiction of that State ... without throwing down the constitutional barriers by which all the States are restricted within the orbits of their lawful authority and upon the preservation of which the Government under the Constitution depends. This is so obviously the necessary result of the Constitution that it has rarely been called in question and hence authorities directly dealing with it do not abound' ") (quoting *Head*, 234 U.S. at 161). Of course, as seen in Chapter 4, this is not true after *Clay v. Sun Insurance Office*, 377 U.S. 179 (1964), and *Allstate v. Hague*, 449 U.S. 302 (1981), but those cases seem somehow to have escaped the *BMW* Court's notice.

employees in Saudi Arabia (a possibility, but one the Court did not invoke or investigate), *Aramco* does not present a potential conflict between U.S. and foreign law. If Title VII reached the relationship between a U.S. employer and employee abroad, the case would be a false conflict. With a foreign employer, however, the likelihood of a conflict is much greater. Assuming the laws differ, Saudi Arabia likely does intend to authorize its employers to engage in whatever conduct it does not forbid. The distinction the Court could not see is the one between true and false conflicts, which did not exist in 1949 but, to put it mildly, was well established in the literature by 1991.

So it seems likely that the Court simply failed to realize it was confronting a choice-of-law question. That failure led it to an anachronistic approach to determining statutory scope, and it did not augur well for the Court's analysis of conflicts between U.S. and foreign law. In *Aramco*, the Court did mention the possibility of a conflict, but it seemed to assume that the only possible course of action in such a case would be to decide the case under U.S. law. (It seemed to think, that is, that if U.S. law "applied" in terms of its scope, courts would be required to "apply" that law in terms of giving it priority over contrary foreign law—a failure to distinguish between the two steps of the choice-of-law analysis that I have suggested may stem from careless use of the word "apply.") In the Court's defense, one could observe that granting universal priority to forum law was indeed Brainerd Currie's initial suggestion. But we have already seen that this initial suggestion was superseded by others and soon modified by Currie himself. In any event, when that issue came up after *Aramco*, the Court performed quite poorly.

The extraterritorial scope of federal antitrust laws had been established before *Aramco* and survived the decision. Because U.S. law may prohibit conduct other countries permit, the possibility of conflict with respect to conduct abroad that has effects in the U.S. is substantial. In *Hartford Fire Ins. Co. v. California*,[16] U.S. states and private plaintiffs alleged, among other things, that English insurers, acting in England, had conspired to restrain trade within the United States. English law permitted the actions of which the plaintiffs complained, and the British Government appeared as amicus curiae to assert that it had intended to authorize such conduct.

From the ordinary choice-of-law perspective, *Hartford Fire* looks like a true conflict. The law of the place of conduct authorizes some acts that cause forbidden consequences in another jurisdic-

16. 509 U.S. 764 (1993).

tion. Section 403 of the Third Restatement of Foreign Relations Law provides that states should not exercise legislative jurisdiction (which, again, it terms "jurisdiction to prescribe") "with respect to a person or activity having connections with another state when the exercise of such jurisdiction is unreasonable." It goes on to explain that reasonableness should be determined by evaluating a non-exclusive list of factors including territorial connections, the nationality of the parties, the traditions of the international system, and the interests of other states in regulation. Section 403, in short, quite closely resembles Section 6 of the Second Restatement, although it is directed to states rather than courts. It says that in cases of overlapping jurisdiction, priority should be determined by an open-ended balancing analysis.

Unfortunately, the Supreme Court simply declined to apply § 403, on the grounds that no conflict existed unless it was impossible to comply with both British and American law.[17] This is, of course, not the standard meaning of "conflict" in choice of law, and it has little to recommend it on practical grounds. It amounts to an implicit decision always to give priority to the more restrictive law if compliance with both is possible. Because the decision was implicit, the Court made no effort to justify it. But it is fairly easy to see that such a rule will not always prove desirable—one might, for instance, consider the case of American speakers subjected to the defamation laws of foreign countries despite the protections of the First Amendment. In fact, the Sherman Act itself seems to recognize that more regulation is not always better. It provides that state insurance regulations may authorize conduct the Act forbids—that is, it contains a rule of priority subordinating the federal prohibition to state authorization with respect to the conduct at issue in *Hartford Fire*. Given that explicit statement of the relative priority of federal and state law, it seems quite plausible that

---

17. It also, bizarrely, cast its inquiry in terms of subject-matter jurisdiction, rather than the scope of U.S. law or the relative priority of U.S. and English law. The idea that subject-matter jurisdiction is lacking if the law the plaintiff invokes does not "apply" is pervasive in choice of law cases. *Aramco*, for instance, affirmed a dismissal on that ground after concluding that Title VII did not protect Americans abroad. The related idea that some law must "apply" if the case is to be decided at all explains why the unprovided-for case struck commentators as such an anomaly. But in both cases, the correct conclusion is just that if the plaintiff's allegations fall outside the scope of the law he invokes, he has failed to state a claim. After *Aramco*, that is, invoking Title VII against an employer abroad would be like invoking it against an employer with fewer than fifteen employees. That, the Supreme Court recently explained, is failure to establish an element of the claim, not a jurisdictional defect. See *Arbaugh v. Y & H Corp.*, 546 U.S. 500 (2006). (Note that this was true only for a brief period after *Aramco*—Congress quickly amended Title VII to make explicit that it does apply to American employees of American employers abroad.)

Congress would also be willing to subordinate the federal prohibition to English authorization for conduct occurring in England.

Because it misunderstood the analytical structure of the problem, the Court never attempted to consider how the interests of England compared to those of the United States. It collapsed the two steps of the choice-of-law analysis into one: decide whether U.S. law "applies." A more recent case offers somewhat more hope. In *Hoffman-La Roche v. Empagran S.A.*,[18] the Court considered an attempt to hold foreign defendants liable under the Sherman Act for foreign harm caused by conduct that also caused injury within the United States. This, the Court said, would not be reasonable. Citing § 403 of the Third Restatement of Foreign Relations and the *Hartford Fire* dissent, which had argued for the correct application of that section, it concluded that the foreign interest was clearly greater than the U.S. one.

Aramco and *Hartford Fire* point in opposite directions. *Aramco*'s sledgehammer use of the presumption against extraterritoriality limits the reach of federal law, while *Hartford Fire*'s narrow definition of conflict expands it. But the cases are similar in that they both essentially ignore the possibility of resolving conflicts by a comparison of interests. They both assume that if a case falls within the scope of U.S. law, it must be decided under that law, foreign law to the contrary notwithstanding. *Hoffman-La Roche* does not entirely free itself from this one-step perspective, nor does it explicitly reject *Hartford Fire*'s view of what constitutes a conflict. But by correctly understanding the Restatement of Foreign Relations Law, it does achieve a more sensible approach to determining the scope of U.S. law.

III. Extraterritorial application of the Constitution

A. Global Due Process

The scope of the Constitution is well settled in some particulars. No one would deny that it protects Americans within the United States. For more than a century, the Court has held that it affords many protections to aliens inside the U.S. as well.[19] And for over fifty years, it has held that Americans abroad can invoke constitutional rights.[20] The difficult question has to do with aliens abroad.

---

18. 542 U.S. 155 (2004).
19. See, e.g., *Wong Wing v. United States*, 163 U.S. 228 (1896).

20. See *Reid v. Covert*, 354 U.S. 1 (1957).

In its most recent decision, the Court adopted a practical and fact-specific approach to determining the extraterritorial scope of the Constitution.[21] This case-by-case inquiry lacks a strong underlying theory. It is guided by "particular circumstances" and "practical necessities" and above all the question whether extending a particular right in a particular case would be "impracticable and anomalous." Because it is so case-specific, it is hard to characterize as a unitary approach, but it shares some affinities with the analysis the Court used to determine whether a particular Bill of Rights guarantee could be invoked against the states through the Due Process Clause. Some Justices have described it that way, and relied on cases about the incorporation of the Bill of Rights to buttress their arguments about extraterritoriality.[22] If we are to give it a name, "Global Due Process" is as good as any.

Global Due Process is of course not the only approach, and certainly not the most theoretically coherent. There are essentially six other possible ways to go about determining the scope of the Constitution. Most have been endorsed at one time or another by at least one Justice of the Supreme Court. Since the Court's decisions have varied so widely in their analysis, and since the current state of affairs is still somewhat unsettled, it is worth spending some time considering the possibilities before proceeding to a discussion of the cases.

B. Other Possibilities

1. Textualism

Perhaps the simplest approach would be to take the Constitution's text as a sufficient guide. Some constitutional provisions specify limitations on their scope, either geographical or personal. The impost clause of Article I, § 8, for instance, applies only to taxes "throughout the United States," and the Fourteenth Amendment's Equal Protection Clause makes specific reference to the "jurisdiction" of the States.[23] Likewise, the Fourteenth Amendment's Privileges or Immunities Clause appears to restrict its protection to "citizens of the United States,"[24] while the privileges

---

21. See *Boumediene v. Bush*, 553 U.S. ___, 128 S.Ct. 2229 (2008).

22. See *Reid*, 354 U.S. at 75 (Harlan, J. concurring) ("one can say, in fact, that the question of which specific safeguards of the Constitution are appropriately to be applied in a particular context overseas can be reduced to the issue of what process is 'due' a defendant in the particular circumstances of a particular case"); *Hawaii v. Mankichi*, 190 U.S. 197 (1903) (relying on incorporation cases).

23. U.S. Const. Art. I, § 8; id. Am. 14.

24. U.S. Const. Am. 14. One might also read the phrase "privileges or immunities of citizens of the United

and immunities of Article IV are guaranteed to "the Citizens of each State." A textualist, or at least one who believed textualism to be the only permissible interpretive methodology, might then approach the problem of scope by reasoning that constitutional provisions without textual limitations are available to anyone, regardless of citizenship or geography.

The textualist model has never enjoyed much support among the Justices, and for good reason. Conflicts problems typically arise precisely because legislatures do not specify the geographical or personal scope of their statutes. To decide that such statutes (or, in the constitutional context, such provisions as the Fifth Amendment's due process clause) are therefore unlimited in scope is abdication, not analysis.

2. Territoriality

Territoriality suggests that as each sovereign is supreme within its geographical borders, its law, all of its law, and only its law, is there in force. The Constitution, then, could be invoked by persons within (some definition of) the United States, and not by anyone else. This model can claim at least a historical ascendance, and perhaps a renewed modern appeal. (There are second acts in the lives of American constitutional doctrines.) Certainly, no rival conception can boast such repeated and unqualified endorsement by the Supreme Court.[25]

But territoriality faces two serious problems. First, the Supreme Court long ago rejected it with respect to Americans abroad, who are protected by the Constitution. Second, territoriality is actually somewhat question-begging with respect to aliens within the United States. Grant that the Constitution "applies" within the borders of the United States. Does that mean that cases involving aliens arising within the U.S. should be resolved as though they were entirely domestic—i.e., as though the alien were a citizen? The conventional understanding of territoriality suggests that the answer is yes,[26] but in fact the territorial premise does not get us to

States" to identify the class of rights protected against abridgement, rather than the class of rights-holders—that is, to indicate that the relevant privileges and immunities were those held against the United States under federal law, rather than the state-law privileges and immunities referenced in Article IV. Cf. *The Slaughterhouse Cases*, 83 U.S. (16 Wall.) 36, 118–119 (1873) (Bradley, J., dissenting) (noting that Bill of Rights guarantees and others "are specified in the original Constitution, or in the early amendments of it, as among the privileges and immunities of citizens of the United States").

25. See, e.g., *Ross v. McIntyre*, 140 U.S. 453 (1891); *American Banana Co. v. United Fruit Co.*, 213 U.S. 347 (1909); *New York Life Ins. Co. v. Head*, 234 U.S. 149 (1914).

26. That makes it fit the doctrine, for the Court has held that even unlawful entrants enjoy constitutional rights. See, e.g., *Zadvydas v. Davis*, 533 U.S.

that conclusion. The reservation of some benefits to citizens is common, and some provisions of the Constitution make that distinction explicitly. Even in the absence of textual limits, judges might plausibly interpret other provisions to deny some protections to unlawful or involuntary entrants, perhaps those who have entered the country in order to make war on it[27] or those we have deemed enemies and brought within our borders for incapacitation or punishment.[28] Or, to look at the matter from the opposite side, if there is a good reason that such people should have constitutional rights within the U.S., it is hard to see why it should make a difference that the government has (fortuitously or strategically) elected to hold them outside its borders. So territoriality is demonstrably false with respect to Americans abroad and at best incomplete with respect to aliens within the United States. It cannot be counted a successful explanation of the scope of the Constitution.

3. Social Contract

Where territoriality focuses on geography, the social contract model focuses on citizenship. As the Preamble states, the People ordained and established the Constitution to "secure the Blessings of Liberty to ourselves and our Posterity." One might, then, suppose that the protections of the Constitution are available only to, as Justice Rehnquist put it in a 1990 decision, "a class of persons who are part of a national community or who have otherwise developed sufficient connection with this country to be considered part of that community."[29] Rights that the text of the Constitution limits to citizens would of course be for them alone, and its references to "persons" would be understood to apply only to persons with a sufficient connection.

678, 693 (2001) (noting that "once an alien enters the country, the legal circumstance changes, for the Due Process Clause applies to all 'persons' within the United States, including aliens, whether their presence here is lawful, unlawful, temporary, or permanent") and cases there cited.

27. Compare *Ex Parte Quirin*, 317 U.S. 1, 25 (1942) (holding, on the basis of petitioners' undisputed status as unlawful belligerents, that they could be tried by military tribunals rather than civil courts).

28. But see *United States v. Verdugo–Urquidez*, 494 U.S. 259, 278 (1990) (Kennedy, J. concurring) ("All would agree, for instance, that the dictates of

the Due Process Clause of the Fifth Amendment protect the defendant."). Justice Rehnquist's majority opinion could in fact be read to suggest that illegal aliens enjoy lesser rights. See *id.* at 282 (Brennan, J., dissenting) (expressing alarm at the implication); compare *Fong Yue Ting v. United States*, 149 U.S. 698, 738 (1893) (Brewer, J., dissenting) ("The Constitution has no extraterritorial effect, and those who have not come lawfully within our territory cannot claim any protection from its provisions").

29. *United States v. Verdugo–Urquidez*, 494 U.S. 259, 265 (1990). For Kennedy's disavowal of this theory, see *id.* at 276.

The social contract model is essentially equivalent to the "self-ish state" Currie hypothesized to illustrate interest analysis.[30] It conceives of the Constitution as existing for the benefit of the People and limits its scope to them. But the idea of the selfish state has serious problems, and the social contract model shares them.

Most notably, it is far from clear that a state interested only in the welfare of its citizens would best promote that welfare by granting rights only to them. Currie himself acknowledged that states might pursue more enlightened policies, and it was soon pointed out that considerations of reciprocity and game theory might lead even the most selfish state to moderate its assertions of authority and restrictions of rights. It is quite likely in the interest of citizens to extend constitutional rights to some categories of aliens.

The People might, for instance, worry that ruthless treatment of aliens by their own government would expose them to equally ruthless treatment at the hands of foreign powers.[31] They might think it beneficial to extend constitutional rights as a means of encouraging commerce and immigration.[32] They might worry that a government that had experienced the exercise of totally unchecked power against aliens would prove a greater danger to citizens. Or they might simply be repulsed by the idea of the government—their agent—acting in their name with no obligation to observe even the most fundamental norms of decency and fairness.[33]

The premise that the Constitution exists only for the benefit of Americans, in short, tells us very little about whether and under what circumstances it extends rights to aliens. And so the social contract model, too, cannot by itself determine the scope of the Constitution. Instead, it directs us to ask what scope best promotes the interests of the American People. I think this is the fundamental question, and later I will suggest that it should be viewed as a choice-of-law problem. For now, it suffices to note that the social contract model will not, by itself, take us all the way to an answer.

30. See Currie, supra note 11, at 89.

31. See, e.g., Brief Amicus Curiae of Retired Military Officers in support of the Petitioners in *Rasul v. Bush*, 2004 WL 99346 at *25 ("the lives of captured American military forces may well be endangered by the United States' failure to grant foreign prisoners in its custody the same rights that the United States insists be accorded to American prisoners held by foreigners"); *Verdugo–Urquidez*, 494 U.S. at 285 (Brennan, J., dissenting) ("By respecting the rights of foreign nationals, we encourage other nations to respect the rights of our citizens").

32. See Neuman, supra note 3, at 59 n. 51.

33. See, e.g., *Verdugo–Urquidez*, 494 U.S. at 286 (Brennan, J., dissenting) ("Our national interest is defined by [our moral] values and by the need to preserve our own just institutions.").

4. Limited Government

If the question of where and whether aliens possess constitutional rights proves knotty, an analysis that does not rely on the concept of rights might seem an attractive alternative. Rather than identifying rights that defeat the exercise of government power, one could seek out limitations on that power. If the government simply lacks the power to take a certain act, considerations of geography and citizenship might seem irrelevant, and the question of who bears particular rights can be avoided.

This idea has been popular with some Justices in the past, and we will see it in some of the cases discussed in the following section. In practice, however, it turns out not to work very well. There are two main problems. First, the Supreme Court has described the federal foreign affairs power as inherent in sovereignty and not dependent on the Constitution for its source.[34] The decision has been criticized, but "[m]ost scholars assume that Congress has a general power to legislate in foreign affairs matters."[35] Thus the idea that limiting the government to its enumerated powers protects liberty, a theme of some of the Court's domestic federalism decisions,[36] will have no effect with respect to aliens abroad.

In consequence, anyone attempting to use the limited government model has to identify not the limits of enumerated powers but constitutional provisions that withdraw power from the government, rather than granting rights to individuals. And that is the second problem. It can probably be done in some cases. Most people would probably agree that when Article I, Section 9, states that "No title of nobility shall be granted by the United States," it means that the government simply cannot do it, regardless of any considerations of geography or citizenship. But on the issues that matter, distinguishing rights from absences of power is likely to be much harder. There is no obvious way to do so, and Supreme Court doctrine constructed with other purposes in mind stands in the way in some important areas. (The First Amendment, for instance, has clearly been construed as granting rights, even though it is phrased

---

34. See *United States v. Curtiss–Wright Export Corp.*, 299 U.S. 304, 315–16 (1936) ("The broad statement that the federal government can exercise no powers except those specifically enumerated in the Constitution, and such implied powers as are necessary and proper to carry into effect the enumerated powers, is categorically true only in respect of our internal affairs.").

35. Saikrishna B. Prakash & Michael D. Ramsey, *The Executive Power Over Foreign Affairs*, 111 Yale L.J. 231, 233 (2001).

36. See, e.g., *United States v. Morrison*, 529 U.S. 598 (2000); *United States v. Lopez*, 514 U.S. 549 (1995).

as a restriction on the powers of Congress.) The model of limited government is not a promising way forward.

5. Mutuality of Obligation

The mutuality of obligation model starts with an idea of reciprocity. If the United States demands obedience to its laws, then it should grant the protections of its Constitution. As Gerald Neuman puts it, constitutional rights "are prerequisites for justifying legal obligation."[37] Thus, "when the United States asserts an alien's obligation to comply with American law as a justification for interfering with the alien's freedom or property, the alien is presumptively entitled to the protection of all constitutional rights in the interaction."[38]

Mutuality flows from a basic idea of fairness, and it certainly has substantial intuitive appeal. But it also has two problems. First, there is the question of what sort of exercise of U.S. power triggers the mutuality requirement. If any federal action counts, then mutuality makes aliens abroad indistinguishable from Americans at home, or at least from lawfully resident aliens. That is an extremely generous approach. If, on the other hand, the requirement is triggered only by a demand that aliens obey U.S. law, it seems to allow the government great latitude to abuse aliens outside the legal system. (It could, for instance, detain and interrogate them at will as long as it rested its authority on national security, rather than claims they had broken the law.)

Second, the source of the mutuality model is not clear. It does have normative appeal, as I have said, but normative appeal is ordinarily not enough to establish a rule of constitutional law. Without some evidence that mutuality was a foundational principle of the Constitution, it is hard to see what warrant judges have for elevating it to that status.

6. Choice of Law (Interest Analysis)

I have suggested that none of the prominent theoretical approaches to determining the scope of the Constitution is fully satisfactory. Our best hope may be to turn to choice of law theory. Choice of law is widely derided as a theoretical failure,[39] but in

---

37. See Neuman, supra note 3, at 7–8.

38. *Id*. at 99. Neuman notes that specific text or other factors may override the presumption. See *ibid*.

39. See, e.g., Lawrence Lessig, *The Zones of Cyberspace*, 48 Stan. L. Rev. 1403, 1407 (1996) (stating that "conflicts of law is dead—killed by a realism intended to save it"); Gerald Neuman, *Extraterritorial Rights and Constitutional Methodology After* Rasul v. Bush, 153 U.Penn. L. Rev. 2073, (2005) (suggesting that "the field of conflict of laws is more

earlier chapters I have attempted to demonstrate a viable under-standing of its analytical structure. Here I will suggest how it could be applied to the Constitution.

Interest analysis suggests that the scope of legal rules should be set by analysis of their purpose. As Larry Kramer puts it, "[t]he basic premise ... is that the court should determine what policy a law was enacted to achieve in wholly domestic cases and ask whether there are connections between the case and the nation implicating that policy."[40] That is, the court should focus on the particular right at issue, and whether its extension to a case with foreign elements will promote its domestic purpose.

This is not necessarily an easy task. A simplistic approach might say that the purpose of the individual rights provisions of the Constitution is to protect particular liberties, and to the question "Whose liberties?" respond, "Those of Americans, of course!"[41] But that is nothing more than restating the question and answering it through a crude application of the social contract model. If we can do no better, the methodology would merit the kind of accusations Lea Brilmayer has leveled against interest analysis: that it simply substitutes a presumptive domiciliary focus for a presumptive terri-torial focus.[42]

I think we *can* do better, both with interest analysis and the Constitution. I have discussed the former in earlier chapters; here I will focus on the latter. Some provisions—for instance, the Fourth Amendment—seem likely to pose a substantial challenge. Without a well-developed theory of what the Fourth Amendment is for, we are left asking whether its application to searches of aliens' property abroad implicates the "right of the people to be secure in their persons, houses, papers, and effects, against unreasonable searches and seizures." I confess the answer to this is not obvious to me, though one might well conclude that a search for items to be introduced at a U.S. trial as evidence of the violation of U.S. laws brings its target within the community of the "people."[43]

Other provisions seem more tractable, which suggests to me that the effort is worthwhile. Consider, for example, the First

in need of methodology than itself a source of methodology").

40. See Kramer, supra note 3, at 213.

41. Compare Currie, supra note 11, at 85.

42. See Lea Brilmayer, Conflict of Laws 85–87 (2d. ed. 1995) (criticizing Currie's domiciliary focus).

43. This would amount to an en-dorsement of some form of mutuality in the Fourth Amendment context. Suppos-ing that the Fourth Amendment does grant aliens abroad some protection, it might also make sense to look to foreign standards to determine what searches are reasonable.

Amendment. The purpose of the speech clause has received substantial scholarly attention, with conventional accounts tending to ring the changes on two main themes: facilitating democracy by informing the electorate and promoting self-actualization.[44] The first of these might be implicated by actions against aliens abroad, most obviously if they are attempting to communicate with Americans. (In such case, of course, Americans would be able to assert their rights as willing listeners under current doctrine.[45] Thus, this analysis might not change results very much, though it would allow the aliens to litigate in their own right. But the very fact that the Court has reached similar results, by whatever rationale, indicates its recognition that the First Amendment is at stake in such communications.) Alien communication to other aliens, by contrast, seems much less relevant to the First Amendment's domestic purpose of facilitating democracy.[46] As for self-actualization, a domiciliary focus seems appropriate: it is hard to see why the Constitution would be concerned with the self-actualization of aliens abroad. Thus it seems possible to conclude that the government should have greater latitude in regulating speech among aliens abroad than it does in the domestic context, at least as far as the First Amendment is concerned.[47]

The Establishment Clause of the First Amendment presents different issues. Again, substantial scholarship on its purpose exists.[48] Suppose that its purpose may be formulated as protecting a community within which neither a particular religion, nor religion in general, is supported by compulsory individual donations or receives the endorsement of the government.[49] Is this purpose implicated by federal action abroad?

---

44. See generally Kermit Roosevelt III, *The Costs of Agencies: Waters v. Churchill and the First Amendment in the Administrative State*, 106 Yale L.J. 1233, 1250–52 (describing "speaker-centered" and "listener-centered" models of the First Amendment).

45. See, e.g., *Virginia State Bd. of Pharmacy v. Virginia Citizens Consumer Council*, 425 U.S. 748, 756–57 (1976); *Lamont v. Postmaster General*, 381 U.S. 301, 308 (1965) (Brennan, J., concurring).

46. Thus, for instance, a federal decision to support a particular foreign political party seems unlikely to trigger the same kind of "funding forum" concerns it might in the United States.

47. This is not, of course, to say that attempts at such regulation would be a

good idea, or that a foreign law protecting the speakers should not be given priority. I am claiming only that on the account of the First Amendment developed in the text, the First Amendment would not be a barrier. If we understand the First Amendment differently—if, for instance, we suppose that it has some moral dimension, reflecting a judgment that governmental restraints of speech are intrinsically abhorrent—then we would likely reach a different conclusion

48. For a recent and comprehensive treatment, see Noah R. Feldman, *The Intellectual Origins of the Establishment Clause*, 77 N.Y.U. L. Rev. 346 (2002).

49. This statement does not do justice to the complexity of Establishment Clause jurisprudence and scholarship, but its accuracy is essentially irrelevant

The answer to this question is probably yes. Federal expenditures in support of religion abroad clearly convey a message of governmental favoritism, and they compel individual taxpayers to support religions with which they may disagree. Thus, the Establishment Clause should operate to restrain federal action abroad. That is not necessarily to say that aliens abroad should be able to bring claims. They are not, generally speaking, taxpayers, nor can they argue that federal endorsement of religion marks them as second-class citizens, for they are not citizens at all. In this case the purpose-based analysis tends to accord with mutuality, as potential Establishment Clause violations are unlikely to involve the assertion of authority over aliens. However, it also answers the question of whether federal action abroad can violate American's Establishment Clause rights, which mutuality does not.

I do not claim that these analyses are authoritative. Others may have different conceptions of the purpose of the provisions I have considered, or different views on what sort of contacts implicate those purposes. But they seem plausible enough to make me think the methodology is sound. Unlike most of the other approaches, it is a methodology that could be incorporated into the Court's current fact-and case-specific approach. Indeed the most recent case suggests that the Court is taking a similar tack. The next section gives a brief survey of the caselaw.

C. Cases

As with federal statutory law, cases assessing the scope of the Constitution began with a strongly territorialist approach. In 1891, the Court stated flatly that "[t]he constitution can have no operation in another country."[50] Early in the twentieth century, however, U.S. colonialism posed challenges to the doctrine. What rights should inhabitants of U.S. possessions such as Puerto Rico be entitled to assert?

The Supreme Court grappled with this question in the Insular Cases, a series of cases decided between 1901 and 1922. The different opinions display an impressive range of methodologies. Different Justices looked to the text of the Constitution, its struc-

---

to the value of the methodology I demonstrate.

50. *Ross v. McIntyre*, 140 U.S. 453, 464 (1891). The petitioner in Ross had been convicted by a consular court in Japan of a murder committed aboard an American ship in a Japanese harbor, and he protested that this process deprived him of the rights to a grand jury indictment and a jury trial.

ture, the nature and purpose of various constitutional provisions, and fundamental theories of government.[51]

In the end, the Court settled on an approach suggested by Justice White. Territories that had been "incorporated into and become an integral part of the United States,"[52] were, with respect to the availability of constitutional rights, indistinguishable from the states of the Union: all constitutional provisions applied. Unincorporated territories lay beyond the scope of constitutional provisions referring to "the United States." That did not mean for White that they lay beyond the Constitution entirely. He offered a backstop of limitations on Congressional power that operated without respect to geography:

> Undoubtedly there are general prohibitions in the Constitution in favor of the liberty and property of the citizen, which are not mere regulations as to the form and manner in which a conceded power may be exercised, but which are an absolute denial of all authority under any circumstances or conditions to do particular acts. In the nature of things, limitations of this character cannot be under any circumstances transcended, because of the complete absence of power.[53]

As the focus on an absence of power indicates, White here endorsed a version of the model of limited government. But as I have suggested, the distinction between rights and absences of power is hard to make out and to maintain, and eventually this alternative came to be understood as a rule that even in unincorporated territories, certain "fundamental rights" applied.[54] The question of whether a given right was fundamental was answered by an analysis that paralleled, and in some cases relied on, the one performed to determine whether a Bill of Rights guarantee could be asserted against the states through the Due Process Clause. Thus, the model of limited government collapsed into a version of Global Due Process.

In 1950, the Court confronted the question of extraterritoriality again when it received habeas petitions from German nationals confined in the Landsberg prison in Germany following convictions by military tribunals in China. The Court's opinion in that case, *Johnson v. Eisentrager*,[55] is hardly a model of clarity. It notes what it takes to be the salient facts about the petitioner: he

51. Justice Harlan, for instance, argued that constitutional rights attended any exercise of United States power. *Downes v. Bidwell*, 182 U.S. 244, 385 (1901) at 385 (Harlan, J., dissenting).

52. Id. at 299 (White, J., concurring).

53. Id. at 294–95 (White, J., concurring).

54. See, e.g., *Reid v. Covert*, 354 U.S. 1, 13 (1957) (describing *Insular Cases* as "conceding that 'fundamental' constitutional rights applied everywhere").

55. 339 U.S. 763 (1950).

(a) is an enemy alien; (b) has never been or resided in the United States; (c) was captured outside of our territory and there held in military custody as a prisoner of war; (d) was tried and convicted by a Military Commission sitting outside the United States; (e) for offenses against laws of war committed outside the United States; (f) and is at all times imprisoned outside the United States.[56]

Without explaining the precise significance of these factors to its various lines of reasoning, the Court then goes on to suggest that the petitioners (a) simply lacked standing to litigate in U.S. courts, regardless of what substantive rights they might have;[57] (b) possessed no Fifth Amendment rights;[58] and (c) had failed to state a claim on the merits.[59] What precisely *Eisentrager* stands for is unclear. Later cases read it to endorse a fairly rigid territoriality, but that is oversimplified, and the Court has recently corrected its mischaracterization.[60]

The morass of *Eisentrager* aside, the Court's midcentury approach to the scope of the Constitution, like its analysis of federal statutory extraterritoriality, stands up well compared to contemporaneous choice of law analysis. In *Reid v. Covert*,[61] the Court slipped the bonds of territoriality, at least with respect to American citizens, a full six years before the first significant judicial salvo of the domestic choice-of-law revolution.[62] *Reid* considered the consolidated cases of American women who had killed their servicemen husbands abroad, one in England and one in Japan. Each was tried before a court martial abroad, and each sought habeas relief on the basis of constitutional rights to grand jury indictment and jury trial.[63] The Court initially rejected the petitions on the theory that the Fifth and Sixth Amendment's jury guarantees did not extend to Americans tried "in foreign lands for offenses committed there" (though the Due Process Clause did).[64]

After granting reargument, however, the Court reversed itself. Accidents of geography, it suggested, should not control the rela-

---

56. Eisentrager, 339 U.S. at 777.

57. See id. at 776–77.

58. See id. at 782–85.

59. See id. at 785–90.

60. Compare *Zadvydas v. Davis*, 533 U.S. 678, 693 (2001) (citing *Eisentrager* for the proposition that the "Fifth Amendment's protections do not extend to aliens outside the territorial boundaries") with *Rasul*, 124 S.Ct. at 2693 (observing that "all six of the facts" about the status of the *Eisentrager* peti-

tioners were "critical to [the Court's] disposition" of the constitutional claims).

61. 357 U.S. 1 (1957).

62. *Babcock v. Jackson*, 12 N.Y.2d 473, 240 N.Y.S.2d 743, 191 N.E.2d 279 (N.Y. 1963), is generally considered the first significant judicial adoption of the new conflicts learning.

63. See *Reid*, 357 U.S. at 3–5.

64. Id. at 5.

tionship between Americans and their government. "When the Government reaches out to punish a citizen who is abroad, the shield which the Bill of Rights and other parts of the Constitution provide to protect his life and liberty should not be stripped away just because he happens to be in another land."[65]

Reid contains no explicit invocation of conflicts theory. But its reasoning echoes (or presages) the domestic rejections of territoriality. Its ringing endorsement of the relevance of citizenship is as forceful as any penned by Brainerd Currie, and its disparagement of geography would become a staple of torts cases involving accidents in the course of interstate travel.[66] Viewed from the conflicts perspective, and compared to contemporaneous conflicts theory, the Court's performance is more than adequate.[67]

This state of affairs did not persist. With respect to federal statutes, we have seen, the Court began a territorialist retrenchment with *Aramco*. And while lower federal courts were relatively adventurous in enforcing constitutional rights in favor of aliens abroad,[68] the Supreme Court seemed to be taking its cue from

65. Id. at 6.

66. Compare *Reid*, 357 U.S. at 6 (arguing that American citizen's rights "should not be stripped away just because he happens to be in another land") with, e.g., *Kilberg v. Northeast Airlines, Inc.*, 9 N.Y.2d 34, 211 N.Y.S.2d 133, 172 N.E.2d 526, 527 (N.Y. 1961) ("Modern conditions make it unjust and anomalous to subject the traveling citizen of this State to the varying laws of other States through and over which they move. ... The place of injury becomes entirely fortuitous").

67. *Reid* also contains other approaches. Some language echoes the *Insular Cases'* conception of a limited government bound always by the Constitution. See *id.* at 5–6 ("The United States is entirely a creature of the Constitution. Its power and authority have no other source. It can only act in accordance with all the limitations imposed by the Constitution"); *id.* at 12 (rejecting the proposition that Constitution is territorially limited as "obviously erroneous if the United States Government, which has no power except that granted by the Constitution, can and does try citizens for crimes committed abroad"). Some takes a textual tack.

See *id.* at 8 ("The Fifth and Sixth Amendments, ... are also all inclusive with their sweeping references to 'no person' and to 'all criminal prosecutions.' ") Still other passages suggest that constitutional rights appertain to the obligation of obedience or subject status, a form of the mutuality model. See *id.* at 6 (observing that English inhabitants of settled colonies "take with them ... allegiance to the Crown, the duty of obedience [but also] all the rights and liberties of British Subjects") (quoting 2 Clode, Military Forces of the Crown 175).

68. See, e.g., *Lamont v. Woods*, 948 F.2d 825, 832–33 (2d Cir. 1991) (entertaining Establishment Clause challenge to federal funding of foreign religious organizations located outside United States), *Haitian Centers Council, Inc. v. McNary*, 969 F.2d 1326, 1342–44 (2d Cir. 1992) (finding serious questions as to Fifth Amendment rights of Haitian refugees detained in Guantanamo), vacated sub nom. *Sale v. Haitian Centers Council, Inc.*, 509 U.S. 918 (1993), *United States v. Verdugo–Urquidez*, 856 F.2d 1214 (9th Cir. 1988) (excluding evidence obtained from a warrantless search of an alien's residence abroad), reversed 494 U.S. 259 (1990).

Aramco. In *United States v. Verdugo–Urquidez*,[69] the Court rejected a Mexican national's attempt to invoke the exclusionary rule as a remedy for the alleged Fourth Amendment violation created by a warrantless search of his house in Mexico.

After *Reid,* pure territoriality was no longer an option for the *Verdugo-Urquidez* Court, and the opinion displays some creativity in accommodating that precedent. Chief Justice Rehnquist, writing for the majority, relied in part on the Fourth Amendment's reference to "the right of the people" to justify a distinction between nonresident aliens and "a class of persons who are part of a national community or who have otherwise developed sufficient connection with this country to be considered part of that community," a form of the social contract model.[70] He also consulted the "available historical data" in an attempt to ascertain "the purpose of the Fourth Amendment,"[71] turned to the practice of the Framers' contemporaries to shed light on the original understanding,[72] and toured the doctrine, giving special attention to the *Insular Cases.*[73]

The culmination of this methodological eclecticism, however, suggests a thwarted yearning for the simple clarity of territoriality: what follows is a surprisingly univocal reading of *Eisentrager* that finds its "rejection of extraterritorial application of the Fifth Amendment ... emphatic."[74] Later cases would repeat that characterization, citing *Eisentrager* (and *Verdugo-Urquidez)* for the simple proposition that the "Fifth Amendment's protections do not extend to aliens outside the territorial boundaries."[75]

Justice Kennedy, however, did not endorse that blanket statement. Though he joined Rehnquist's opinion, he also wrote a separate concurrence. He expressed doubts about the social contract model and instead applied the global due process approach set forth by Justice Harlan in his *Reid* concurrence. Because he found that the "conditions and considerations of this case would make adherence to the Fourth Amendment's warrant requirement impracticable and anomalous," he agreed that the government should not be bound by it.

69. 494 U.S. 259 (1990).

70. Id. at 265.

71. Id. at 266.

72. Id. at 267.

73. See id. at 268–69 ("And certainly, it is not open to us in light of the *Insular Cases* to endorse the view that every constitutional provision applies wherever the United States Government exercises its power").

74. See id. at 269.

75. *Zadvydas v. Davis,* 533 U.S. 678, 693 (2001).

In the most recent decision, *Boumediene v. Bush*,[76] this global due process analysis won majority support. *Boumediene* featured habeas petitions from foreign nationals detained at the naval base in Guantanamo Bay, Cuba. After an earlier decision held such detainees entitled to file habeas petitions as a matter of statutory construction,[77] Congress passed the Military Commissions Act of 2006, purporting to revoke those habeas rights and suspend the writ. The *Boumediene* Court thus confronted the issue of whether the Suspension Clause protected aliens held in Guantanamo.

In an opinion by Justice Kennedy, the Court concluded that it did. The analysis rested on two main points. First, the Court was plainly concerned about strategic behavior by the government. Guantanamo had been chosen as a detention site in significant part because it was believed to be beyond the reach of federal judicial power. But allowing the government to avoid judicial oversight by strategic selection of detention facilities would allow "the political branches to govern without legal constraint." In rejecting this possibility, the Court observed that maintaining the separation of powers was one of the purposes of the writ of habeas corpus, an observation that fits well with an interest analysis-inflected approach to constitutional scope.

Second, *Boumediene* re-emphasized the importance of what it called "objective factors and practical concerns." It identified "at least three factors" that were "relevant to determining the reach of the Suspension Clause:"

(1) the citizenship and status of the detainee and the adequacy of the process through which that status determination was made;

(2) the nature of the sites where apprehension and then detention took place; and

(3) the practical obstacles inherent in resolving the prisoner's entitlement to the writ.

To a large extent, these factors are familiar. Citizenship and geography are the primary factors in most choice of law analysis, so the inclusion of citizenship and the location of apprehension and detention is not surprising. The concern with practical obstacles is also predictable; it flows naturally from the global due process model, for due process is a flexible concept that takes its contours from particular facts and circumstances. It is somewhat more surprising to see the adequacy of the process through which the

---

76. 553 U.S. ___ (2008).   **77.** See *Rasul*.

status determination was made as a factor to be considered in deciding whether the Suspension Clause grants rights. This factor seems somewhat more like an element of deciding on the merits whether due process has been accorded, or whether the government has offered an adequate alternative to habeas petitions. Still, *Boumediene* is easily recognizable as a product of the global due process model Justice Kennedy endorsed in *Verdugo-Urquidez*. Future cases will presumably be decided on their particular facts, but *Boumediene* is encouraging for those who would like to see the Court's approach to constitutional scope incorporate the insights of interest analysis, in particular in its invocation of the domestic purpose of the habeas writ and the Suspension Clause.

IV. Recognition of Foreign Country Judgments

While the judgments of states command respect in state and federal court by virtue of the Full Faith and Credit Clause and its implementing statute, foreign country judgments do not. Each state is thus free to choose for itself what its approach to recognition in such cases will be. Whether this is sensible is not clear. Arguably, recognition of foreign country judgments touches upon foreign affairs and therefore should be governed by federal law. And even if foreign affairs concerns are not involved to an extent sufficient to justify preemption of state law, uniformity seems obviously desirable.

As a practical matter, substantial uniformity exists. The vast majority of states, as well as the District of Columbia and the U.S. Virgin Islands, have adopted the Uniform Foreign Money–Judgments Recognition Act (UFMJRA), which provides that foreign money judgments are enforceable in the same manner as a sister-state judgment to which full faith and credit is owed. With respect to other judgments and on questions of preclusion, most states follow an approach close to that recommended by the Restatement, Second, of Conflict of Laws, which provides in § 98 that foreign country judgments will be recognized "so far as the immediate parties and the underlying cause of action are concerned" if they are valid and rendered after a fair trial in a contested proceeding. Thus, states will typically require as prerequisites to recognition the participation of both parties, an exercise of jurisdiction consistent with United States due process standards, and a fundamentally fair proceeding.

The American Law Institute, in an effort to ensure uniformity, has recently proposed a federal statute that would preempt inconsistent state laws. The proposed statute departs from the practice of the majority of states by imposing a reciprocity requirement: it forbids United States courts from recognizing foreign-country judgments if the foreign country's courts would not recognize a comparable U.S judgment. (The Supreme Court embraced a reciprocity requirement in the 1895 case of *Hilton v. Guyot*,[78] but the requirement has become increasingly uncommon since.)

For judgments within its scope (it excludes domestic relations and bankruptcy judgments, and also arbitral awards), the proposed statute requires recognition subject to the reciprocity requirement mentioned above and several other possible defenses. Judgments "shall not be recognized" if the proceeding was not fundamentally fair, if the judgment was obtained by fraud, if the underlying law is contrary to federal or state policy, notably including the First Amendment speech clause, or if jurisdiction is based on certain prohibited grounds or is otherwise unreasonable or unfair. Recognition of some other judgments is neither required nor prohibited; examples are judgments where the rendering court lacked subject-matter jurisdiction or where the foreign proceeding is a race to judgment against a pending or possible U.S. proceeding.

At approximately the same time as the ALI was completing its draft statute, the National Conference of Commissioners on Uniform State Laws was revising the UFMJRA, producing the Uniform Foreign Country Money–Judgments Recognition Act (UFCMJRA). Like the UFMJRA, the UFCMJRA does not include a reciprocity requirement. Whether the ALI's proposed statute is ultimately adopted by Congress will thus determine whether reciprocity is a part of U.S. law on the recognition of foreign judgments.

78.   159 U.S. 113 (1895).

TABLE OF CASES

References are to Pages.

247

INDEX

References are to pages.

ADOPTION, 218–219

"APPLY"
Meanings of, 58–59, 103, 106, 143, 224

BAXTER, WILLIAM
Comparative impairment, 67–68, 93–94

BEALE, JOSEPH
Classical legal thought, 33
Contracts, 39; see also Restatement (First)
Application of foreign law, 28–29
Generally, 3
Views on renvoi, see Renvoi
Vested rights, 3, 5, 18, 25, 33, 99, 213

BETTER LAW, SEE LEFLAR, ROBERT

BRANDEIS, LOUIS, 24–25, 116

CARDOZO, BENJAMIN, 24

CAVERS, DAVID
Test for depecage, 98
Disagreement with Brainerd Currie, 96–97
Principles of preference, 69, 137

CHILD CUSTODY, SEE JURISDICTION

CLAIM PRECLUSION
Finality, 191, 202
Generally, 190, 206

COLLATERAL ESTOPPEL, SEE ISSUE PRECLUSION

COMPARATIVE IMPAIRMENT, SEE BAXTER, WILLIAM

COMPLEX LITIGATION
Capacity to sue, 106
Class action, 101, 104, 200
Class Action Fairness Act, see Statutes

CONDUCT–REGULATING RULE
Generally, 52
Interest analysis and, 52, 53, 54, 55

CONSTITUTION, SEE DUE PROCESS; FULL FAITH AND CREDIT; PRIVILEGES AND IMMUNITIES; SUPREMACY CLAUSE; SUSPENSION CLAUSE

CONTRACTS
Acceptance, 9
Choice of forum clause, 180
Futures, 192
Invalidity of, 39
Lex loci contractus, 8, 9, 14–17, 28, 50
Mailbox rule, 10
Majority rule, 10
Minority rule, 10
Party autonomy, 38, 39, 40, 86–87
Place of performance, 10, 179
Settlement agreements, 205
Surety contracts, 44
Unilateral offer, 10

COOK, WALTER WHEELER
Criticism of Joseph Beale, 41

CORPORATIONS
Internal affairs, 14, 112, 121
Minimum contacts, see Jurisdiction

CURRIE, BRAINERD
David Cavers and, see Cavers, David
Forum preference, 48, 49, 57, 136
Generally, 41, 43, 220
Governmental interest analysis, see Interest analysis
"Moderate and restrained interpretation", 61, 68
Selfish state assumption, 45, 46, 76, 133, 230

DAMAGE MULTIPLIERS, SEE JUDGMENTS

DEPECAGE,
Generally, 9
Interest analysis and, 49, 96
Second Restatement and, 84, 95, 96

DOMICILE
Co-domiciliary immunity, 105
Definition of, 13
General jurisdiction and, 180

249

†